McCoy
1060 Harvest Lane
Mattituck, NY 11952

D1256815

JOYFULLY
SHATTERED

A Physician's Awakening at the Crossroads of Science and Spirituality

RICK SHEFF, MD

Innergy Publishing
Manhattan Beach, CA

by Rick Sheff, MD

Dr. Sheff weaves together his personal journey of spiritual awakening with accessible, compelling scientific and philosophic insights. In so doing, *Joyfully Shattered* provides a significant contribution to the growing integration of science and spirituality, as well as a roadmap for all seekers of truth on their own journey to joy.

Larry Dossey, MD
Author of *One Mind: How Our Individual Consciousness Is Part of a Greater Mind and Why It Matters*

In *Joyfully Shattered,* Dr. Sheff takes us on the inner journey that is the true mystical path, revealing a universal spirituality that transcends all denominations and all religions with the deep ring of ageless truth.

Dale Allen Hoffman
Translator of the Aramaic words of Jesus
Author of *Echoes of an Ancient Dream*

Dr. Sheff, in *Joyfully Shattered,* has accurately and with an open heart portrayed the extraordinary healings, the mission, and work of this amazing man, John of God, and the miracles of the Casa de Dom Ignacio.

Heather Cummings, John of God Translator
Co-Author of *John of God: The Brazilian Healer Who's Touched the Lives of Millions*

Innergy Publishing
952 Manhattan Beach Boulevard, Suite 200
Manhattan Beach, CA 90266

Library of Congress Cataloging-in-Publication Data

Sheff, Rick
Joyfully Shattered:
A Physician's Awakening at the Crossroads of Science and Spirituality
1. Spirituality   2. Science   3. Love   4. Religion   5. Healing   6. Paranormal

ISBN: 978-1-4951-4209-3

Cover Design: Frank Parker

First printing

© 2015 Rick Sheff

This book is dedicated to Ron Roth, a Roman Catholic priest, modern-day mystic, and founder of Celebrating Life Ministries, and to João Teixeira de Faria, known to the world as John of God, for his lifelong loving and generous ministry of healing.

"For one who believes, no proof is necessary.
For the nonbeliever, no amount of proof is sufficient."
—Saint Ignatius of Loyola

"Must it always be so?"
—Richard Sheff, MD

"Someday, after mastering the winds, the waves, the tides and gravity, we shall harness for God the energies of love, and then, for a second time in the history of the world, man will have discovered fire."

—Pierre Teilhard de Chardin

Table of Contents

ACKNOWLEDGMENTS

Neither this book nor the personal journey it depicts would have been possible without generous, wise, and loving gifts from so many. My parents, Ron and Janet Sheff, gifted me with so much, including a commitment to justice and caring for my fellow human beings. But most of all, their love created the foundation for my own lifelong commitment to love others as openly and courageously as possible.

Numerous academic teachers challenged, taught, and inspired me to strive for the truth with disciplined intellectual integrity. They, as with all teachers, do not know the ultimate fruit their labors have borne. I wish they could know how much they have contributed to this book. To the spiritual teachers who have most touched me and shatteringly transformed my world, I express gratitude beyond words. Caroline Myss, Reverend Ron Roth, Sri Bhagavan and his wife Amma, the dasas of Oneness

University, the yoga instructors at Kripalu, and the man known as John of God deserve special mention, but so many others have contributed in ways both small and large. I owe much to the generous love and teaching I've received from Master Chi'ang, a humble yet profoundly wise Bon Po monk, who, to the best of my understanding, has not been in a human body for four thousand years.

And a special thanks goes to all the fellow spiritual seekers with whom I have had the honor to share the road on this journey. That each of you has had the courage to pursue your own path to living the most loving, enlightened life you can has both taught and inspired me to do the same.

I also thank my publisher, Paul Karasik, for seeing in this book and in my work a message that needs to be shared with the world. And thank you to Michelle Hutchinson who put countless hours into the challenging task of editing my initial manuscript into a much better read.

This book would never have become a reality without the steadfast encouragement of my wife, Virginia. She has been my most ardent supporter and toughest critic. Her clear thinking and honesty in critiquing every page have made this a much better book than it would have been without her by my side. But far more, Virginia's wisdom and guidance can be found woven throughout the pages of *Joyfully Shattered*. Thank you, Virginia, my partner and sometime guide on this extraordinary journey we share.

AUTHOR'S NOTE

The events in this book took place over a more than forty-year period in my life. The names of all individuals in this book, other than the author and a handful of people who have given permission for me to use their real names, have been changed to protect their privacy. Occasional details have been modified to allow for a coherent telling of some of the stories. With these minor exceptions, all of the stories in the pages that follow are true.

Chapter I: A Seeker is Born

Glimpses of Truth

I am a scientist and a skeptic. I have studied philosophy at Oxford, the sciences at Ivy League universities, and medicine at the oldest medical school in America. I have deeply questioned everything we think we know and how we think we know it. After more than four decades in the ardent pursuit of truth, I have come to the surprising conclusion that the world is a far more wondrous and mysterious place than most of today's scientists are telling us.

* * *

Slowly I approached Ryan's tiny bed. A low, hissing sound escaped from the ventilator that forced air in and out of his young lungs. Swollen lips, eyelids, nose—every feature had grown distorted beyond recognition. He laid so still, his skin mottled with dark purple blood oozing beneath the surface from infection-ravaged capillaries. The tips of each finger had blackened where blood could no longer flow.

Just two weeks earlier I'd seen Ryan with his mother, Christie, for a routine six-month well-baby visit. He'd cooed sweetly as I'd examined him. "He's healthy as can be," I'd pronounced. Christie had smiled proudly. In that moment, we'd tacitly shared all the fears and difficulties of her pregnancy, the labor that had stretched on for days, the moment of unspeakable joy when I'd placed Ryan, bloody and wet from birth, on her breast to nurse for the first time.

As her family doctor, I'd shared all this with Christie, and more. Countless calls early on as Ryan had not been easy to nurse. His first ear infection. Her struggles with Tom, Ryan's dad, and their final decision not to marry before the birth. At each important moment she'd turned to me, asking for my judgment as her doctor and Ryan's doctor. Then the call.

"Dr. Sheff, Ryan just woke up from his nap. And something's just not right."

Years of medical practice had taught me that those words, when spoken by a mother, needed to be taken seriously. "What seems not right?"

"Well, he's a little warm, but I'm concerned because he's just not himself."

"Is he fussy and irritable?" I asked, thinking we were likely dealing with another ear infection.

"No. If anything he's the opposite. Nothing bothers him. He's just quiet."

Again, listening to patients over the years had taught me to be alarmed at these words. A lethargic baby might be a very sick baby. "Take him to the hospital. Dr. Chandler is on call right now. She'll see him in the emergency room."

Ryan's exam was normal except for the fever and a few tiny red spots on his skin. Those concerned my partner, Amy Chandler, who began a work-up for a possible bloodstream infection from meningococcal bacteria. Over the next two hours her worst fears were confirmed as those few tiny red spots blossomed into cascades of black-and-blue blotches. Being in a community hospital, she quickly started him on high-dose antibiotics and called the transport team from Children's Hospital, who whisked him away to their pediatric intensive care unit. The next call from Christie was heartbreaking. "Dr. Sheff, Ryan's so sick. They think he might die." With a meningococcal infection, I knew they were right.

"He's in the very best place he could be," I tried to reassure her. "Children's Hospital has the best of whatever he needs."

"Dr. Sheff, will you come see him?"

I paused. A trip into Children's would drain at least two hours out of my already crammed day. And for what purpose? I didn't even have clinical privileges there, so I could do nothing to help treat Ryan. "Of course I will," I heard myself answer.

Now, as I approached Ryan's bedside, I wondered what I had to offer as a family doctor that the experts at Children's didn't. Christie needed something from me. Did Ryan, too?

Unlike at my own hospital, these nurses did not know me, didn't exchange the usual pleasantries, and did not seek my medical opinion. In fact, they completely ignored me as they raced from bed to crib. I had nothing to offer the world-renowned expert doctors and highly trained nurses caring for Ryan. But Christie had called because I had something to offer her. She wanted me there to face Ryan's death with her.

The Children's doctors had been open, telling Christie and Tom that this might be Ryan's ultimate fate, but as all good doctors do, they had kept alive hope that Ryan's treatment might produce a miracle. To most if not all of them, the miracle would be the result of their science. But our medical science has limits. And when these are reached, something else is called for. It was that something else that Christie, and Tom, needed now.

Standing over Ryan, I sensed his tenuous grasp on life. Death hovered near, almost at my shoulder. As a doctor, I'd come to know death, to feel a strange comfort in its presence, as I did now. Christie and Tom needed me to help them find a parcel of that comfort, a solace that would come only when they could make sense of this moment, of Ryan's terribly brief life, and their overwhelming grief. That's what they needed from me now—not pat answers—but to stand with them with an open heart and to lend them courage as they faced this searing heartbreak.

"Ryan's gonna make it, isn't he, Doc?" Tom desperately implored before I could even sit down. Then he turned to the extended family that had come to rally around him and Christie in the ICU waiting room, proudly announcing, "This is the doc who delivered Ryan. He knows 'im better 'n anybody. He'll tell us when Ryan's gonna get better, won't you, Doc?"

I looked from face to face, pausing, trying to find the words to say what I knew, that Ryan was dying. I could tell from Christie's resigned sadness that she had come to the same conclusion. She looked lonely amid her own family, all of whom held onto Tom's misplaced optimism.

"Yeah, they got the best doctors here at Children's. They'll fix 'im up," one volunteered.

"I know he's gonna make it, I just know it. God wouldn't have brought him into this world to take him out so young like this," another added.

God...the word hung in the air. How could a good and loving God take a six-month-old from his parents? I thought of the atheism of my upbringing that had sustained me into my twenties with easy answers to such questions. Raised in a culturally Jewish family, we had carried our atheism with passion and pride. Hearing God mentioned instantly transported me to my family's Passover seder. I could see my grandfather at the head of the table, his dark, receding hairline punctuated with gray, his bushy eyebrows that never seemed to end, and the fire in his eyes as he recounted the Jews' escape from slavery. For him and my entire family, it was not God who had enabled the exodus (for we knew with certainty God did not exist), but the political courage of Moses, the courage of an entire people to risk standing up to oppression. I thrilled to this story each year, learning before I knew the words that politics, not religion, is how we determine what is right and just.

Each year the conversation would eventually turn to some rational explanation for how the Jews got across the Red Sea, because we knew with equal certainty it could not have been by a miracle. With his usual irreverence, my father would call out, "I'm sure Moses knew the tide charts." One year my uncle informed us, "I read scientists think an island may have sunk in the Mediterranean, causing the level of the Red Sea to go down." Another year my aunt said she had read they had really crossed the Sea of Reeds, not the Red Sea. And so the kibitzing would go on. I enjoyed the fun and laughter while learning at an early age that science held the answers to how the world really works, soon joining in my own reflexive defense against all references to God.

A voice brought me back, "Doc, why did this happen to Ryan? He didn't do anything wrong. He's just a baby."

If there is no God, there need not be a reason for suffering, for the unfathomable pain Christie, Tom, and their family now confronted. Facing death as a doctor with my patients had stolen from me the easy answers of my upbringing. I needed to respond.

"Ryan's very sick," I began, waiting for the next words to come. "He has an infection that's spread throughout his bloodstream, a bad one." All the faces continued to look at me expectantly. Christie's was the only one with fresh tears. She seemed so strong in that moment, accepting what I knew to be unbearable pain. The others waited for my pronouncement that all was not as bad as it seemed, that this nightmare would have a happy ending. I would fail them. "Though there is always a chance for a miracle, I don't think Ryan's going to make it."

"Aw, Doc," Tom moaned, "it can't be that way. I don't accept it. Ryan's gonna make it. He's got to make it. He's just got to."

"I am so sorry, Tom, but my whole medical experience tells me Ryan is not going to be able to recover from this overwhelming infection." I paused, letting the finality of my statement sink in, but it didn't.

"Doc, you could be wrong. I feel it in my bones that you just might be wrong."

Now I had to pause, because I knew I had been wrong before. Occasionally one of my patients had experienced a miraculous cure not explainable through current medical understanding. Such experiences always gave me pause at a moment like this. Yet there was a quiet knowing I'd felt standing next to Ryan's bed in the ICU. Over the years of training and practice, I'd learned to honor when my medical intuition spoke with such clarity.

As I sat with Ryan's family, that intuition told me it was time for Christie and Tom to say good-bye. Christie knew as well. We sat and talked quietly about the many precious moments in Ryan's short but blessed life, the joy he had brought to their entire family, and the unspeakable pain of having to let him go. Christie cried softly. Tom stared at me with wide, disbelieving eyes. Christie was the first to go back to Ryan's bedside to say good-bye. Tom refused to join her.

"I ain't ready to accept that he's leavin' us. I just can't," he kept repeating. I knew this would make it harder on him when Ryan did die, but I felt there was nothing more for me to offer them that day. I hugged Christie and Tom and told them they could call me at any time.

The call didn't come. All day as I saw patients in the office, images of Ryan kept returning. His puffy little hands, his swollen face, the black tips of his fingers. Despite my lack of a religious upbringing, I experienced an unexpected urge to utter a prayer that Ryan's death be swift and painless, that his suffering not be prolonged, nor that of his family. As I drove home from the office that evening, I couldn't help but think of the few patients who had experienced miraculous cures. Could I be wrong? Could it not be Ryan's time to die? Should I allow myself to feel the hope to which Tom clung so desperately?

But I knew if Ryan survived, the chances of him having severe brain damage from long periods of low blood pressure and the bacteria that had invaded his brain were high. Tragic as it was, I sensed it would be best if Ryan passed quickly.

Morning came without any call from Christie and Tom or from Children's Hospital. I made the early morning trip to see Ryan and again found him hovering on the edge of death. His condition had worsened, and nobody on the ICU's team of doctors and nurses could explain why he had not already died. My heart sank as I saw that his fingers had now blackened all the way up to the first knuckle, the cells in those fingers dying before my eyes. Even if he survived, he would do so without the use of his hands.

I sat with Christie and Tom one more time, freely sharing with them my bafflement at how long and tenaciously Ryan clung to life. At that moment a thought formed that I'd never considered before. Given my upbringing to believe in rational solutions to every problem, and my training as a scientist, I hesitated to give it voice. But in the silence of that ICU waiting room, the thought would not leave me. "Tom," I began haltingly, "I…I don't know if I can even say this, but I wonder if there is a reason Ryan is hanging on."

"What's that, Dr. Sheff?"

"It's you."

"Me? I don't understand what you mean."

"I have a gut sense that Ryan may be hanging on because he somehow senses that you won't be all right if he dies." Was it possible that this six-month-old child, too young to have learned to talk, possessed a consciousness that could understand his dire condition and then hold off death out of love for his grieving father? To have formed this thought felt like a stretch beyond anything I'd previously considered rational or possible. To have given it voice was a leap founded on nothing more than intuition. If shown somehow to be right, it would force me to question so much of what I'd previously known to be true.

Tom's response told me I might be on the right track. "You know how much I don't want little Ryan to die." His face began to contort with rising grief that threatened to overwhelm him. "But I understand what you've been telling us, Doc." Then, barely able to get his quivering lips to say the words, he got out, "I know it's most likely Ryan will die. And I know I'll have to deal with it." And finally, "I certainly don't want Ryan hanging on 'cause of me."

"He may be doing just that. I've never said this to anybody in all my years of practicing medicine, but I am saying it to you. I believe the best thing, the most loving thing you can do for Ryan, is to go to his bedside and tell him you will be OK if he leaves."

"Dr. Sheff, you know I'd do anything for Ryan." Tom was crying now.

"If you think that's the best thing I can do for him now, I'll do it." With that, Tom disappeared into the ICU.

A few minutes later he returned. "I did it," he said, heaving with sobs. "I did what you said. I told Ryan I loved him so much. I told him I loved him, but I didn't want him to stay just 'cause of me. I told him if he needed to go, he could go, and that I would be all right. I told him again how much I loved him, and how much I would miss him, but that I'd be OK if he went where he had to go. I just held his little hand, with those fingers...I held him real gentle not to hurt him. And then I said good-bye."

Tom wailed, and Christie joined him. I sat with both of them, knowing all I could do now was be with them as they felt a pain I could do nothing to lessen. The wails gave way to muffled sobs. Eventually I felt there was nothing more for me to do there.

As I got up to leave, Tom said, "Doc, you've done so much for us. I trust you. I'm going back in and telling Ryan again it's OK for him to leave." After embracing them both, I drove back to my office. The call came two hours later. It was Christie, her voice choking through tears.

"Dr. Sheff, Ryan's gone. Tom sat with him the whole time after you left, telling him he loved him but that it was OK for him to go. He promised Ryan he'd be OK." Her voice trailed off.

"I'm so sorry, Christie. Please tell Tom he did the bravest, most loving thing he could."

As I hung up the phone, I wondered how this had all happened. The scientist in me wanted to say the timing of Ryan's death was just a coincidence. Sometimes it just happens that a person stays alive for days beyond when their physicians expect them to die. It wasn't as if Tom had talked to Ryan and moments later he'd died. Two hours had intervened. Was Tom's releasing Ryan the cause of his time of death or just coincidence? Labeling it a coincidence would preserve my faith in the science in which I'd been trained, but I found that far from a satisfactory scientific explanation. Two hours. This window of time loomed large as I yearned to make sense of Ryan's death, to grasp the truth behind these events. Sitting alone, I wondered if I'd been gifted a glimpse into how our world works, a glimpse that told me the atheism of my upbringing must be called into question. The scientist in me yearned for certainty. The seeker in me knew certainty was not the path to truth.

* * *

I can pinpoint the very moment my journey as a seeker began. My best friend, Bobby, and I had felt our favorite rock beckoning. With the heroic impulsiveness of teenage boys, we had not waited quite long enough for the tide to go out. Each jump from one boulder to the next above the dark, swirling waters of the bay became a test of courage. Finally we clambered up the side of that massive rock, settling into the safety of the saddle at its top, gleeful in our shared audacity. Our heavy breathing slowed almost in unison as we took in the sun's multicolored descent toward the horizon.

Bobby finally broke the silence. "Do you believe in God?"

"Of course not," I answered with a certainty from the upbringing I'd never questioned.

"I'm not so sure," Bobby replied. "What if God actually exists?"

I paused. Until that moment I hadn't really given the question any serious consideration. "Belief in God," I responded, "is just that, a belief, an irrational, unfounded belief. Science will eventually make God obsolete."

"Are you sure?" he persisted.

"Sure I'm sure," I answered but wavering for the first time.

Bobby sensed the shift. "I wish I knew somebody who believed in God, somebody I respected." He paused. "I'm not talking about a person who's always believed in God. Someone who has never profoundly doubted the existence of God can't answer my questions. I'm talking about a person who's deeply questioned whether God exists, who's faced a crisis of faith. Better yet, someone who believed like you, who was sure God didn't exist. If that person could come from there to believe that God exists, now that's something. That's enough to make me consider God just might exist."

We settled back into a shared silence watching the last blazing edge of the sun disappear beyond the darkening bay. *Was such a thing possible?* I wondered. Though I didn't recognize it at the time, in that moment a small door opened somewhere inside me. For the first time in my life, instead of dismissing the existence of God, I pondered it.

* * *

As a family physician, I delivered babies during my early years of practice. That's how I had come to deliver Ryan and become so close with his family. I thought I understood pregnancy and childbirth, at least medically. But when my wife, Marsha, became pregnant, I was not prepared for what I was about to learn.

Marsha and I met at the University of Pennsylvania when I was in medical school and she was studying social work. As I scanned the sea of people at a friend's party, Marsha's fiery eyes and vivacious laugh caught my attention. "Do you want to dance?" I asked as I approached her.

She paused, our eyes locking together. A broad smile lit up her face as she replied, "Sure."

Our first dance…the conversation that followed…everything felt perfect, even though we were very different.

"You're not Italian, are you?" she asked between dances.

"Nope. Jewish." I had an impulse to try to explain to her how I could be both Jewish and an atheist but was too caught up in the growing chemistry between us to quibble over such a distinction.

"I thought so," she responded, taking in my beard and mane of dark curly hair.

"From your question, I take it you're Italian."

"Yup. Italian Catholic, with the emphasis on Italian. You know what that means, don't you?"

"Not really."

"When anyone in my family stubs their toe, everybody says ouch. No boundaries."

"That's about the opposite of mine. Very rational, dinner conversations about science and politics. Too many boundaries to the point of growing up feeling lonely in my own family, even alienated."

Her eyes widened. "You don't seem that way. It must have been hard for you." I wanted to fall into her arms right then. She understood me. After that night, we were almost never apart.

That was the thing about Marsha. She was truly intuitive. She connected with other people. But what happened when she got pregnant with our first child took this to a whole new level. Her best friend, Susan, had gotten pregnant two months before Marsha. While they'd been close before, over the ensuing months it seemed as if each already knew what the other was feeling and thinking.

Then came a moment that changed my life. Susan had gone past her due date and had become increasingly depressed, worried that something might be wrong. One morning at four thirty, Marsha sat bolt upright in bed. "Rick, wake up! Susan is in labor! I know it. I feel tingling energy running up and down my whole body. It woke me up."

"If you think she's in labor, call her," I mumbled, still half asleep.

"What if I'm wrong? I don't want to wake her." This rational perspective finally won out, so Marsha tried going back to sleep, which took some time due to how energized she felt.

The next morning Marsha paced the floor, wondering if she should call Susan. At ten o'clock the phone rang.

"Marsha," Susan's voice exclaimed into the phone, "I'm in labor!"

"I know," came the surprising response.

"What do you mean *you know*?"

"I woke up at four thirty this morning absolutely sure you were in labor."

"That's really strange. I was awakened at four thirty with my first contraction. But I didn't know I was in labor until five."

Marsha had known before Susan. I had witnessed this event. As a scientist, I knew this had to have a rational explanation. But nothing in all the science I'd learned at the university and in medical school could explain it. Marsha had been awakened out of a sound sleep through some kind of connection with Susan who lived seven miles away. This was a fact. Because of this fact, I *knew* the world was not as I had been taught, either by my parents or my science professors. I suddenly knew people could communicate at a distance. Nothing would convince me otherwise. It stood out as an incontrovertible data point that changed everything. I wanted to share it with everybody.

"It's not data. It's just coincidence," one of my fellow physicians replied when I excitedly told him the story.

"What do you mean *coincidence*? The statistical chances of Marsha awakening at precisely the same moment Susan was awakened with her first contraction and Marsha being flooded with energy and knowing that Susan was in labor at that moment are so vanishingly small that something had to cause it. To call this simple coincidence is an outrageous act of faith. It's not good science."

"I believe in Occam's razor, the principle that when faced with multiple possible explanations of the same event, the simplest explanation is the best one. It's certainly simpler to attribute what you've described to coincidence than to start positing that human beings can communicate at a distance telepathically."

Just a coincidence. Occam's razor. I had used those same arguments with others in the past. Yet now I had a data point that couldn't be explained away with these rationalizations. They were frankly not rational. I could see that my friend had a stronger emotional attachment to his current theories about the world than to the truth. I realized he was in good company.

Even scientists fall prey to this problem. Before going to medical school, I had received a scholarship to Oxford University in England to study politics and philosophy. While there, I'd read the work of Thomas Kuhn who recognized that most of the time, scientists work within what he called a dominant paradigm, a way of making sense of the work in any particular field. As fellow physicians, my friend and I shared just such a paradigm at this moment. Scientists go to great lengths, including sometimes acting irrationally, to defend their dominant paradigm, the one in which they trained and within which they had built their careers. My friend, whose career as a physician had been built on the current medical paradigm, was doing just that.

As I reflected on why my friend couldn't see this astounding event as data, I had an aha moment. He and I were both scientists, both believed the world works according to the modern scientific paradigm. We believed the material world is all that exists, so all events in the material world must have a cause in the material world. I now had a data point that had no plausible material-world cause or explanation. Telepathic communication just doesn't fit anywhere in the paradigm of modern science, a paradigm I had fully bought into, at least until now. But any scientific theory or paradigm is just that, a theory. When data and theory don't agree, a good scientist knows the data wins.

What my friend did was not good science. He let his theory win over the data. He reminded me of something else I'd come across during my studies at Oxford. A Harvard philosopher named Willard Van Orman Quine had coined the term *web of belief* to describe the phenomenon I'd just witnessed in my friend. Each of us functions within our own personal web of belief, a network of mutually reinforcing knowledge claims about the way the world works. My friend and I had a shared web of belief. It included agreeing on the truth of what today's science tells us about the world and faith that applying the scientific method will elicit greater knowledge about the "real" world.

Part of our individual and shared webs of belief was the claim that only material phenomena exist, a core claim of the modern scientific paradigm. We now confronted a data point that didn't fit our web of belief, and we each had three choices. My friend chose one option, to not see this as data. He chose to label it coincidence. This meant he could keep his web of belief intact. I had chosen a second option, to recognize this as data, so it took up residence somewhere near the periphery of my web of belief, but it didn't impact any of the core portions of my web. I still believed the world was made of material things and phenomena, but I had this one data point that potentially contradicted it. I realized part of human nature is the capacity to tolerate this kind of inconsistency in our personal web of belief. A third option happens when the number and significance of anomalous data points reaches critical mass, producing a shift in a central portion of the web.

Kuhn said that when this happened in a particular scientific field, scientists working in that field entered a period he called *revolutionary science*. That's when scientists propose and fight over what the new paradigm will be, what will become the organizing structure of the new web of belief in that discipline. We experienced such a period of revolutionary science when Copernicus proposed that the sun, not the earth, was in the middle of the universe. It happened again when Einstein taught us that time and space are not as we thought they were.

As I sat with the knowledge that I'd witnessed Marsha communicate in her sleep over a distance of miles, I confronted a data point that called out for a response, a response based on good science. Was it possible it would require a period of revolutionary science, a time of letting go of the old paradigm and ushering in a new paradigm for all of us? I did not know at the time that this experience with Marsha would be joined over the years by many other challenging experiences, data points that would require the courage of a seeker to recognize them for what they were, glimpses of truth that one day would not just shift my web of belief but shatter it. Marsha's experience with Susan had given me a first glimpse of the new period of revolutionary science into which we are all heading. The seeker in me stirred with anticipation.

CHAPTER II: CRACKS IN THE ARMOR OF CERTAINTY

"You don't believe this crap, do you?"

Marsha and I married in 1982, about a year after I graduated from medical school. We navigated our considerable family and cultural differences by having an Ethical Culture minister officiate. By that time, I had entered my family medicine residency training at Brown University.

During the second year of residency, Tony and Hillary, two physicians married to each other, rejoined our residency group after having left the program several years earlier.

Tony had developed a recurrence of lymphoma, a cancer in the blood. Ten years earlier, when it had first occurred, he had been treated with conventional chemotherapy and had gone into remission. But when the lymphoma recurred during their second year of residency, they left the program to seek the best treatment.

Their search took them into complementary and alternative medicine because conventional medicine had nothing to offer except toxic chemotherapy with little to no chance of a cure. Eventually a strict regimen of diet, herbs, and homeopathy had produced remission, allowing Tony and Hillary to return to our program to complete their training.

Hearing their story brought my ever present skepticism to the fore. The experience of Marsha knowing Susan was in labor would not happen for another three years, so I was not yet prepared to see Tony's healing from his alternative treatments as a data point. Instead I wanted to argue his healing wasn't data, and argue I did.

Tony and Hillary were extremely bright, perhaps even brilliant. They'd gone to Stanford as undergraduates and Johns Hopkins for medical school. I couldn't comprehend how they could consider unproven, alternative treatments when Tony's very life hung in the balance. Besides, I had my own education at Cornell, Oxford, and the University of Pennsylvania School of Medicine to draw on, so I couldn't hold back. One day I decided to ask what to me was an obvious question.

"You two are intelligent. You've had the same medical training I've had. You don't believe this crap, do you?"

They looked at me with completely straight faces as Tony responded, "Of course we do."

"Even homeopathy? Homeopaths dilute their remedies one part in ten to the tenth, ten to the twentieth, and even ten to the thirtieth power." With great self-assurance that I was about to put an end to this nonsense, I concluded, "Based on the chemistry we all learned in high school, there's no chance even one molecule of the original substance can be in one of those remedies. You have to admit they can't possibly be anything but placebos."

Tony and Hillary looked bemused. "Are you familiar with the term *scientism*?" Hillary finally responded.

"No," I replied, wondering how they could not accept the finality of my argument.

"Scientism is the use of the trappings of science in defense of dogma," Hillary went on. "In this case, you assumed, without adequate proof, that matter, the substance all around us, is *only* made up of molecules."

"But that's because it is."

"How do you know this with such certainty? Einstein shocked the world by suggesting matter and energy were interchangeable, something we all now take for granted. What if the energy inherent in matter could be tapped to produce healing?"

"You'd still need molecules to be present for that energy to have any effect," I said.

"Really? How do you know?"

I thought of all the science courses I'd taken, all the experiments conducted by the giants of science over the past four hundred years that had confirmed the molecular and atomic nature of matter. I knew with certainty I was on solid ground. So I pressed the attack. "Matter *is* composed of molecules, which in turn are composed of atoms. Science has predicted how these molecules would interact, and these predictions have been proven true. We're even using electron microscopes to see smaller and smaller particles. Every time we have, we've confirmed the molecular nature of matter."

"We agree with everything you've said. But none of that proves the energy associated with any particular substance cannot have healing effects when the number of molecules is diluted. Your argument against that idea appears to be a matter of faith, faith that molecules and their constituent parts are all that exist. That's an assumption, not something proven by science. Basing your contention on faith in that assumption is a perfect example of scientism, and it's not good science."

Bristling at the suggestion that scientific truth could be based on faith, I marshaled my next argument. "What if homeopathy is based on a claim that is not testable? It then could not be proven or disproven, which makes such a claim inherently unscientific."

This, too, called forth another rejoinder from Tony and Hillary. So the cycle continued, not only long into that evening, but almost nightly for six months. Through our debates, I gained a deeper understanding of the value and limits of science as it is carried out. I came to realize that the medicine I'd been taught was only partially based on science. It was still very much an art. I also came to realize that so much of what I thought was true about health and illness, about what makes people sick and how we try to heal them, is founded on limited and deeply flawed science.

This recognition did nothing to devalue the great strides of modern medicine, such as saving millions of lives through vaccines; astounding, life-saving surgeries; and sanitation improvements.

But I came to see the medicine in which I was training as possessing only a part of the truth about health and illness and what constituted effective treatment. Other healing disciplines, like osteopathy, massage therapy, homeopathy, acupuncture, naturopathy, herbal medicine, nutrition, and chiropractic, also held some truth. Each of these disciplines had developed its own coherent, mutually reinforcing web of belief, theories and knowledge claims about health and illness, just as had the conventional medicine I'd been learning. Some of the theories of these complementary and alternative healing disciplines seemed extremely farfetched, given what I thought I knew about the human body and disease. But I realized I did not have to accept the theoretical explanations promulgated by each healing discipline to consider the possibility that its diagnostic and healing modalities might offer some degree of effectiveness.

When I accepted with humility that everything I thought I knew with certainty would always be embedded in my personal web of belief, and that even what I took to be unshakeable scientific truths turned out to be embedded in the shifting, evolving public web of belief shared by scientists, my world expanded. I came to see all healing disciplines as holding a piece of the truth about health, illness, and healing.

One night, when relating all of this to Marsha, I said, "I owe it to my patients, to my future career in which I seek to become the most effective physician and healer I can, to responsibly explore and apply these other healing disciplines." From them on, I practiced what came to be called integrative medicine, drawing on the best of conventional, complementary, and alternative medicine in an ever-changing mix, always seeking the most effective modalities available to help my patients heal.

* * *

"Why is it so hard for you to accept that reincarnation might be possible?" Hillary asked during one of our epic battles.

I recoiled at the very word. The year was 1983, and to most westerners, including me, reincarnation was an exotic belief belonging to a distant culture. "It's one thing to recognize that diet, herbs, or acupuncture might promote healing of the human body," I protested, "but remember, I was raised an atheist, and I haven't found anything in all your arguments to convince me to believe in God, not to mention believe in a soul that rein-carnates a gazillion times."

"Why is the conviction with which you defend atheism any less an act of faith than someone else's belief in reincarnation?"

"Because I haven't seen evidence of anything spiritual at any time in my entire life. Evidence is what makes a knowledge claim about something different from an act of faith. What people call *spiritual* I have always found to be one of two things. The first is a mystery, which at that point cannot be explained scientifically. Over the past four hundred years, one mystery after another has given way to a clear, provable scientific explanation. So here may be my act of faith: that up until now, science has been so remarkably successful at understanding and explaining our world that it's a good bet that what can't be understood scientifically today will be at sometime in the future. As far as I'm concerned I have evidence to believe that.

"The second set of events that people call spiritual are subjective, in-dividual experiences that can't be validated by anyone else. Part of what defines science is that all data is public and can be critically examined and validated or invalidated by others. It is this public nature of scientific knowledge claims and data to support or refute them that gives science its unique position of getting closer and closer to the truth over time."

"That's a pretty persuasive argument," Tony replied. "But what would happen if *you* had one of those subjective experiences you couldn't explain away scientifically? What if you had a personal experience that showed you our souls live on past death or some other experience that showed past lives were at least possible? Would you be open to reconsidering your current opposition to reincarnation?"

I paused. If I said no, I would be showing just how much my refusing to believe in reincarnation was an act of faith. But I was troubled by allowing an individual subjective experience, even one of my own, to constitute evidence for how the world works. This felt distinctly unscientific. "I suppose so," I answered noncommittally.

"Then I suggest you ask for a sign."

"A what?"

"A sign. Put out a request that you be shown a sign that reincarnation is possible, if not downright probable. If you're uncomfortable asking this of God, however you may understand God, then put it out as a request to the universe," Tony suggested.

The very thought of asking the universe for something felt absurd. The universe as I understood it wasn't capable of responding to a question from any individual. But I was even more uncomfortable asking for something from God because I thought I knew with certainty no such God existed. "Are you telling me to conduct an experiment?" I finally replied.

"If you want to see it that way, it's fine with me."

I mulled the possibilities. If I put out such a request and nothing happened, I could remain comfortably sure reincarnation was a fiction. If I were to be shown a sign, even if I couldn't imagine what a sign might look like, I wasn't sure how such a sign would impact my web of belief. And further, what, if anything, would such a personal experiment have to do with science? Yet I was intrigued. So far Tony and Hillary had been right in helping me see how unnecessarily restrictive my thinking had been. Could they possibly be right about this one? "I'll do it," I said.

Later that night, while Marsha was brushing her teeth, I lay in bed.

Awkwardly I began to formulate the request for a sign. Against great inner resistance I half mumbled the words, "I put out to the universe a request that you show me a sign, a sign that we as human beings reincarnate, a sign there is a realm of the spiritual that is beyond all that we see and know at this time."

Marsha had heard my unintelligible muttering, so when she came into the bedroom, she asked, "Who were you talking to?"

A bit embarrassed, I explained to her the deal I had made with Hillary and Tony.

The next morning nothing happened. The following day nothing happened. In fact, nothing happened for so long that I forgot about my request for a sign. I resumed my busy routine as a family medicine resident. Three weeks later, Mary Sue, an eighteen-year-old woman, showed up on my schedule in the family care center, the outpatient clinic in which all the family medicine residents saw patients. She was there for a pre-employment physical. After recently graduating high school, she had moved to Rhode Island from a rural part of West Virginia, didn't have a doctor, and needed a physical examination to show she was healthy to start her new job. As I went through her medical history, nothing seemed out of the ordinary, except that she said she had nearly drowned three years earlier. She'd recovered without any aftereffects. As I completed the paperwork for her employer, she shifted uneasily in her seat. I looked up, and she looked away. I sensed she wanted to ask a question but was hesitating. As a family physician, I had learned to be on the lookout for questions not asked, as these usually held the key to what was really going on for a patient, often holding the real reason for their visit.

"I get the feeling there is something else you want to ask," I said, creating the opening.

"Thay…Thay is. But I's a little embarrassed askin' it." She hesitated. "I ain' never told nobody this. It's kine a hard to talk about."

"I understand that some things can be hard to talk about, especially if you've never told anybody before," I said. This was often how experiences of abuse, suicidal thoughts, or homosexuality came to light, so I was prepared for any of these. I was not prepared for what occurred next.

"I ain' never told nobody what happen' when I almos' drown."

"Go on," I said, not knowing where this was headed.

"When I's under water, I done wen' somewhere."

"What do you mean you 'went somewhere'?"

"It was like I wasn' under the water no more. I was in some kine a tunnel. At the end of the tunnel, I done seen a light. As it got closer, I felt like everythin' was gonna be OK. It felt amazin'. I just stayed in the light awhile. Then suddenly I was back. Not under water no more, but thay was workin' on me, an' I woke up. When I got better I started tellin' people what happened, but in my little hometown they all thought I's crazy, so I din't tell nobody the whole story. Nobody done heard the whole story 'til today." She looked at me hesitantly. "You think I's crazy?"

"No. No. I don't think you're crazy." I had trouble getting the words out. Here was a young woman from rural West Virginia telling me a classic life-after-death story that she had personally lived through. I'd heard about such things but had never met anybody who'd actually experienced one. Before I could decide what to make of this, I needed some questions answered. I knew that articles in the popular press had been written about near-death experiences, including descriptions of individuals seeing light and a tunnel, so I asked, "Have you ever read anything about near-death experiences?"

"No. I ain' knowed thay's any such thin'," relief already beginning to show on her face for my not condemning her for what she had shared.

"Have you heard anyone else talk about their experiences with near death, the tunnel, or the light?" I persisted, seeking some bias.

"No. No. You mean other people who jes' 'bout died like me go through a tunnel an' see that light too?" Her reaction told me her experience hadn't been tainted by reading a book or article or hearing about near-death experiences on TV or radio. She had been too isolated for that. And in the early 1980s, discussions of a tunnel and light were not nearly as widespread as they are in pop culture today. Having adequately determined that Mary Sue's description of the experience had not been influenced by reports from others, I had to conclude it was authentically her own.

Though I was fascinated with Mary Sue's story, it wasn't until later that night that its potential import struck home.

"Perhaps this is the sign you asked for," Marsha said.

I'd practically forgotten about asking for a sign, but this certainly could qualify as a sign that something about us lives on after death. Until that point, no other patient had ever shared a near-death story with me. "I don't know, Marsha. Perhaps the tunnel and light images experienced by near-death patients are a result of the physiology of the dying brain. Am I reading too much into this because I want this to represent proof of something that could be called spiritual?"

Marsha didn't answer, knowing that I had to mull this over for myself, but in that moment, a crack opened in the armor of certainty that had surrounded the atheistic worldview in which I'd been raised. But it was only a crack.

CHAPTER III:
DIALOGUE WITH OTHER HEALERS

"Dad! Dad! Something inside my ankle is moving!"

Marsha had given birth to a beautiful boy we named Sam. Now three years old, he loved wrestling with me. I had just picked him up and thrown him onto the couch, one of his favorite games, when his squeal of glee was interrupted by the phone ringing. I found my old college roommate, Ezra, on the other end of the line. "Rick, what are you doing next weekend?"

"Nothing's booked. What do you have in mind?"

"I've been invited to join a group of healers from different disciplines to share our perspectives on what healing is, and I thought you and Marsha would be great additions."

A few days later, sitting on the lawn of a rolling estate in central Massachusetts, I looked around at the unusual group of individuals who had gathered to explore the nature of healing. This gathering was the brainchild of Peter, an open-hearted man in his sixties, and his physician, George. They had felt frustrated with the limitations of the biomedical model and wanted to explore health and illness, and caring and healing, from as broad a collection of perspectives as possible.

It appeared they would succeed. The group included two physicians, George and me; a half dozen mental health specialists of various types including Ezra, as well as Marsha who was now a licensed clinical social worker and practicing therapist; and several energy healers. The energy healers strained my credulity, and I could only roll my eyes when one woman introduced herself as a psychic. Images of a turban-wrapped, old matron sitting in a dark room, reading palms, came to mind. It was hard to take her seriously.

The discussion began with an obvious opening question: What is healing? The therapists joined in first.

"Healing is about becoming a whole person," one of them began.

"For me it's less about becoming a whole person than an authentic person," Marsha responded. "When one of my clients trusts me enough to drop their false persona and let their true self out, they literally blossom into their authentic selves."

"Why do they trust you?" I prompted.

Marsha paused to reflect before answering. "They know I accept them, that I won't criticize them as others in their life have. At its deepest level, it's love. I love them unconditionally as they've always wanted to be loved. That's what allows the therapy process to be a form of re-parenting for them, providing the love they had missed at critical moments in their past."

"So their response to love from you is their own healing," I chimed in.

"Yeah, that's a good way of putting it," Marsha responded.

"You're on to something," I kept going. "For me, healing is about love."

"Say more," came the response from Peter.

"Like Marsha, I sit with patients, but in the role as their family doc. I ask them to tell me their stories. On one level, I'm listening for information to diagnose their physical condition so I can prescribe the best medical treatment. But on another level, when I'm doing good doctoring,

I'm offering something similar to what Marsha is. Part of my training as a family physician is to ask the question behind the question, to get to the deeper reason the person before me is seeking help." I thought of Mary Sue, the young woman who had wanted to tell someone what she had experienced when she had almost drowned. "More often than not I find that question. The result is a similar blossoming to what Marsha portrayed. I sometimes describe the response I see in my patients as the joy of being truly listened to. Every patient wants this from their doctor. It doesn't replace technical competence, but it's critical for their healing."

"Rick, you've helped me realize I try to do the same thing with my patients," George said, "but I've never put it in those words before."

"But there's something more." I paused, an image of Tom holding Ryan's tiny hand rose before me. "I've had patients suffer a terrible loss, have their hearts broken. I've helped some of them through the grieving process. Their extraordinary capacity to heal from the greatest tragedies fills me with awe. A crucial ingredient for this healing to occur seems to be love."

This triggered an animated exchange among all members of the group as each shared experiences of times when love had played a critical role in healing for their clients and patients, and even for themselves. At one point I made an observation. "It's clear that for each of us these moments when love played such an important role in healing have been some of the most gratifying moments in our careers as healers. I can sense that for everyone here, we each experience a calling to love our fellow human beings. The question is why? Why *should* we love another person?

"At some level, both individually and as a society," I went on, "we base our ethics, our moral choices, on something like the Golden Rule, to love others as we love ourselves. But why? I was raised an atheist. I'm still an atheist, though with a few more questions. I'm not prepared to accept the 'reason' to love another is because God said so. I know of too many instances in history when someone's interpretation of what God said was used to justify acts that couldn't be further from love or the Golden Rule. Yet something inside me feels like it almost *calls* me to love all others. In fact, you could say this calling, this belief in love, comes as close to a belief in anything as my atheist upbringing has allowed. For as long as I can remember, I have felt this sense that loving others is what I am here to do."

I felt an urgency now and couldn't seem to stop talking. Since no one interrupted me, I continued. "At the age of five, while walking to kindergarten, a stray cat started to follow me. It looked cold and hungry, so I stopped to pet it. As it rubbed its shivering body up against my hand and then my leg, I was overwhelmed with an impulse to do something to relieve this poor animal's suffering. Instead of walking on to school, I turned around and brought the cat home. My mother was more than surprised to find me at the front door saying, 'Can we give this cat some milk? She's hungry and cold.'

"Whatever the source that impelled me to do something caring in the face of the cat's suffering, that is what I am talking about. I chose a career in medicine because of that drive inside me. It literally hurts me to see another suffer, and I immediately want to do something to help. I sense you all feel the same way. But why? Is it just the conditioning of our upbringing? Is it some personality trait we have and others do not, or perhaps something in our DNA that provides a survival advantage for our species? Is it a rational choice because we recognize that if we all make the same choice we will all be happier? Or is it something deeper? Until now I've found an answer to this question in *existentialism*, in the perspective that everything we do is a choice and that we define ourselves by the choices we make. I believe whether or not to love another is always a choice, a moral choice. I'm not talking about loving another romantically. That's driven by whether or not the other person pleases me. Romantic love is far too conditional and ephemeral, and it's proven not to be a source of lasting happiness for so many. I'm talking about something that could be called existential love, that arises from the freely made choice to love another because they are a fellow human being, or, in the case of the cat, a fellow being.

"The question I've struggled with most of my life is, Why *should* I, why *should* each of you, or why *should* anyone choose to act this way? I went to Oxford with the burning need of a young man to find an answer to this question. I yearned to know the truth about all that is, and from that truth, how we can establish an unshakeable foundation for ethics, for this kind of love, with the answer not depending upon proclamations from a willful God. The same source of authority, God, has been claimed both for the Golden Rule and for so many heinous acts throughout history. So 'because God said so' cannot be an adequate answer for how we know the truth and why we should love another. I left Oxford realizing the academic study of such questions generated ever more questions, but not a satisfactory foundation for truth and ethics. Yet the urgency to find such a foundation has never left me."

Without skipping a beat, and with what I thought was a bizarre response to my outpouring, Valerie, the psychic, asked, "You see that smiling woman under the tree over there?"

I didn't see anyone under the tree.

"You mean the old woman with the white shawl and black hat?" Leah, one of the energy healers, asked.

"Yes, that's her. She's been sitting there smiling at us for a while, clearly approving of all that's been happening here."

"That sounds like my grandmother," Peter said perfectly naturally while I gaped. "We've got pictures of her in the house."

Minutes later my mouth still hung open as Peter turned the pages of the family album. "That's her. That's who's been watching us," Valerie said.

"I remember her sitting under that tree when I played here as a child," Peter responded. Then, as if it were an afterthought, he added, "She's been dead for forty years."

I wasn't sure if I had suddenly been shown an outrageous new data point or if half the people in this group I'd just joined were nuts.

* * *

Our son, Sam, was an unusual child. Verbally precocious, he stunned us when, at the age of twenty months, he used the word *actually* correctly. But that was not as stunning as the series of events that unfolded shortly after our first meeting with the group of healers.

One day Marsha was working in the kitchen when she heard Sam talking in the hallway. When he entered the kitchen, she asked whom he was talking to.

"The little boy," he casually answered. As he had never previously had any imaginary friends, Marsha's interest was piqued.

"What little boy?" she asked.

"The little boy whose mommy and daddy died." As a therapist, this certainly increased her interest.

"Which little boy is that?" she asked, wanting to draw out whatever fears or anxieties she assumed underlay this fantasy he had created. But her psychological training had not prepared her for his response.

"A long, long time ago when I was a grown-up Indian, I knew a little boy whose mommy and daddy died," he responded matter-of-factly.

Marsha was astonished. Before she could say anything else, Sam walked out of the room and went back to playing with his toys. He never again mentioned the boy, being an Indian, or anything else related to this incident.

Several months later, Sam sat drawing pictures with his babysitter, Alice. She was a good artist, and he enjoyed describing a scene and asking her to draw it. "Alice," he said, "draw a picture of a little boy."

"What is the little boy doing?"

"He's holding a bird."

Alice drew the scene of a little boy who looked remarkably like Sam standing in the grass, holding a small bird. Sam looked at the picture for a while, finally breaking the silence by saying, "Write 'Hold a bird, see its life, then let it go.'" Alice dutifully wrote these words at the bottom of the picture, not sure what they meant.

Marsha and I stared at the picture as Alice told the story, feeling it represented another moment whose import we could not grasp. We placed the picture on our refrigerator.

There it sat for several months until one day when Sam, playing in the garden, came upon a small bird. Through the sliding glass door in the kitchen, Alice watched Sam approach the bird cautiously.

"Cheep...cheep...cheep," he quietly cooed. The bird hopped a few feet away and looked back at him. "Cheep...cheep...cheep," he repeated, getting closer. It stayed where it was. Sam bent down and cupped the bird in his hands. Bursting with excitement, he ran to the house calling, "Alice! Alice!"

"What is it, Sam?"

"A bird! A bird!" he shouted, barely able to contain himself. Alice felt sad for the bird, assuming it had been injured, which would be the only way Sam could have caught it. As Sam opened his hands to show Alice the precious prize, the bird spread its wings and flew away through the open glass door.

Alice stood dumbfounded. Sam had caught a perfectly healthy bird in his bare hands, held it for a moment of sheer glee, and then let it go. She stared at the picture on the refrigerator she'd drawn months earlier. The words, "Hold a bird, see its life, then let it go" jumped out at her from the picture. Later that day when she and Sam recounted the story, Marsha and I could do nothing but shake our heads in wonder. Labeling these events a coincidence was not even an option. I did not know how to connect them to everything else I took to be true. The feeling was both unsettling and exciting.

* * *

Looking at my patient schedule for the morning, I smiled seeing Christie's name. It had been eighteen months since Ryan had died. Christie had come in for a few appointments soon after his death, and our talks seemed to have helped her through her almost overwhelming grief, but I hadn't seen her for a year. In that time, Marsha and I had had our second son, Michael. He had been very much wanted, though his being a terrible sleeper had made our lives challenging and exhausting. Christie was glad to hear the news of our new son and had news of her own.

"Dr. Sheff," she began a little hesitantly, "when you do my exam today, can you take out my IUD?"

"Is it causing cramping or heavy bleeding?"

"No, it's not that." She paused. "I think I'm ready to have another baby."

"Really? You're ready?"

"Tom and I talked about it. It's time we got back to building the family we wanted when we had Ryan. Tom's a lot older than me, and we thought we shouldn't put it off any longer."

"I'm so happy for both of you," I said, handing Christie a tissue as a tear fell down her cheek. We laughed softly together. No further words were needed. I was aware of love hanging in the air between us and wondered at its power—from me to Christie, between Tom and Christie, and from so many others—to have helped accomplish this healing. With their own courage and with love from those myriad sources, Christie and Tom had healed enough from Ryan's death to fully open their hearts again.

This time she had an easy pregnancy. Tom stayed by her side throughout the birth of their beautiful baby daughter, Shannon. Again, I served as Shannon's doctor. All was well until Christie brought Shannon in for her well-child visit at nine months old. "Dr. Sheff, can you check Shannon's hearing? I'm not sure she's hearing so good."

I went through the initial screening tests, starting with making a noise behind Shannon and to the side. She didn't turn her head. I increased the volume of the noise. When she didn't respond, I grew concerned. With a sinking feeling, I finished the last of my screening tests and confirmed Christie's fear. "I am so sorry," I began. As a doctor, I'd delivered bad news many times, yet few had felt so personal. "It breaks my heart…," I couldn't continue.

"No need to finish," Christie said in a quiet voice. After giving her a referral to the best pediatric hearing specialist I knew, we hugged each other without words.

I stepped out of the exam room, turning to go into the next room for the patient waiting for me there, but instead I slumped into the nearest chair, grief for Christie, Tom, and Shannon threatening to overwhelm me. "Why?" I whispered half out loud. Instinctively I looked up, though I still held no belief in God or any power guiding our lives. "Why...?" No answer came.

* * *

"Want to go to a channeling?" Marsha asked. "Valerie, from the healing group, told me about it."

"What's a *channeling*?" I asked.

"It's when somebody serves as a medium, allowing the voice of a person who is no longer alive to speak through them."

I resisted the urge to roll my eyes because I didn't want to upset Marsha, so with a bemused sense of adventure, I responded, "I'm game." Not long after, we gathered with a dozen others in an unpretentious living room, studying the man who had been introduced as Mark Johnson, our channeler for the evening. A modestly attractive man in his mid-forties, he spoke with a friendly ease. Nothing about him seemed odd. Absent were the dark curtains I'd remembered from grainy old black and white movies with séances. Absent was the heavy table that might rise mysteriously. Everything about this man and this moment seemed normal, at least until the channeling began.

Mark closed his eyes and took several deep breaths. When he opened his eyes, a completely different voice emerged. "Da yeh hev any questions?" the voice asked congenially. The accent was odd and hard to place, a cross between an Irish brogue and an eastern European inflection. The pitch was somewhat higher than Mark's natural voice with a pleasing lilt. I studied him carefully and wondered if he was acting. I watched for an occasional minor slip in the consistency of the accent, but it never happened. Slowly I found myself drawn into the content of what I was hearing.

"My son and I seem to be caught in a pitched battle," a man in the group was saying. "I don't understand why we fight over everything."

"Ah," the voice replied, "yeh and yer son hev come t'gether in this life to work through en event that occurred meny lifetimes ago." This voice, or the being generating it through the channeler, seemed to take reincarnation as a given. "The two of yeh hed a chance encounter 'n the desert. You fell inta a quarrel. At the end of the fight he staked yeh ta the ground, leaving yeh ta die from the sun, the heat, and the fire ants. That is why everything between yeh feels like a fight ta the death. Hev yeh not been heving dreams of this?" the voice asked.

"I have had a recurring dream...a nightmare...I am struggling... afraid...I always see a harsh line in the dream, but I can never make sense of what I'm seeing."

"That line, as yeh call it, is the horizon as yeh saw it when staked ta the ground. Yeh and yer son have much karma ta work out between yeh. Yer work in this lifetime is ta forgive him. His work is ta accept what he's done and ta forgive himself. Until yeh each do this, yeh will continue ta fight. Yeh understand now why it feels like a fight ta the death each time, do yeh not?"

"Yes..."

"And yeh wish it ta be different, do yeh not?"

"Yes...Yes I do."

"Then open yer hart ta yer son. He knows nothing o' this, yet he reacts ta yeh from it every day." The voice paused. "Opening yer hart is the work we are here ta do. We are all imperfect. We do much ta hurt each other. Yet it is through opening the hart in the face of our imperfections that we grow."

During the ride home with Marsha, I gave voice to the cascading questions this experience provoked. "I'm trying to figure out what we just witnessed. Is Mark simply an excellent actor, capable of pulling off a flawless accent for hours at a time?"

"Rick, even though I'm no longer a practicing Catholic, I'm fine accepting we have a soul and that after we die, a soul could communicate through a channeler like Mark."

"Clearly I'm not there. I'm wondering if he made up that story on the spot about the man and his son having had a chance encounter lifetimes ago that would explain the intense fights between father and son. Such fighting is not uncommon, and perhaps Mark has a supply of similar alleged past life stories upon which to draw in response to this common situation. What I can't explain is the knowledge the voice seemed to have of this man's dreams...Wait a minute. Perhaps that man who asked the question about his son was a shill in collusion with Mark to create the illusion of channeling."

"Rick, don't you think you may be taking this skeptic thing a little too far?"

"I'm struggling to figure out what to do with that...that...whole thing we just saw. I can't get the image out of my head...two men in a chance encounter provoking each other into a lethal fight, one leaving the other staked out in the desert to die a painful, tortured death. I'm sure that kind of stuff did and still does happen. It's the same story for all the pain and suffering we humans inflict upon each other again and again. Why do we do this if we are here to learn to open our hearts? There's certainly enough suffering in the world to open everyone's hearts without us adding to it." I suddenly saw an image of Christie holding Shannon, feeling her heart break upon hearing her child was deaf. I wondered if Ryan's death and Shannon's deafness might have provided lessons for Christie, Tom, and even me, to open our hearts. Could this be the reason for human suffering? Do our hearts need to break to grow?

Sensing the thoughts I was not sharing, Marsha added, "The voice speaking through Mark implied that encountering our own imperfections and the imperfections of others is how we learn to open our hearts."

"Seems a strange and cruel way to teach someone about love...," my voice trailed off. We drove the rest of the way home in silence, each taking in what we'd just experienced. I could only wonder where this data point would eventually come to fit in my now shifting web of belief.

* * *

Shannon laughed as she rapidly signed to Christie her response to my question. At the age of five, she'd already shown herself to be bright and a very fast learner of both sign language and lip reading. She sat happily in Christie's lap for her well-child visit. Despite bilateral hearing aids, she had profound hearing loss, making her almost completely deaf. Yet once Christie and Tom had gotten over the initial shock of learning of her deafness, they'd shown amazing resilience in adjusting and creating a family filled with love. Each time I saw them in my office, I felt I was being shown another lesson in how hardships can help open our hearts to love. I was about to be shown another.

"Dr. Sheff," Christie began as we were finishing Shannon's visit, "I'm worried about Tom. He's got a cough that just won't go away."

"You know I've talked to him for years about quitting cigarettes. Please tell him to make an appointment to see me."

A few weeks later, I sat alone with Tom in an exam room. "How long has this cough been going on?" I started.

"A few months," he responded.

"Any shortness of breath?"

"Nope."

"Any chest pain?"

"Nope."

"Coughing anything up?"

"Nothin' more than usual. You know I've been smokin' for years, so coughin' stuff up isn't anything different."

"Do you ever cough up any blood?"

"Sometimes."

I stopped. Until now, this had been a routine assessment for a cough. Coughing up blood was anything but routine. My concern rose. That concern turned to alarm when his chest X-ray revealed a mass. Further tests showed it to be lung cancer, and it had already spread to his liver. Christie joined him for the follow-up appointment to learn the results of his tests.

One more time I sat with Christie and Tom. One more time I had to share heartbreaking news. Tom was the first to respond.

"Doc, I kinda suspected somethin' like this. I had a feelin'…"

I looked over at Christie. It was clear she'd suspected it as well. Again, a silent tear made its way down her cheek, yet she communicated that quiet strength I had seen before. Sad as the news was, I knew she and Shannon would be OK. But that did not lessen the pain of sharing the news or receiving it.

At the time, the type of chemotherapy Tom received was given in the hospital, so I had the chance to visit with him each time he came for treatment. He lost more and more weight, making it clear he would lose this fight with cancer. One morning as I entered his hospital room, Tom seemed agitated.

"Doc…Doc…I don' know what happened. This mornin' I was lyin' in this bed and the wall over there," he pointed to the opposite wall of his hospital room, "that wall wasn't there. It like melted away. Standin' there I saw my mom and dad…you know they're both gone…and my older brother who died…they're all there…" His voice trailed off, as if he were seeing them again.

I waited a moment, not sure how to respond. I certainly didn't see anything different in his hospital room. Finally I said, "How did it feel to see them?"

"Kinda OK. I know which way this cancer's goin'. It sorta felt like they were lettin' me know where I'm headin' ain't so bad." I waited, a question forming, but I wasn't sure I should ask. The answer came without my prompting. "I…I was hopin' I'd see little Ryan…" He paused, fighting back tears. "But I don' think he was with all those people I saw…" Again he drifted off, as if he were seeing something I could not.

Tom died six weeks later. When I received the call, sad though it was, I felt grateful for the privilege practicing medicine afforded me, the privilege of sharing with my patients the journeys of birth, life, illness, and death in their raw, most honest expression. Tom, along with my other patients, gifted me with moments like the one we'd shared in his hospital room, moments that touched me and taught me, moments that gradually accumulated as data points that stripped away the simple answers of my youth and showed me truth is not so easily discerned.

* * *

By this point, I found myself eager for new experiences that would further challenge my old beliefs. So when Tony and Hillary invited us to a weekend retreat with a gifted spiritual teacher, Marsha and I gladly accepted.

As the weekend came to a close and we gathered to say good-bye, the teacher turned to the facilitators who had helped lead the retreat to ask if they had any final thoughts to share. When it came her turn, a soft-spoken woman began, "I am of Jewish background, raised on the stories of the Torah. I have been struck by those stories that speak to moments in our own lives. When Moses stood before the burning bush and the voice of God called his name, he responded with one word. '*Hineni.*' No one expression in English can capture the meaning of this Hebrew word, but hineni is best translated as 'Here am I.' God was calling upon Moses to lead the people of Israel out of slavery. Moses did not feel up to the task to which God called him, yet he still answered, 'Hineni.' When God called to Abraham, he did not know what God would ask of him, yet he responded, 'Hineni.' God asked Abraham to sacrifice his only son, Isaac. Rather than shrink from what God asked of him, his response remained 'Hineni.' Then, just as he was about to lower his hand to take the life of his son, God again called out Abraham's name, and again he responded, 'Hineni.' It was then that God asked him to spare his son.

"I cannot claim to have heard the voice of God. But I have experienced moments in my life when I have faced a challenge that felt beyond me. In those moments I have set my intention to respond, 'Hineni. Here am I,' for it is in those moments that I experienced God calling me. When I adopt the stance of hineni, I find myself in an undefended state, open to what will come next without any foreknowledge of what that will be. When I respond, 'Hineni,' I experience a complete presence in the now to say yes to whatever the universe is going to ask of me, no matter what it may be. I am no longer afraid of what will be. I surrender to it. Hineni."

Her soft voice and diminutive stature belied the strength of spirit that spoke through her. Her words left me shaken, unsure if I could adopt hineni if called to do so by events beyond my control. Raised on a steady diet of parental guidance that had emphasized hard work and self-reliance, the ego I'd invested a lifetime honing to great effectiveness was not prepared to take a back seat to anyone or anything. Yet through this woman's expression of surrender, the word *hineni*, with roots in an ancient heritage into which I'd been born, became planted in the consciousness of this rational scientist.

* * *

Marsha and I struggled over whether to raise our sons within any religious tradition, and if so, which one. My harsh atheism had softened only a little, and I still had scant experience with the Jewish religion to pull me in. Marsha had turned her back on Catholicism after the nuns in her Catholic school had shown so little compassion and so much vicious blame during her parents' divorce when she was nine. Neither of us felt drawn to raise our sons in the religion into which we had been born.

My younger brother, Daniel, had married into a family with deep connections to Judaism, so a few years after he and his wife had wed, I found myself in a reform Jewish temple attending a baby-naming ceremony for his daughter. Sam, now six, had been excited to dress up in a jacket and tie for the first time. He readily added a yarmulke as we entered the synagogue, wanting to look just like the adult men who milled about waiting for the service to begin.

Marsha looked up and saw Sam walking across the back of the temple with his other cousins. "That's it!" she called out almost a little too loudly.

"That's what?" I asked.

"That's the look…Sam…Looking like that…all dressed up…with the yarmulke. It's just somehow right. We're supposed to raise the boys Jewish."

"Really?"

"I'm sure of it."

So the decision was made, and in a manner that allowed me to preserve all my ambivalence. That ambivalence faded a little when we found a nearby temple that embraced interfaith couples. I was even more pleased to discover they held a pickup softball game every Sunday morning. For the rest of that summer, playing softball each weekend became as much of a religious tradition as any I'd experienced before. I also developed great relationships with the men and women who came out each week to participate.

When it came time to attend temple services for Rosh Hashanah, the Jewish New Year that occurs in the early fall, I had a new experience. For the first time as I entered a synagogue, I found myself warmly greeted by people I knew, people who cared about me and I about them. It gave a completely different feel to sitting through services. I felt a sense of community that made me want to learn the prayers, learn Hebrew. The temple had a wonderfully loving, warm rabbi who had a great sense of humor. His sermons proved thought provoking and entertaining. Gradually, I claimed my first connection with the religion of Judaism.

I was still not comfortable with any belief in God and felt gratified to find a surprisingly large number of fellow members in this reform temple shared the same discomfort. I also found the language I kept hearing in the services about the Jews being a chosen people, somehow different than all others in the eyes of this God, clashing with my deep sense that we are all equal, all equally deserving of love and respect, and that no one group could or should lay claim to being preferred over any other. In spite of these misgivings, I came to look forward to each experience I shared with this caring community, even religious services in a temple.

* * *

At the next meeting of our healers' group, Peter introduced Arthur, a round-faced man in his fifties who was purportedly a highly accomplished energy healer, whatever that was. "I assume you are all familiar with the *chakra* system," he began.

"That would not be an accurate assumption," I interrupted. "What's a chakra?"

"Chakra is a Sanskrit term for the energy centers in our subtle body," he responded.

"What do you mean, 'our subtle body'?" I said, somewhat incredulously.

"Each of us has a subtle body that is part of who we are."

"How do we know this subtle body exists?" I pushed back. "We can't see it, and our scientific instruments can't measure it."

"Some people see the subtle body through auras. Others feel the subtle body."

"But why doesn't everyone see and feel this subtle body if it is there all the time? Why don't I see or feel it?"

"Though some people have a natural capacity for seeing and feeling this energy, everyone is capable of it. It's not an exceptional trait. It does take some training, and the sensations for seeing and feeling it are, as the name implies, subtle compared to other sensations."

Positing a subtle body I couldn't see or feel didn't sit right. I only humored Arthur as he invited us to work on Barbara, one of the other members of our group who was battling a severe illness that had not been adequately diagnosed despite many medical tests. I found myself standing at the edge of a massage table on which Barbara lay.

"Leah, you can work on her feet," Arthur instructed. "Peter, come up to work at the head of the table. Rick, you can work in the middle. For now, simply hold your hands about one to two feet off her body and see if you can feel her energy field."

Feel her energy field? I didn't feel anything. I moved my hands above her abdomen. Nothing. But as I moved my hands about eighteen inches above Barbara's chest, I felt something push back. Moving my hands along the surface of whatever was pushing back, I felt a rounded contour. I had my eyes closed but sensed that I was somewhere over her heart. I could push down on whatever this was, and I could feel it pushing back up at me. Yes, the sensation was subtle, but it was definitely there. A smile broke out across my face. I was feeling energy! I let my hands float up in response to the force and pushed against it in return. My hands slowly moved up and down one to two feet above her body, engaging in what seemed like a dance with her subtle energy. I let myself take in this powerful data point, and my smile widened.

Suddenly Arthur was at my side. He pushed me away from the table. "I'll explain later," he said abruptly. With a look of concern on his face, he rushed to the head of the table, moving his hands in what appeared to be a purposeful manner, but I had no sense of what he was actually doing. Next he moved to the feet. Then he returned to the head. After about ten minutes, he seemed to relax.

Later he pulled me aside. "Rick, I had to stop you. You were draining her energy badly."

"I was what?" I said alarmed.

"While you were playing with her energy, you were pulling more and more of it away from her. Whatever her illness is, it's resulted in her having very low energy in her subtle body. Though she had enough energy to push against your hands, this effort drained energy from elsewhere in her energy field, and that energy drain was taking a big toll on her. I recognized the mask of death on her face. That, too, is something with training you can recognize in the subtle body because it is unmistakable. I had to run energy back into her, building up her depleted subtle body. It took me a while to stabilize her and get her energy back up to a level that was no longer dangerous."

Dangerous? Even eighteen inches away from Barbara's body my hands were dangerous? My exhilaration turned into alarm. Could this subtle energy be that powerful?

"The energy of another human being is not something you play with. It is their vital force," Arthur explained. "Treat it with respect. Learn to work with it and you will deepen the healing you can offer to others. You have started on a lifelong journey to understand and work with the subtle energy field of the body. Undertake this journey with the seriousness and integrity it deserves."

I wondered what journey he was talking about. Having felt energy, having experienced a force I could not explain by science, I was forever changed. Whatever this energy might be, it was real. I did not need a controlled study published in a peer-reviewed scientific journal to prove it. My personal experience already had.

* * *

Sam's scream launched me into a full sprint to the backyard. As I cradled him in my arms, he wailed, "It hurts! It hurts!"

"What hurts?"

"There! My ankle! Owww!"

"What happened to it?" I asked as I carried him into the house.

"When I jumped off the fence, my foot got caught under it. I rolled, but my foot didn't roll with me," he finally got out.

I held him in my arms on the couch, his head buried in my shoulder, still sobbing. Reaching down with my free hand, I gingerly examined his ankle.

"Owww! That's it!" he cried out when I pressed lightly, confirming my fear that he had likely broken his ankle.

I wanted to do something, anything, to take away my son's pain. Only weeks earlier, I'd felt subtle energy while working on Barbara. I now wondered if that newfound ability could help my son. Without any sense of what I was supposed to do, I held my hand a few inches away from his ankle and envisioned pulling out the energy of the pain. With my hovering hand, I made a pulling motion, consciously forming the intention to draw the pain energy out of his ankle. Sam's head remained buried in my shoulder. His sobs quieted to soft crying as I continued the pulling motion.

Suddenly he said, "Dad! Dad! Something inside my ankle is moving!"

I had not touched his ankle. It had been perfectly still. Yet my son had felt something move! With his head buried in my shoulder, he couldn't have seen my hand moving. His X-ray eventually showed a hairline fracture, but nothing displaced or that could account for his sense of movement. My simple intention and pulling motion had created the sensation of movement. Once again calling this coincidence felt completely out of place. I could not conceive of a mechanism that would link my intention and actions to my son's sensation, but I knew with certainty that he had felt it. Another data point took up uneasy residence in my web of belief. That web was shifting, and the inexplicable data points began moving closer to the center of the web.

CHAPTER IV: CRISIS

"You, Marsha, and Nancy got together before this life and decided to do the dance this way."

I am not the first person to experience the searing pain of betrayal by learning that my spouse had had an affair and fallen in love with somebody else. But that did not make the moment of Marsha's telling me any less heartbreaking. That she had fallen in love with a woman added confusion to my anguish, her explanation that she was bisexual, equally attracted to men and women, providing no comfort. With the pain and confusion came an intolerable sense of public humiliation. I felt the whole world saw my shame and judged me for it. I could not stay in Marsha's presence. Though six inches of snow covered the ground, I raced out of the house. I needed to be alone.

In a wooded area near our home, I plodded through the snow, up and down hills, seeking some way to be with the new reality of my life. I reached down and lifted a large, fallen branch. With a sudden surge of energy, I swung it against the nearest tree. The shattering thwack and exploding pieces physically expressed the roiling emotions that threatened to overwhelm me. I lifted another large branch and smashed it against a tree. The impact shot through my body as a three-foot section broke off and flew through the air. I swung another, and another, and another. My arms tired, but I could not stop. The cold air burned my lungs, and my legs ached as I pushed on looking for more tree limbs to destroy. Two hours later, finally spent and exhausted, I trudged back home to face a new truth.

As a weary numbness began to surround the pain, fear emerged, fear that if this crisis ended our marriage, Sam and Michael, now only six and three, would be scarred by the divorce of their parents. As I opened the door to our home, their gleeful shouts of "Daddy, Daddy, pick me up!" and "Daddy, let's wrestle!" tore open a new wound more intolerable than the pain of Marsha's revelation.

I needed time and space. I'd heard of Kripalu, a yoga and healing center in the Berkshire Mountains. It seemed the best place to care for myself and prepare for helping my sons. I booked three days of rest and renewal. I needed both.

* * *

Struggling to bend backward in the camel posture, I groaned. It hurt.

"Feel the *prana* flow through you," intoned the yoga instructor to my class. "It is the source of true bliss."

I felt anything but bliss. The rain falling on the windowpane seemed to amplify my misery. What did this angelic young woman who moved so effortlessly know of my heartbreak? Not only could I not feel the prana, whatever that was, but I could not stop my mind from racing. Thoughts of Marsha with…what was her name? Oh yes, Nancy. Thoughts of Marsha having passionate sex with Nancy played over and over in my mind, opening again the fresh, hot wound of my humiliation. Hadn't she freely taken the marital vow to forsake all others?

"Let your mind melt into sensation," the instructor encouraged. I felt plenty of sensation...aches in my chest, hips, and back. "Go to the edge of what you can tolerate. But do so with gentleness. Feel the sensations, but know they are only energy."

I focused on the stretch through the front of my thighs. They began to quiver. Was that what she meant by *energy*?

"As you bend backward, let your head drop, and open your chest to the sky. Feel the release of all the pain you have stored here, in your heart chakra. Feel your heart open...allow yourself to become fully vulnerable to love."

Become fully vulnerable to love. The words brought renewed pain. Yes, I had been vulnerable to love, to loving Marsha and to letting her love in. What had it brought me? Pain. Intolerable pain. I felt a tightening around my heart, protecting it, so I would never have to feel this much pain again.

"Whatever pain you're holding in your heart, release it. Let it go..."

Let it go. I don't need to hold onto the pain anymore. Tears filled my eyes. *Let your mind melt into sensation*, I repeated to myself. As the sensations emanating from my chest filled me, I noticed that for almost a minute, I hadn't thought of Marsha and Nancy. Then the gnawing thoughts intruded once again. *Let your mind melt into sensation.* The ache in my chest, back, and thighs filled all of me. I was nothing more than the ache. For the briefest of moments my thoughts went silent, only to intrude again.

"Release the posture," the instructor finally said. "Fold your body over your knees. Allow your forehead to drop gently toward the ground, and drape your arms behind you in the child pose."

As I assumed the near-fetal position, a glow enveloped me from deep within. My breathing slowed.

"Feel the energy coursing through you. This is prana, the energy of all that is and the source of all healing."

Healing. I longed for it, longed to be released from thoughts of Marsha's infidelity. Thoughts of the pain that might lay ahead for Sam and

Michael. Thoughts that had been so intolerable earlier seemed to have lost a little of their power for a moment.

"Let the energy, the prana, wash over you and bring you peace."

Peace. For a moment, curled up like an infant, peace was mine. That fleeting peace soon evaporated. As the session came to an end, the thoughts returned in full force. But in that moment I had glimpsed something I hadn't known to be possible. Sensation had displaced my mind, and the result had been healing.

As I left the room, my steps drew me to the shop where I could buy all I needed to bring this experience home. With the schedule of a busy physician, I knew I would not have time to go to yoga classes. So in addition to collecting a yoga mat and meditation pillow, I purchased several audio and videotapes of complete yoga sessions.

With a full bag hanging at my side, I made my way back to the main meeting room for *satsang*, an evening ritual of song and movement. But as I approached the solid double doors, I felt pulled to turn away. The rain had stopped, and a beam of sunshine from the nearly setting sun poured through the glass doors that led outside. Stepping through those doors, my breath caught; I gazed across the valley to see a rainbow arched over the hills beyond. Whether meant for me or not, that rainbow filled me with hope that somehow I could heal.

* * *

I looked forward to the next gathering of healers. Marsha was noticeably absent because she and I had agreed to alternate meetings and spare our colleagues from the tension between us. Through a series of weekends stretching over several years, these healers had come to feel like family and seemed the natural group from which to seek support. The response I got from Valerie felt like anything but support. "You, Marsha, and Nancy got together before this life and decided to do the dance this way," Valerie announced calmly after I'd poured out the miserable experience of learning of Marsha's affair.

"What the hell are you saying? Are you saying I chose to marry some-one I knew would have an affair, betray my trust, and shatter my heart?"

"That is exactly what I am saying. You chose this experience for the lessons your soul needed to learn. You can't blame this simply on Marsha. The two of you have entered a new stage of your shared journey. The final chapter won't be written for a long time. How you do this dance together and what chapters are written in between are what this journey is all about."

"You are so wrong! I can't accept that I chose to have my heart broken," I sputtered in exasperation and anger. At the time I had no way of know-ing that one day I would find truth in Valerie's words, and do so with joy.

* * *

Let your mind melt into sensation, I repeated to myself. Standing with right leg bent forward—thigh parallel to the ground—left leg stretched back, and arms pointing to the sky, I didn't think I could hold the warrior pose much longer. "Stay in the posture even when your mind tells you to get out." The voice of the instructor came from my small tape recorder, seem-ingly reading my thoughts. "You are capable of more than your mind tells you that you are." My thigh began to quiver. *Relax into the posture*, I told myself. The quivering stopped. A moment later I thought I couldn't hold the posture any longer, but I let the thought go and found new strength to keep holding the warrior pose.

The warrior seemed an apt image. Marsha and I were trying to make our marriage work. The pain had lessened only a little, yet I was trying to keep my heart open, to stay vulnerable to the love I still felt for Marsha. Holding a yoga posture, feeling the pain yet staying open and relaxed in the presence of the pain, became a perfect metaphor, a practice that day by day was teaching me to be in the world differently.

Finally the instructor's voice said, "Come back to standing vertically. Slowly bring your arms down by your side. Now lie on the floor with your eyes closed. This is the time to relax. Receive the benefits of all your hard work."

As I lay quietly, my breath moving slowly in and out, I released all remaining tension and melted into the mat. Thus I entered the only moment each day in which I experienced peace and well-being. Even special moments like playing with Sam and Michael had become bittersweet as I knew uncertainty lay ahead. Each day brought another opportunity to awaken to the truth that all of life is uncertain, that *if I choose to love, it will always mean keeping my heart open in the face of perpetual uncertainty.* Perhaps this is the lesson we are here to learn.

The lesson we are here to learn. That language seemed to make more sense than it ever had before. I had no data to make me believe in reincarnation, in each of us having a soul that inhabited one body after another, with each lifetime serving as an opportunity for our soul to learn new lessons. But during this time I was left to wonder if there really was a lesson for me to learn from Marsha's revelation and the painful process of trying to stay open when my heart wanted to shut down and pull away. For the first time, I found myself considering this just might be possible.

* * *

Marsha and I tried for almost two years to put our marriage back together. During that time yoga became my salve and my salvation. I would tiptoe downstairs before anyone was awake, turn on one of the tapes, and become transported into an experience that increasingly took me beyond words.

"*Namaste*," the instructor's voice would begin. When I'd asked what this word meant during my time at Kripalu, I was told it was a Sanskrit word that meant "the light in me acknowledges the light in you." Each time I heard this word, I sought to touch that light within.

On several occasions I had tried sitting meditation, watching my breath and releasing thoughts as they came into my mind. But I had never been able to quiet my mind enough to get anything out of these experiences. An hour of physical exertion from the yoga postures did more to quiet my thoughts than any amount of sitting meditation.

Upon releasing the final posture in one of my favorite taped sessions, the instructor's voice would say, "Bring your hands up slowly to touch your face." Each time I did, I had the impression of touching something several inches away from my face, a subtle body that extended beyond my physical body. I moved my hands toward and away from each other, sensing a pressure in the empty space between them. This always brought a smile, as I'd remember I was feeling an energy I once thought did not exist.

As each session came to a close, I recognized I'd entered a state I could not have experienced through my mind alone. An hour of vigorous yoga postures that took me to the edge of exhaustion was required to quiet my mind. It allowed me to walk the path of the life I found myself on with greater peace, acceptance, and grace. Whatever pain life might throw at me, I felt I had resources to accept that pain and work with it in a way that would not overwhelm. The love I could give to others seemed to now come from a deeper place within me that in turn touched others in a deeper place within them.

It dawned on me that I could not have reached this different way of being had it not been for Marsha's affair. Valerie might have been right. Perhaps Marsha, Nancy, and I had gotten together before this life and decided to do the dance this way. From my new perspective, I could see what a wise choice this would have been.

* * *

After two years, we both knew our marriage was over. I loved Marsha, so releasing her was bittersweet. But she was still in love with Nancy, and there was nothing I could do to change that.

We prepared to tell Sam and Michael and separate our lives. The children's pain now eclipsed my own. As much as we would do to soften the blow—joint custody, a commitment never to allow the children to become pawns in our relationship, and letting the children stay in the house for the first year while Marsha and I moved in and out for our assigned days of responsibility—I still knew the scars we were inflicting on the boys would go deep.

* * *

In the early morning darkness, alone in the house the day after separating from Marsha and with the two boys sleeping upstairs, I lit a candle. Coming into a seated position on my yoga mat, I closed my eyes. For the first time in my life, I yearned to pray. Never having learned to pray as a child, I could find no words to express the longing for help that now filled me, the desire to connect with something greater than my isolated self.

In the absence of my own words, I quietly recited the words of the prayer used by some of the Kripalu instructors to open each yoga session, seeking to somehow make them my own.

> *I open my heart to explore the Divinity within me.* (The word *Divinity* did not come easily to my lips, but somehow I got it out.) *I acknowledge that my body is a temple of the Divine. I accept that I am not just this body, but the embodied Spirit itself.*

I took a deep breath in and slowly let it out. *Let your mind melt into sensation*, I recited silently. "Come to a standing position," came the voice from the tape recorder. "We will now move into the warrior pose." Ah, the warrior. How appropriate.

CHAPTER V: FREE FALL

My Wife Died When She Was Nine

"Michael, it's time for bed." I dreaded saying these words because I knew what would come next.

"Can't we play a little more?" Michael responded in his plaintive, six-year-old voice.

"We can play 'Where's Michael?' one more time, but then you have to promise to go straight to bed."

"I will. I will."

One more time I hoisted Michael up onto my shoulders. He flopped backward, with my hands holding his lower legs so he could hang from my shoulders down my back. "Where's Michael?" I said, tiptoeing a few steps.

"Here I am!" exclaimed Michael.

I spun to look where the voice was coming from, holding tightly to Michael's legs so his small body flew outward as he squealed with glee. "Where are you? I can't see you. I don't believe you're there," I said in mock frustration.

"I'm over here," called Michael.

Spinning again in the direction of the voice behind me I said "Gotcha! Hey, you're not here either. Where are you?"

"Over here. I'm over here," came the giddy reply.

Repeatedly I spun looking for him, and each time his body would fly outward, almost parallel to the ground, landing with a soft thud on my back again. Each time he would call out, "Here I am!" and each time I would fail to find him, resulting in another round of joyful taunts. Finally we collapsed in each other's arms on the couch amid peals of laughter.

"Now it really is time for bed," I began.

"No. No. One more time," he pleaded.

"Michael, you promised you'd go straight to bed."

There was more hurt than defiance in his eyes. "I don't wanna go to bed. Can't I stay up longer with you?"

"You know it's your bedtime, Michael…" Then the shift happened. Though he now spent half his nights with me, each one ended the same way.

"No! No! I'm not going!" he said, throwing himself at me, arms flailing in instant rage.

"I know you don't want to go to bed, Michael. I know you don't want our time together to end, but it has to. We go through this every night."

"Nooooo! I won't! I…I…I can't!" he howled through his tears.

And so it began yet again. Our bedtime ritual had become Michael's extended tantrums, usually lasting from forty-five minutes to two hours. Nothing I tried prevented them. Nothing I tried consoled him. I felt as if all I could do was allow him to vent his pain and rage at experiencing the fracture of the only family and home he'd known.

"Michael, please, please just let me put you in bed," I pleaded, trying to set firm, consistent limits with him as our family therapist had instructed.

"Noooooooo!" he screamed.

"Michael," I screamed back, frustration and exhaustion sapping my self-control, "you know you have to go to bed!" Then with more blame in my voice than I wanted, "You make this so hard!" Forcefully I picked him up, carried him to his bed, and raced him to the door, holding it shut from the hallway as he wailed helplessly on the other side. Tears poured down my face as I held tightly to the doorknob he pulled frantically against, wanting with all my heart to rush in and scoop up my son in my arms. But experience had taught me even that would lead to further escalation.

When the tantrums first started, I had thought they were a natural reaction, one that would soon transition to something else once his initial anger received expression. But that transition never happened. The tantrums persisted for years.

Soon he developed crippling phobias, first of wind, but then also of thunderstorms, and spiders, phobias that filled him with inconsolable terror and restricted his life.

Until then I had mastered everything in my life I'd ever set my will to do. Marsha had taught me the painful lesson that I had been unable to master our marriage. Michael was now teaching me the even more painful lesson that I could not master being the father I had always hoped to be. The more I tried, the more I failed. I not only failed, but felt each time I added to Michael's pain in spite of wanting so much to do just the opposite. Each nightly tantrum tore me apart, as it did Michael. I felt powerless to end my son's suffering.

Yet in our struggles each night, a part of me seemed to come alive, to feel I was doing what I'd somehow agreed to do when I'd chosen to become a father. By hanging in with Michael during each descent into pain, by loving him with all my heart when he most desperately needed to be loved, I met my son in a place where our hearts joined. Each tantrum ended with Michael, exhausted and spent, nestled in my arms. He always apologized. I always told him there was nothing to apologize for, that I knew he was doing his best. And then I would quietly sing his bedtime songs, often with unseen tears in the dark.

Living every day with the rawness of my son's pain brought me to my knees as nothing in my life ever had. For the first time, I glimpsed the wisdom of the words, "Not my will, but Thy will," for my will was utterly failing.

Each morning I would come to my yoga mat, light a candle, and attempt to pray. Over time, the words I had learned from my yoga teachers slowly morphed into my own. Keeping my heart from shutting down, allowing my heart to remain open and vulnerable in the presence of the pain rather than closed and protected, became the metaphor through which I was able to tolerate all I was experiencing, much like holding a yoga posture. Despite my desire to pray, my roots as an atheist did not leave me with any being to beseech. As I groped for language to express the anguish and desire in my heart, my words became a prayer to be open and loving in the face of the pain I could not conquer. Eventually, I found words to ask for help. From what source that help would come, I did not know.

> *I open my heart—fully, willingly, completely—to be vulnerable to love. I open to do not my will, but Thy will. Help me to act in the most loving way at all times, even when my heart is breaking. Amen.*

* * *

"Rick, I keep getting the message I'm supposed to introduce you to my friend, Virginia," Leah said during a weekend meeting with our group of healers. I had only recently separated from Marsha, and my wounded male ego wanted desperately to get out and play the field, to date as many women as I could. So with some newly bachelorized motivation, I accepted the invitation to Leah's home one evening, hearing that Virginia might show up that night.

* * *

"Who's Rick?"

Virginia was surprised by this question posed to her twenty years earlier, when she had consulted a spiritual counselor for guidance. Having grown up in a family whose members had taken for granted that souls and spirits constituted part of the tapestry of the world, it had been natural for her to seek out spiritual counseling from time to time.

"Rick is over in England right now. I don't know in what way, but he will be important in your life."

The only Rick she knew was her brother's old college roommate. The image of this shy, awkward accountant-to-be came to mind, and she just couldn't see a future with this man. The year was 1975, the very year I had gone to England to study at Oxford, but Virginia had had no way of knowing this at the time. As there was no other Rick in her life or on the horizon, Virginia let this information go and went about her life.

Seven years later, a different spiritual counselor to whom Virginia had turned asked, "Who's Rick?"

Not again, she thought.

"He has dark hair and a beard. He will be important in your life."

Still Virginia knew of nobody named Rick, and again the information receded from her awareness. Yet several years later, a third spiritual counselor asked, "Who's Rick?" When Virginia replied she didn't know anybody named Rick, he went on, "This man will take you on a trip to Florida. When you enter his house, it will feel familiar because it will be painted the same colors as yours."

These seemed odd details, and since Virginia still didn't know anybody named Rick, one more time, the information receded into a forgotten memory. So when Leah told her she kept getting the message to introduce Virginia to a man named Rick from the healing group, she didn't register anything unusual. But when Virginia walked into Leah's house, she took one look at me, recognizing something beyond the dark hair and beard, and instantly the thought exploded in her head, *It's RICK!* Though shaken to her core to be looking at the very person whose entrance into her life had been foretold by three different spiritual counselors over twenty years, she did not show any outward signs of the immensity of what she was taking in. We talked off and on during the night, but neither of us felt any chemistry. Nothing happened between us that hinted at a future relationship. Yet years later Virginia told me she knew that night she had just met her future husband. She added it was more than a little odd for her to hear me go into the bathroom at Leah's house and begin flossing my teeth. She said she drifted off to sleep with the unromantic thought, *I'm listening to the man I am going to marry floss his teeth.*

I was oblivious to all that stirred within Virginia that night. In the absence of any chemistry between us, I was ready to move on to the next prospect. But months later, feeling lonely and not having had much luck in the dating scene, I called Virginia to ask her out.

Given that our connection had been through the group of healers, our conversation over dinner quickly turned to questions of healing. It turned out she had studied for more than ten years with some of the most respected energy healers in the country, had completed a master's degree in holistic counseling that included a thesis about working with personal energy fields, and had a thriving, full-time practice as an energy healer. Though I'd already bumped into energy, I still found the idea of sensing and therapeutically working with the energy field of another to be a little too out there. Because of my resistance, she seemed to hesitate at something she was about to say. In response I said, "You don't have to worry about sharing anything. I don't scare easily," words that over the years would come to take on ever more challenging meaning.

"All right," she replied. After a quiet pause she said, "I died when I was nine."

Now it was my turn to hesitate. This well-educated, articulate, highly intelligent woman was about to share the single most important moment of her life. That it had happened when she was nine years old, long before anything about near-death experiences had been written in the popular press, long before the media could have influenced her, made me instantly engaged. In that moment I knew something was about to shift, something near the core of my web of belief. "Go on," I responded.

"I had meningitis. My mother was home with me and had gone downstairs. She had told me she was going to get me some tea but later admitted she'd gone to call the doctor because she knew something was terribly wrong. While she was gone, I stopped breathing. I knew I was dying. It didn't hurt at all. There was no pain. I was at peace. I found myself in the presence of LIGHT...brilliant, luminous LIGHT...completely enveloped in LIGHT and LOVE...enormous LOVE...beyond what we experience on earth. LOVE was all around me and in me. I was part of LOVE. It was like breathing LOVE. I was aware that I carried my self with me, somehow knowing that I was still me. A being of immense LOVE and LIGHT came towards me. I recognized this being. We communicated through mental telepathy. It was very easy. We don't have any mouths on the other side, you know." Virginia smiled at this and continued. "I made a vow with this being. I said, 'I want to come back to remind people of the LOVE and the LIGHT...because people forget.'"

I sat stunned. The scientist in me was taking in a powerful data point. The man in me felt I was being offered an opportunity to be with an extraordinary woman. And the seeker in me hoped every word she'd said spoke a deep truth about our reason for being on this earth.

"What happened next?" I finally got out.

"I had a perspective from above my body. I saw the doctor slapping me and calling my name, since this happened before CPR had been invented. My mother stood distraught beside the doctor. I found out later the doctor had pronounced me dead three times, but my mother kept refusing to accept it, saying 'No! No! She can't be!' I felt my consciousness being larger, more expansive, than my nine-year-old child self. I hesitated about reentering my body. To this day I feel guilty about the suffering I caused my mother by not coming immediately back in. I hesitated because I knew when I came back into my body, I would have to let go of that expanded consciousness and beautiful LIGHT and be treated like a child again. With resolve, I reentered my body. It was like an airplane's rough landing. Now aware of lying in the bed, I kept my eyes closed for one last moment, knowing that when I opened them, I would be a child again, and my mother would tell me I had to go to the hospital. I opened my eyes, and yes, my mother told me I had to go to the hospital. I spent the next two weeks in the intensive care unit at Children's Hospital in Boston with hushed teams of doctors and nurses worrying over me. The doctors told my parents I might die or be paralyzed. It all seemed like a lot of unnecessary worry. I had already died, made my commitment, and come back. I knew I would be fine. But nobody asked me."

I could picture the scene perfectly. The doctors with all their scientific knowledge testing for the exact bacteria that caused the meningitis and knowing with self-satisfied certainty that the only chance Virginia had to survive was their great skill. That she needed their science and skill is true. That a nine-year-old girl, surrounded by technology and tubes, knew something all the experts didn't know also seemed true. I realized that each truth could exist without making the other false. Truth, I was discovering, was far more complex and nuanced than most scientists and those who defend them seem to understand.

* * *

"What are you doing here?" Virginia asked when I stopped by her office late one afternoon.

"I love visiting you in your office. Even a guy as dense as I am can feel the extraordinary energy in this place."

"I don't think you're as 'dense' as you let on," she retorted smiling.

"Maybe some of you is rubbing off on me." Then after a pause I added, "I also stopped by to see if you are free tomorrow evening. I'm hoping we can get together since Marsha has Sam and Michael."

"I'll be at my weekly healing group," Virginia responded.

"What do you do in that group?"

"The four of us, all women, open with a prayer to Spirit, a prayer of intention for the highest and best for all...," she began.

"What do you mean by *Spirit?*"

"Spirit is…the energy behind all that is…the compassionate intelligence…the source of all…"

"So you mean God," I interrupted.

"Yes…"

"Then what do you mean by *God?*" I persisted, still feeling uncomfortable with the "G" word.

"God is Love. God is Light…"

"I'm really trying to understand this," I interrupted, "but I have a problem making sense of it. Love is something I understand. Light is something I understand. But I don't understand why you need to invoke God if you're really just talking about love and light?"

"*Love* and *Light* are words we use to point to what I'm talking about, but they aren't adequate in themselves to capture what it is. Spirit, or God, is…is the essence of all that is. It's…Look, Rick, you're asking me for a rational definition, a left-brain explanation of something I don't experience in that way. I certainly can think rationally or analytically, as you are doing now. But when it comes to something like Spirit or our healing group, I experience them in a more holistic or right-brain way. The left brain functions in a rational, logical, linear, and frankly critical mode. In fact, I'm feeling you looking at me in that critical way right now, challenging, looking for the flaw in my argument. But holism doesn't make arguments. It makes connections…connections among everything and everyone."

As she paused, still groping for logical words to describe something that did not fit readily into logical language, I realized she was right. I had spent a lifetime seeking left-brain answers to questions like, "What is truth?" and "How should we live?" But I was learning there's no logical answer for how to heal from the humiliation that had come from Marsha's betrayal. There was no left-brain answer for how to be with the pain and frustration I felt at my son's suffering and my impotence to help him. And slowly I was coming to understand there was no fully satisfying left-brain *only* answer to "What is truth?" Knowing, I was coming to learn, is a complex activity. Grasping truth, it seemed, might require both left- and right-brain functioning, essentially whole-brain functioning.

Pulling me back from my thoughts Virginia went on, "If you want a rational 'data point,' as you are so fond of calling them, you might want to look at this series of pictures one of the women in our group took last week using a small, hand-held film camera. We were coming together, taking our places, and beginning the flow of energy. She snapped the first picture as we were setting up. She took the second just as she asked me about you and our relationship, and I had started talking about opening my heart to you. We then continued to establish the flow of energy around the circle, opening our hearts together to create a loving space in the middle of our healing group. Take a look at what the camera caught."

I stared. The first photo showed three women (the fourth was taking the picture) sitting cross-legged in a circle. Everything in this photo appeared normal. In the next photo, a partially formed and clearly discernible pink and white band of light could be seen in the spaces between the women. In the third photo, a clearly delineated band of pinkish red light ran in a swath around the circle linking the hearts of each of the women.

The year was 1994. Digital photography and Photoshop had only recently been invented and hadn't made their way into widespread use. Nobody had taken these images into a darkroom to create special effects. But somehow the film had caught a glowing light that now stared back at me from the photographs, a light that I could only explain as a physical manifestation of love. Another data point forced its way into my web of belief, bringing a smile to my face. The world truly did not work in the way I had been taught.

* * *

In the still of a dark morning, I lit a candle. Seated cross-legged on my yoga mat, I tried to quiet my mind. *What was this Spirit Virginia spoke about?* I wondered. What was the phrase she had said was their opening prayer…to set an intention in the highest and best for all and for Spirit itself? Was this another way of giving voice to the passion I had felt all my life to love and heal others? I had always wondered if this passion arose only from my personal desires, from seeking the approval of others, or from otherwise satisfying my own ego. Something in me wanted my life to be about more than just myself and my personal needs. I wanted…no…it was not just about my wants. I experienced this as a calling, something that would make me untrue to myself if I did not follow. This almost burning drive I had felt for most of my life, a drive that had led me to bring home a shivering cat and to choose a career in medicine…I wanted now to shed any remnants of doing these things for my own ego gratification. I wanted to do them to be of service to something greater than myself…But to what? Might there truly be a source of all that is, a compassionate intelligence, as Virginia had described it, that held knowledge of what was in the highest and best for all? I was not yet prepared to believe in such a source, but for the first time found myself open to the possibility.

I took a long slow breath and released it. If something greater than myself existed, imbued with a truly loving intelligence, did I feel prepared to give over my own will to that intelligence with the intention that all my actions—indeed my entire life—be for the highest and best for all? This felt in part like giving new words to who I had already been and in part, a radical, new commitment.

I paused. Was I truly prepared to cease making all decisions in my life with my personal will and instead open to the will of an entity, an intelligence, I was not sure existed? If I turned over my will, if I kept my heart open to love in the highest and best for myself and others, the path ahead would not be easy. I had already learned opening to love also meant opening to pain. I hovered on the cusp of ambivalence.

For a moment my eyes were drawn to the light of the flickering candle, and then they closed. Holding before me the image of a vast, unknowable, loving source of all that is, my words shifted to become a prayer to hold my heart open in the face of pain—to the pains I had already experienced and those yet ahead—I could do nothing to change, and to do so for some higher purpose I could not know or name. The words came out haltingly.

I open my heart—fully, willingly, completely—to be vulner-able to love. I ask for help to do not my will, but Thy will, in the highest and best for myself…for all those whom my life touches…and for Spirit itself.

Then I paused, a word forming in my mind. Half out loud it came.

Hineni. Here am I.

* * *

Six months later, Virginia and I were finding it challenging to be together. Our left-brain/right-brain differences were just the beginning. Constitu-tionally we could not have been more different. I was an extrovert, Virgin-ia an introvert. I loved to talk about our relationship while Virginia want-ed to just live it. Every one of my natural tendencies in intimacy seemed to push Virginia away. The cultural differences between my Jewish roots and her Quaker/Episcopalian/Irish upbringing played out in almost every in-teraction between us. Together these differences created barriers to deeper intimacy. On top of this, stepfamily and ex-wife challenges threatened to drive us apart. Virginia had already shared with me her experiences with "Who's Rick?" giving us both the impression that we were in some cosmi-cally arranged relationship and that it was up to us not to screw it up. But if we were supposed to be together, towards what end we did not know.

One day Virginia came to me and said, "I've been meditating on why we are together, and I received a clear answer. I know in my heart I am to help you open spiritually, and I know it is for a purpose greater than me. I'm supposed to expose you to all the information I can, and expose you to

Spirit, because you will have an impact on many, many people. Whereas I will only touch others on a one-to-one basis, you will reach thousands on a national and perhaps even an international level."

By this point I had come to simply accept that Virginia got knowledge from a source I could neither fathom nor access. Yet I hesitated. I was still practicing family medicine, touching people on a one-to-one basis, though I'd become responsible for more administration and leadership at the hospital at which I worked. How might I have an impact on such a large scale? The words "I don't scare easily" came back to me. I had said them a little flippantly during our first date. They now seemed to take on a new meaning I could not fully grasp.

* * *

"You're looking for me to be something I cannot be." Virginia's eyes looked pained. We had been together for more than two years now, yet because of our differences, we each still struggled to find a way to the other. The stresses of trying to make a stepfamily work accentuated these differences. "You want me to love you. I do. But my loving is not enough for you. You want me to fill something deep and wanting inside you. That scares me because I know I will fail. I will fail because the kind of love you seek cannot be found with another person. That place can only be touched, can only be filled, by your connection with God."

I wanted to argue with her. I wanted to blame her for a lack of courage, a lack of willingness to engage in an authentic, raw relationship with another. I wanted to be loved unconditionally. I wanted to be touched in that place deep inside that longed to be touched. But once touched, I wanted that place to *always* be held tenderly, lovingly by another. I knew that was not possible.

Could Virginia be right? Was a God I did not believe existed the only thing that could ultimately meet my desire? Virginia could speak of such a connection with God because she had experienced it herself at the age of nine. But I had had no near-death experience to convince me of that possibility. Was Virginia pointing me toward the only possible source of what I most deeply desired? My left brain sought a definitive answer. My right brain seemed content to wait.

* * *

In spite of our differences, Virginia and I stayed together. When Michael's interminable tantrums and other stepfamily challenges made leaving attractive, Virginia remembered the guidance she'd received about this man named Rick. She chose to trust that guidance and stick with the relationship a while longer. At the same time, I felt a growing sense that forces greater than myself might be working in my life, giving mounting import to the words "not my will, but Thy will." So I, too, hung in. Eventually, we found our way to a growing love and connection between us. After five years together, we began to talk of marriage. But this became a challenging time when Virginia's two closest friends, Patricia and Carol, each developed cancer. Both were beautiful, vibrant women in their late forties. Patricia's diagnosis came first: breast cancer. Despite a lumpectomy and chemotherapy, her cancer spread. Almost at the same time Carol was found to have metastatic ovarian cancer. She went into remission with aggressive chemotherapy, but we knew recurrence was likely.

One January day, as we discussed wedding plans for the coming summer, Virginia informed me that Carol would be moving to California in a month. I asked, "Once Carol moves to California, do you think she'll come back east for the wedding?"

"I don't know…" Virginia left hanging the unspoken thought we had previously shared, namely that it was likely only a matter of time before Carol's cancer recurred, and neither of us was sure she would be alive that coming summer.

We were interrupted by a phone call from Patricia. Virginia's face turned ashen. Her hand shook as she hung up the phone.

"What is it?" I asked, suspecting the worst.

"Patricia's cancer has progressed faster than we feared. It's now in her brain. They've scheduled a bone marrow transplant in three weeks."

I gave words to the question we were both thinking. "What are the odds Patricia and Carol will be at our wedding this summer?"

After a somber pause, Virginia quietly answered, "Not good."

"How would it feel to get married without them there?"

"It would leave a huge hole in my heart."

Without hesitating, I blurted out, "Then we need to get married sometime in the next three weeks."

"You'd do that for me?" she asked, tears rising in her eyes.

With more love than I'd realized I held for her I responded, "Yes... Yes...I would."

So began a rapid-fire process to plan a wedding. The first calls went to the minister at the Unitarian church Virginia had been attending and the rabbi at the temple I'd joined. Both were available Sunday afternoon in two weeks. We grabbed the opening.

Invitations went out by phone because of the short notice. We decided to make the wedding a surprise, so as we called family members and friends, we told them we were engaged and invited them to our engagement party. We said we would announce the date of the wedding at the party. We obviously told my sons we were getting married. We also told Patricia and Carol, as we wanted them to be part of the wedding preparations.

I arranged a tuxedo rental while Virginia found a full-length white dress in the evening gown section of the third store she tried. Sleeveless with thin straps and a white wrap, it wasn't designed to be a wedding dress, but the price was two hundred dollars and it was available without a wait. It would do. Over the next week she sewed the wrap into sleeves and had a surprisingly beautiful wedding dress. Perfect wedding bands showed up in the first store we visited. Virginia, Patricia, and Carol prepared hors d'oeuvres, and Virginia ordered flowers that she and her mother arranged the day before (though her mother thought she was arranging them for an engagement party).

In front of our guests, we toasted our engagement with champagne and announced the date of our wedding was…today! We informed everyone the minister and rabbi would be arriving shortly and invited them to enjoy the food while Virginia and I changed. Thirty minutes later, the ceremony began.

To this day, every time I see my niece she exclaims, "I can't believe I came to your wedding in my jeans!" That's just how we wanted it.

Patricia died six weeks later. Carol died three months after Patricia. The hole in Virginia's heart went deep, but we both held the warm glow of their presence at our wedding.

* * *

Virginia continued over the years to keep her part of the bargain to expose me to new and often startling information about spirituality. One mind-bending book after another made its way over to my side of the bed. I read each with a mixture of intellectual curiosity, willingness to suspend disbelief to take in new possibilities, and scientific rigor to assess their potential validity.

One quiet evening, Virginia handed me a book that would change my life forever: *Journey of Souls* by Michael Newton, PhD. The subtitle, *Case Studies of Life between Lives*, spoke volumes about how challenging the book's subject would be. I looked at Virginia somewhat incredulously. She simply responded, "Read it."

Newton used hypnotic regression with his patients to generate content about experiences from previous lives. That in itself was challenging enough. But to his surprise, he found his subjects spontaneously generating content about what happened between lives. For millennia, human beings had wondered and imagined what happens after we die. It seemed Newton had some answers.

Newton recorded the words of his subjects as they pierced the veil that separated the living from the unliving. Initially they reported the familiar tunnel and white light. Many reported being met by loved ones who had died before they had. Then Newton's subjects went on to describe a stage after dying in which they were bathed in energy that gradually healed them from whatever traumas had accompanied their previous lives, including how they had died. This was followed by another stage in which the souls joyfully reunited with their cluster group, other souls with whom they shared deep relationships built through many lifetimes together. At one point the souls participated in life reviews to reinforce lessons learned during previous lives. Instead of experiencing harsh judgment, countless moments from previous lives were examined, each with an eye toward helping the souls learn how to be more loving.

Upon reading this I sat bolt upright. For more than twenty years I had been seeking a foundation for why we should love others. Was it possible that science could answer this question through the tool of hypnosis? I read and reread the session transcripts looking for evidence that Newton was leading his subjects, suggesting the content to them rather than ensuring the subjects generated the content on their own. And I wondered if he would have edited out from the transcripts any evidence of doing such leading. Yet if some or even most of the content Newton reported was contaminated by his leading the subjects, the *possibility* that under hypnosis subjects could generate content of their time between lives held enough credibility that dismissing it because it didn't fit my current web of belief felt like bad science, like scientism. I was left with the sense that if only a tiny fraction of what Newton reported was true, this book marked one of the most significant scientific and spiritual achievements of the millennium.

So how has the scientific community responded to this astounding research? With silence. There have been no scientific debates about the protocols for conducting such research to minimize inadvertent hypnotist influence, no well-controlled attempts to replicate his results, no scientific symposia. These are the tools of science done well. I could only conclude that the scientific community did not see Newton's findings as data, data that had the potential to challenge, if not shatter, the dominant scientific paradigm. Kuhn's work on scientific revolutions applied aptly here. If there was *any* validity to Newton's work, I knew we stood at the threshold of a paradigm shift, one that could change the debate between science and religion forever.

* * *

The plain white envelope seemed an odd Christmas present. (I will set aside the oddness of someone raised both Jewish and atheist opening a Christmas present at all, but having been in two interfaith marriages—first with Marsha who was raised Catholic and now Virginia, raised a combination of Episcopalian and Quaker—I had long since accepted that my evolving ecumenical approach to spirituality aptly applied to celebrating the holidays as well.) "What is it?" I asked.

"Just open it," Virginia answered.

The words inside initially didn't make sense. Virginia…er…I mean Santa, was giving Virginia and me consultations with someone who had studied with Michael Newton. I looked at Virginia in disbelief. I hadn't known Newton had trained others to do the same work. I certainly hadn't known one of those trainees lived less than two hours from our home. The possibility that I would be able to experience life between my past lives was intoxicating.

The process required two hypnotic sessions. The first was a one-hour session to demonstrate to me that I could be hypnotized and that I could generate content about a past life. The second would be a half-day session in which I would delve into my experiences between lives. At the first session, I found myself in the home of a soft-spoken, pleasant woman named Ann. She offered me a cup of tea before the session, which I politely refused, wanting to get started.

In medical school I had taken an elective course on hypnosis, so I understood a fair amount about the hypnotic process intellectually. But I had never personally been hypnotized. All subjects enter the experience of hypnosis wondering, *Can I be hypnotized?* I was no different. Ann anticipated this and explained that this was one of the reasons she carried out the process in two sessions. With some trepidation, I settled back in the reclining chair in her office with my eyes closed.

"Breathe slowly…with each breath feel yourself relax deeper and deeper…," she began. After some time she went on, "Become aware that you are experiencing a sense of comfort, calmness, inner peace…Your eyelids are relaxing…" After several more steps in deepening my relaxation, she said, "I will count backward from five to zero. When I arrive at zero, you will find yourself in one of your past lives. Five…four… three…two… one…zero. What do you see?"

At first my mind stayed blank. I could sense myself consciously not trying to force any content to come to mind but waiting for something to arise spontaneously. After what seemed like a minute or two but may have been longer, a scene began to form in my mind. "I…I am in a forest somewhere," I began hesitantly.

"Go on," was all Ann said. Even in a hypnotized state I realized part of me was watching for how much leading she would be doing that might contaminate the content that arose within me.

In my mind I looked down. "I'm wearing leather leggings and my chest is mostly bare but not completely…there is something hanging around my neck. It feels like I am in a Native American life."

"What happens next?" she asked.

Time passed as I waited for more content to arise without my forcing or fabricating it. "I…I'm waiting…waiting for something…for someone… who is supposed to meet me here in the woods…" I didn't know whom I was waiting for, so again I paused, not wanting to force any content. "I'm seeing an image of a woman…she has long, black hair…a slim figure…I see her coming toward me. She, too, is wearing leather clothing. Her face is beautiful. Love shines from her face. We are lovers…We embrace…We are going to make love here in the woods…" I eagerly awaited the details of what happened next, but when they didn't appear, I reported, "The scene is beginning to fade."

"Then move onto another time in that same life," Ann prompted.

After some time another scene arose in my mind. "I'm standing in the middle of a clearing. There are some structures around me…teepees… There is a firepit in the center of the clearing. I sense others around… There is another man in the middle of the clearing with me…I look at my right hand. I'm holding a weapon…some kind of hatchet…The other man also has one in his hand…We are here to fight…We are here to fight to the death…" My breaths came faster. "We each attack and parry… Then…I feel his hatchet strike my chest…There is pain, but it is not over-whelming…my chest breaks open…I am dying…I feel a calm awareness as I begin to die…No fear…Whatever pain I may be feeling fades into the background…I…I simply know I am dying…" The scene dimmed.

"It is time for this session to come to an end," Ann said. "I will count backward again from five to zero. When I arrive at zero, you will again be in the present. Five…four…three…two…one…zero. Open your eyes."

For a long time I sat in silence. I could remember everything that happened. I felt a warm glow from my encounter with the beautiful woman, an awareness that this was a great love, even if short-lived. But the most powerful experience was that of dying. In spite of the drama I imagined would have accompanied the preparation for the fight, the fight itself, and the moment of my death, I was at peace with how it had all unfolded. There was no sadness. No regrets even though I had died at a young age.

I left Ann's house in a daze. Did I now have knowledge of a past life, or could the vivid scenes have been the result of my imagination? I reviewed Ann's words and could not see how she contributed anything to the content. Was there something a little too pat about conjuring up a scene with the beautiful woman who would be a fulfillment of any man's fantasy? Even if this were possibly the case, I was left with the haunting experience of the hatchet plunging into my chest, the sensation of dying, the inner peace that came with it. These I could not see as fantasies from an imagination eager to conjure something pleasing. I accepted that I now had one more startling data point. I anticipated the next session with Ann would bring more.

Six weeks later I was back in her office preparing to find out what happens after we die. Again she carried out the hypnotic induction. "When I count down to zero, you will find yourself in the life that immediately preceded the one you are living now," Ann instructed. "Five…four…three…two…one…zero. What do you see?"

Again for some time my mind remained blank. Gradually a scene arose…a garden. I looked down as I had done in the previous session. "PARTY SHOES?!" I blurted out. "I'm wearing girls' black party shoes…" It took a moment for this to register. Above the shoes I was equally shocked to find a small dress that rose to cover my entire body…the body of a little girl…perhaps around the age of six or seven. "I'm in a garden…there is some kind of party that I've dressed up for…"

"What happens next?" Ann asked noncommittally.

"I sense someone nearby…a man…not a friendly man…he approaches…I feel his hands around my throat…I can't breathe…He is strangling me…" Again I experienced the sensation of dying without distress. "I am floating up out of my body at the same time he continues to strangle me…For a moment I look back at my body and then float on…As I do, I know my father will be very sad that I've died…My heart pours out love for my father and then this too recedes."

"What happens next?" Ann quietly asked.

I let my mind stay blank, waiting for something to arise. "I'm still floating…I see some figures…I recognize them as familiar…but I don't know who they are…I sense myself in a kind of cage or shower…the figures are all around me…bathing me in some kind of energy…Bathing me with love…I sense the negativity of what has just happened to me gradually receding…being washed away…I am aware of a tightness in my throat easing…releasing…healing…The sadness I felt at leaving my father slowly fades…I feel myself growing lighter…brighter…I don't want to leave this place…It feels wonderful."

Eventually Ann prompted, "It is time to move on."

"I don't want to move on…I'm not ready…Just a little longer…," but I heeded Ann's instructions. I left the shower of healing and love. "I'm floating again…seeing other…other…I don't know what to call them… they are balls of energy, some with figures discernible within them…I am floating towards a group of these beings…They are familiar to me…" I became aware of thinking that this is what Newton called one's *cluster group*, though I didn't say this out loud.

"Do you recognize anyone?" Ann asked.

"Yes…Yes…I recognize my younger brother from this life…he is welcoming me warmly…and Marsha." I realized Virginia was not in my cluster group. Perhaps this explained why Marsha and I had instant chemistry and Virginia and I took years to develop ours.

"It is time to move on to the life review," Ann said. For the first time, I sensed she was directing the content rather than simply prompting me with "It's time to move on." Those five words had allowed me to generate whatever content would arise next.

"This was a life cut short…I am seeing moments from it…moments I could have acted differently…I feel sad when I see how I could have treated people differently, especially my family…" The life review did not seem to go on very long, and I became silent.

"It's time to prepare to come into this life," Ann said, again being more directive than before. "Individuals will come before you who will play a role in the life you are living now. Who are they?"

"I see someone floating toward me…It is my father in this life…Oh!… Oh!…He was my father in my immediate past life…He is so sad he could not protect me in that life…His commitment in this life is to protect me…to protect me and his other children. He will do whatever it takes to protect us…" I suddenly took in all of my father's admonitions in a different way, all his warnings about how many things could go wrong and how to protect myself from them. I realized his diligent efforts over a lifetime to provide financially for each of his children and grandchildren came from such a deeply injured place within him. Ironically I knew that as a dedicated atheist, he would never accept that his drive to provide for his family and keep them safe might come from a past life experience. But to me this recognition held the deep ring of truth.

One by one, individuals from my current life floated before me, and in each case I had instant recognition of that particular soul's journey and our contract in this life. Not everyone I had hoped to encounter came before me. But for those who did, the information I grasped about them and our relationship resonated as true and provided valuable guidance.

"It is now time for you to be born into this life," Ann guided. "You see your parents in your current life. A fetus is growing in your mother's womb. You are now descending down…down…down…and at the right moment you enter that fetus."

As I experienced my "self" enter that small fetal body, I blurted out, "Oh! A restless mind in a restless body," instantly recognizing an essential truth about the being I had been all my life but had never articulated.

"It is time to bring this experience to a close and come back to the present. When I count down from five to zero, you will again be back in the present. Five…four…three…two…one…zero. Open your eyes."

The furniture in Ann's office came into focus. The familiar sense of being in an altered state returned. As Virginia drove me home, we sat in silence. I turned each piece over and over in my mind. I felt I'd been gifted with sacred insights that deserved honor and respect. There would be a time for sharing. That time was not now.

* * *

Weeks later Virginia and I listened to the tapes of each other's sessions with Ann. Though the stages of what we saw were fairly consistent, the content was dramatically different. Virginia's time before dying in her previous life had been far more difficult, requiring much greater time in the shower of love and healing to be ready to move on. Her cluster group had her own familiar members. And she, too, had the experience of instantly recognizing the contract with key individuals in her current life.

Virginia was left puzzled over what she'd seen for one member of her cluster group, a lifelong friend from high school with whom she'd been in relationship for several years before meeting me. He had a darkness about him the others in the cluster group did not. This left her shaken, as she still cared for this man and did not understand what that darkness meant. (Only years later did this darkness make sense when she received news that he had killed himself under tragic circumstances, creating yet another inexplicable data point.)

I strained to make sense of our hypnotic regression experiences and their content. Was this simply the work of our creative imaginations influenced by both of us having previously read Newton's book? I was a little frustrated with the amount of leading Ann had done, especially in the latter part of the second session, as this made the information generated more difficult to evaluate. Yet the spontaneous emotional intensity of some of the scenes experienced under hypnosis, the knowledge gained during my alleged time between lives, and the stunningly accurate insights into my relationships in this current life all made compelling data points.

As I pondered where these data points fit in my web of belief and how they impacted other knowledge claims about how the world works, Tony's words from a debate during our residency came back to me. "What would happen if you had one of those subjective experiences you couldn't explain away scientifically?" he'd asked. "What if you had a personal experience that showed you our souls live on past death or some other experience that showed past lives were at least possible? Would you be open to reconsidering your current opposition to reincarnation?" Shortly after that debate, I'd listened to Mary Sue, an eighteen-year-old patient, recount her near-death drowning experience. Since then, I'd married a woman who had died at age nine. But now I had had my own experiences that spoke to me with an authority the experiences of others never could. What should be the appropriate scientific status of this information?

A fundamental tenet of the scientific method mandates that all information that supports scientific "truth" must reside in the public domain where it can be replicated and rigorously validated or invalidated by others. That is what purportedly allows us to know something scientifically and what gives scientific knowledge claims preferred status over other types of knowledge claims. In this view, subjective experiences can never be considered scientific evidence. For many years I had agreed with this line of reasoning. But now the same logic troubled me because I *knew* things to be true based upon my subjective experiences. I *knew* people could communicate at a distance (and while sleeping) through experiencing Marsha's awakening at the moment her friend went into labor. I *knew* we have palpable energy fields extending beyond the physical body because I had bumped into such a field. I *knew* by simple intention I could impact my son's experience of something moving inside his broken ankle. And now I had startling personal experiences that seemed to give me knowledge about past lives and the time between lives through hypnosis. Denying the truth status of these knowledge claims solely because they were based upon subjective experiences felt wrong.

More than wrong, it was unscientific because it ignored important data, data that couldn't be explained by the current paradigm. The subjective data points I'd directly experienced as well as countless other similar data points experienced by others constitute the kind of data that can and should serve as a spark for igniting the period of revolutionary science we have already entered. Yet the testing of any proposed new paradigm need not give up science's appropriately heavy focus on public information that can be replicated by others. The greatest challenge for science in this revolutionary period will not be generating creative hypotheses or conceiving candidates for the new paradigm. It will be developing the means for testing each hypothesis against the gold standard of publicly shared, reproducible data when so much of the phenomena to be explained arise as subjective experiences of individuals. I have faith that science, done well, will be up to this task. I also strongly suspect that the distorting biases of entrenched webs of belief will make this a rocky course for us all.

* * *

If I am honest with myself, I must admit that I, too, carry distorting biases in my personal web of belief. I did not realize the next step on my path would bring me face to face with two of my most deeply held and distorted biases: what I *thought* I knew about Jesus of Nazareth and what I *thought* I knew about God.

Chapter VI:
A Spirit-Directed Life

"There is only one religion, the religion of love."

"This little light of mine," the singer's deep voice rang out in a gospel rhythm, "I'm gonna let it shine." I sang along…sang from my heart. "This little light of mine, I'm gonna let it shine." Clapping, swaying, I joined two hundred others. "Let it shine, let it shine, let it shine," she finished. We all clapped and cheered.

It was easy to feel the joy and love everyone had brought into the room at the start of this four-day workshop. "You've got to come with me to the next Celebrating Life Ministries retreat," Virginia had said the previous year. "You're gonna love it." As a child I'd gone to folk sings and hootenannies in the 1960s. In my days as a camp counselor I'd led many evenings of singing, playing my guitar. This felt familiar. Virginia was right. I was loving it, at least so far.

Then one by one the ministers of Celebrating Life Ministries greeted us. "Welcome. Welcome all of you," said Emily, the first of the ministers, with a smile that made me want to hug her. She seemed so normal, at least compared to the outsider's view I held of ministers of all religions from having grown up not attending organized religious services of any denomination. Dressed along with the other ministers in street clothes rather than a formal robe, she talked as if we had been friends for a long time, as apparently many of the workshop participants were. "I thought my past days as a corporate trainer would have prepared me to coordinate a four-day retreat like the one I thought we had been planning for the last many months. But I wasn't prepared for how this morning began. Ron Roth—our founder and spiritual leader for those of you new to Celebrating Life Ministries—got up this morning and said, 'Throw out whatever you thought we were doing. They are telling me to just turn it over to God and he/she will do the rest. My job is to get out of the way and let the Holy Spirit work through me.'"

There was the G word already. I had previously encountered many startling data points that had come to reside uneasily within my shifting web of belief, reincarnation and channeling counted among them. But none had cracked the belief at the core of that web, that God did not exist. Was I ready to question even this? The image of a bearded man on a cloud floated before me. I felt myself pull back, instinctively looking toward the exit doors. But I had picked up on the "he/she" reference. This seemed an attempt to acknowledge that God, whatever that may be, has masculine and feminine aspects. So at least the beard was gone, and hopefully the guy on the cloud. This was a start.

I was also unnerved by Emily's reference to the Holy Spirit. Despite my Jewish and atheist upbringing, I was certainly aware of the Trinity of the Father, the Son, and the Holy Spirit as essential elements of Christian theology. Was I not only going to have to struggle with God over the next four days, but with trappings of the Christian faith as well? Apparently so, since Virginia had already shared with me that Ron Roth had been a priest for many years until making the wrenching decision to leave the Catholic Church because his spirituality and teachings had not been acceptable to the ecclesiastical hierarchy. The final straw had come when his bishop had told him he could only provide Communion to Catholics. Ron believed God's table should be open to everyone. Forced to choose between obeying Church leadership and living, practicing, and teaching his faith, he chose the latter but clearly maintained a connection with his Christian roots.

And who were the "they" he was talking about who had overturned months of careful planning for this retreat? I leaned over to Virginia, who was sitting next to me, and said half jokingly, "I'm not sure I want to spend four days listening to somebody who hears voices."

"Trust me," she responded. "You'll appreciate Ron soon enough."

For the moment I was willing to suspend disbelief, as I had done whenever Virginia had given me something to read or exposed me to a new experience. She was still keeping her part of the bargain. It seemed my part was not to dismiss out of hand whatever she was sharing because it didn't readily fit into my then current web of belief. I would do the same for the next four days, though I would continue to evaluate the data points as they presented themselves.

The other ministers added their welcomes to Emily's. Gary shared some of his journey, which had begun in the 1960s with explorations of Eastern religions, but surprised me when he talked about the recent death of his wife whom he so clearly still loved. As he described her persistent presence, a presence he felt palpably in the room at the start of our retreat, I wondered if I would ever feel such a presence. With a start, I realized that I did not doubt that she was present, only that I had difficulty sensing her presence. My personal experience of the hypnotic regression into time between my own lives had left me accepting that some part of us continues after we die, so the thought that that part might be felt by her husband did not seem a far stretch.

Next Paul, a minister with a cherubic face, who had devoted most of his adult life to assisting Ron, spoke of his journey from doubt and skepticism. He had not believed in Ron's teachings when he had first met Ron. Instead Paul had adopted a prove-it-to-me stance, which I not only recognized but still embraced. One day Ron Roth had performed a hands-on healing with him, and a lifelong medical problem resolved. Since that time, Paul reported, he had come to experience a force in his daily life he could only describe as the Divine. What was that lifelong medical problem? Warts.

That's it? I thought. *Warts?* I'd heard about healings that had resulted from the laying on of hands, heard of miraculous cures of the lame and the blind. But warts? Somehow curing warts didn't seem dramatic enough to justify belief in hands-on healing, not to mention belief in God. Yet Paul spoke from an earnest place in his heart, and I could not help but be touched by that.

Martin, soft-spoken and the oldest of the four ministers, openly shared the depth of his faith. He had found in Ron Roth and Celebrating Life Ministries an expression of authentic prayer and access to the Holy Spirit that had called him to his highest self. I found myself wondering if one day I might experience such a calling. After the welcome and sharing from the ministers, the singing resumed, building the energy in the room until the moment was right for Ron Roth to enter. All turned to the back of the room, and we continued to sing as a tall, stout, white-haired man made his way slowly up the center aisle, eventually taking his seat at the center of the stage in the front of the room.

"Namaste to each of you," he began.

Why is a former Catholic priest opening his teachings with a Sanskrit word I'd learned from yoga? I wondered.

"That word, *namaste*, means that the light in me, the Divine in me, the Christ in me honors and acknowledges the same in you."

So it didn't take long for me to have to deal with Christ in this retreat, but somehow Ron's reference to Christ felt universal rather than sectarian. While this stretched my prior understanding of the word *namaste*, I was ready to hear more.

"We are all not only children of God, but we partake of God. Each of us has a spark, an essence that is of the Divine. Each of you is holy. Each of you is deserving of love. And I honor the holiness in each of you as we start our time together. Welcome."

I had never heard a minister of any faith begin a religious service with words like these. Ron's voice, his demeanor, his heartfelt smile, and his message of celebrating the Divine in every human being opened my heart. My thoughts flashed to a moment many years earlier when I'd attended a musical concert by two brothers, Nathan and Joseph. These men sang beautiful Jewish spiritual music from their hearts. I'd been told spending an evening with them would be special. I had been running late and arrived at the entrance to the concert hall after the doors had closed. As I hurriedly bought my ticket from the sweet-faced woman sitting behind the makeshift table, she said, "Oh, here are Nathan and Joseph now. Would you like to meet them?"

"Yes...Yes," I stammered, surprised at the informality and naturalness of the moment. Two tall, bearded men turned to me with a shared smile as we were introduced, their eyes twinkling. I reached out my hand to shake theirs and said, "I'm so glad to meet you. I hear you are quite special."

First Nathan reached out to take my hand with his two hands, and then Joseph grasped both of ours with his. Our eyes met, and his warm voice said softly, "Everybody is special. Welcome." Instantly my heart opened and tears came to my eyes. His words and warmly clasped hands touched a place within me, vulnerable and yearning, that had been seeking this experience of acceptance, love, and belonging.

Now Ron was delivering the same message, the same energy, and with the same effect. Did the source of this connection lie dormant within us all the time, the capacity of the human heart to open to and love another? Or did we need God and a sense of the spiritual to achieve this goal? Perhaps this was the question I'd brought to Celebrating Life Ministries, to Ron Roth, in search of an answer.

I was struck that Ron's use of the words *God* and *Christ* in his opening welcome did not seem jarring to me as they so often had when heard through the ears of my culturally Jewish and atheist upbringing. Had I changed, or was it something in Ron's message? I sensed both played a role.

Ron expressed a view of God and Christ as not just supreme beings but also as something personal, something within each of us, something to be honored in ourselves and in others. And he linked all of this with love, with the central message that we should love others, a message I had been struggling a lifetime to justify. Yet that message seemed to flow effortlessly and with grace from this man.

"As many of you know," he went on, "I used to be a Catholic priest. I find so very much in the Catholic faith that is to be valued. My most important teachers are Jesus and the great Italian spiritual leader, Padre Pio. But I have learned over the years that all great spiritual masters have taught the same message, whether in the Jewish, Christian, Islamic, Hindu, Taoist, or Buddhist traditions. These are the traditions I have studied, so I can speak of them and know the truth of what I am saying. But if I were to study others, I'm sure I would find the same message in all of them. There is one God, with many paths to God." He paused for emphasis. "There is only one religion, the religion of love."

Yes! I wanted to say. Yes! If there is truth in any religion, this is its essence. Each organized religion may have its own way of expressing this truth, but if it is to be authentic, to serve a higher calling rather than to further the agenda of any particular religious institution or individuals, it is not about the rightness of one set of rituals over another. Ritual should be a tool for bringing practitioners of a religion into the state of love. Any religion missing this kernel of truth has lost its way in the hands of its leaders.

"Jesus understood the truth that love forms the core of any authentic spiritual path. His was a universal message. In the hands of the church leaders that followed him, something about the universal nature of this foundation has been lost. Take for example the phrase, 'In Jesus's name.' So many prayers, both Catholic and Protestant, begin or end with that phrase. I have studied Jesus's words all my life. I have studied them in the original Aramaic rather than the Greek in which we initially received the Bible and which still serves as the primary source for what Jesus actually said. The problem is that the Greek language frequently cannot express important concepts inherent in the Aramaic language in which Jesus lived and taught. So we must go back to the original Aramaic, we must study his words in Aramaic to understand what Jesus was trying to tell us.

"After a lifetime of studying Jesus's words as best we can know what they were, I have found no evidence that Jesus believed there was anything magical about his name. The Gospel of John does include the following words in chapter sixteen, verses twenty-three and twenty-four: 'In that day you will not ask me for a thing. Truly, truly, I say to you that anything you may ask the Father in my name, he will give it to you. Until now you have not asked for a thing in my name. Ask and you will receive so that your joy may be complete.'

"Whenever I try to understand Jesus's words, I have always found it helpful to look beyond their surface meaning, because that is how Jesus taught his disciples. This is where understanding the Aramaic points us in the right direction. The Aramaic term translated as *in my name* is *beshmi.* But the meaning of this word in Aramaic is closer to *according to my way,* or *with my kind of understanding.* So what has been translated as *In Jesus's name,* I find to be a mistranslation, a misunderstanding of the essential teaching Jesus wanted his followers to grasp. The words are more accurately translated not as *pray in my name* but as *pray in this manner, in the manner I am trying to show you.*"

Listening to Ron's words, I felt another barrier fall. In spite of being raised atheist, growing up in a culturally Jewish home left me with an inner experience of feeling personally excluded every time I heard a minister or priest open or close a prayer with "In Jesus's name." To hear that the historical Jesus likely did not believe his personal name held unique power, and that instead his was a universal message about how to pray, left me hopeful that I might find wisdom in Ron Roth's teachings…and even in Jesus's.

"The best example of Jesus teaching his disciples how to pray is the Lord's Prayer. But before we talk specifically about the Lord's Prayer, I want to say a few words about how Jesus understood prayer in general. Again, we need to go back to the Aramaic, to the meaning of the word we translate as *prayer, slotha.* The root of this word, *slo,* literally means *to trap* or *to set a trap.* So when Jesus instructed his disciples to pray in the manner he was showing them, he wasn't telling them to tell God what to do. God doesn't need your help or mine to figure out what to do. God doesn't need our help to be more loving. Oh no. Jesus was showing his disciples how to open their own minds so God can change them, showing them how to open themselves in a manner that sets a trap for God's thoughts."

Setting a trap for God's thoughts? How can God, whatever that is, have thoughts? Why would I need to trap them? With an act of will, I set aside my failed left-brain attempts to make sense of Ron's words as he continued.

"Now let's turn to the Lord's Prayer. The most common translation in English is as follows:

> Our Father, who art in heaven,
> hallowed be thy name.
> Thy kingdom come.
> Thy will be done, on earth as it is in heaven.
> Give us this day our daily bread,
> and forgive us our trespasses,
> as we forgive those who trespass against us,
> and lead us not into temptation,
> but deliver us from evil.
> For thine is the kingdom, the power and the glory, now
> and forever.
> Amen.

"This is a beautiful prayer when stated in this manner. As one of the central prayers of Christianity, it holds great meaning for many Christians, and I want to do nothing to diminish this for them. Yet to my careful reading of Jeṣus's words in Aramaic, this translation misses the essence of the message he was trying to teach us. I want to share with you what I believe is a much more accurate translation of the Lord's Prayer that is closer to the intention of Jesus's teachings, to what he meant by 'Pray in the manner I am showing you.'

"First of all, it is important to understand that Aramaic is a vibrational language. By this I mean that the meaning of the words is only part of what the speaker intends to communicate. There is an energy in the words, a power to the vibrations they carry. So even the words I am about to share with you will not do justice to the vibrational or energetic communication Jesus intended. The Greek language does not have this vibrational dimension, and neither does English, which makes going to the original words of Jesus in Aramaic even more important. So I invite you to listen to the prayer as translated from the Aramaic, and know that even these words do not carry the full power of Jesus's teaching.

Our One, Absolute, Eternal Being, of which we are borne forth from the Realm of the All and the Only.
I am empty within the awe of Your Presence and the purity of Your Name
Empower my Creative Beingness through Your expansion from the ever-present Realm
As I realize Our strength and virtue as One
On the manifest earth as in the un-manifest Realm
Provide my nourishment and shine Your insight and understanding through me now and in every present moment
Release my hidden past as I cancel my past concerns with others
Do not let me lose my True Self in forgetfulness, but wholly release me from my errors of perception
For Thy Realm is the Absolute, the All and the Only

And Our strength of virtue and magnificence
From cosmic gathering to cosmic gathering, From Age
to Age
May these be the rooted center from which all my actions flow – Ahmeyn"[1]

I listened to these words, or more accurately, they flowed over me, bathing me in something I did not have language to express.

"This is authentic prayer," Ron went on. "This is what Jesus meant when he said, 'Pray in this manner.' Authentic prayer means praying from a place deep inside you, with an intention to open yourself to the Holy Spirit, to your personal connection to the Divine, and to let the Holy Spirit flow through you." Even his use of the term *Holy Spirit* felt universal. His voice built in power. "Now let that Spirit flow through you. Pray from the deepest place within you. Pray for what is most precious and important in your life."

My thoughts instantly turned to Michael. On my yoga mat I had sought words of prayer, words asking for help for Michael to ease the pain and suffering that still drove him to nightly explosions. These bedtime episodes had already torn my heart and family apart, but until now, no words had been adequate to express what I felt. I had wanted to pray for Michael, but no words of prayer had come. In those moments I had realized that the deepest desire of my life was for Michael's healing. Yet nothing I or anyone else had tried had worked. No amount of love or therapeutic skill had made a difference. My human capacities had failed again and again.

I thought of his earliest years, the years before the divorce. Michael had been such a happy child, at least during the day. But at night, he would often awake screaming with what the doctors called night terrors. I would run to his bed and find a little child of two or three sitting upright, eyes

---

[1] Hoffman, Dale Allen. Translation © 1997. Asheville, NC, www.daleallenhoffman.com, used with permission. Note: Ron Roth utilized several different translations of the Lord's Prayer from the Aramaic, this being one of them.

staring forward but not seeing, crying out with an intensity, a suffering, I could not fathom. I would hold him in my arms with as much love as I could, but he would stay rigid, screaming as if I were not there. These episodes went on for twenty minutes or longer until slowly, he would begin to recognize his surroundings. Eventually, exhausted by the ordeal, he would lay his head upon my shoulder, allow his little body to melt into my arms, and drift off to sleep. I would feel relief that his suffering had ended, at least for that night.

What was it that tormented him so? With my newfound belief in past lives, I now wondered if he had been reliving a tortured past-life experience. No amount of love from me or others was up to the task of healing such a place within him. The night terrors had eventually subsided, but he continued to suffer daily, venting from an explosive place within him. I would do anything, even learn to pray, to help my son heal.

"Dear God," I found myself praying in a whisper. "Please…Please help Michael. With all my heart I ask…" I'd never wanted anything in my life as much this. I fell to my knees in prayer to ask for his healing. "I ask that whatever Michael came into this life with, whatever his suffering, please… please help him. Heal his fears, his anger, his pain. Heal his soul." The words kept pouring out, along with the tears streaming down my face. Everything I'd kept inside during all those years of holding Michael through his pain and rage broke open. "Help him live a life filled with love. Help him fulfill all that he came into this lifetime to do." My chest heaved with sobs. "Above all, God, please help him heal that he may know love, feel loved, and be whole."

As my cries slowly subsided, I heard Ron say, "Now open yourself. Open yourself to let the Holy Spirit, the loving Presence that is the Divine, come to you. Let us all sing together 'Come Holy Spirit.'"

Music began and voices around me in unison sang a song I had never heard. At first I let the music wash over me. Then, as I realized the song repeated a single verse, I, too, sang out with words I'd never thought would come from me.

Come Holy Spirit, I need Thee.
Come sweet Spirit, I pray.
Come in Thy strength and Thy power.
Come in Thy own gentle way.[2]

The morning session came to a close. I sat still, not ready to move. A lightness came over me as I realized that Ron Roth, in a few short hours, had taught this scientist and skeptic to pray.

* * *

"You've got to see this," a woman said as we exited the morning session. "I snapped this picture with my digital camera just as the session was ending. Can you see the orbs in the photo?"

"What orbs?" I asked.

"Here. You see that one above Ron? And these others floating over the whole group?"

As I stared at the image on the small camera screen, I saw a translucent, white, round shape a few feet over Ron's head. I could make out four others of varying sizes scattered throughout the rest of the small picture. "Can you make this any larger?" I asked, wanting to see if the orbs contained any detail. With maximum enlargement, I could make out a faint lattice-like pattern in the largest of the objects. As I looked closely, I noticed the pattern was different in each of them. "What if you take a picture of us standing here right now?" I asked, clinging to my last vestiges of skepticism and wondering if there was something within the camera that made these light-like objects appear. She snapped a picture, and we all looked at it. No orbs. There was no escaping that I had just been shown another data point.

---

[2] Lyrics to "Come Holy Spirit" reprinted with permission.

Four days later, as the retreat came to an end, this data point took on even greater significance when I looked at a new picture taken with the same camera from the same angle of the same people in the same room. This time the image contained hundreds of white orbs. The only thing that had changed was that for the past four days, the room had been the site of hours of spiritual teaching, joyous songs, and open-hearted prayer. This was an ordinary digital camera. No trick lenses. No trick lighting. No special effects in developing the images. Moments after the picture was taken, I stared at an image that forced me to accept that beings of light exist and that they are drawn in large numbers to an environment in which love, fellowship, and prayer filled everyone's hearts. The scientist in me had a one-word response. Wow!

* * *

Another wow happened during day two of the workshop when I witnessed Ron perform healing by the laying on of hands.

"I didn't believe in hands-on healing," Ron began, "even though I was a Catholic priest. I certainly knew Jesus had healed the sick, and there were stories of other saints able to heal by laying on hands. But that was all in the past, or so I thought. Then one day I received an invitation to be a guest speaker at a large religious gathering. I had already given my sermon to the crowd when the pastor leading the event asked if I would minister to the people. I responded that of course I would. Then to my amazement, he announced that I had graciously agreed to perform laying on of hands for all who sought healing. I'd had no idea that's what he had meant by *ministering to the people*! It was too late to turn back. As the crowd surged to the front, I found myself confronted with a woman pleading for healing. For an instant I wondered if I should use the sign of the cross or invoke the Holy Spirit. From somewhere I heard the words, 'Give 'em double or nothing.' So I made the sign of the cross and placed my hand on her forehead as I said, 'I invoke the Holy Spirit to heal this woman now!' To my surprise she fell down at my feet. I did this again and again, and to my amazement people fell down one after the other as I waded through the crowd. When I was finished, I high-tailed it out of there before anyone could figure out I didn't know what I was doing.

"Six months later a woman waited for me at the end of one of my services. She said, 'You probably don't remember me, but I was at your service six months ago.' I recognized her as that first woman who had approached me for healing, so I waited to hear how badly I had disappointed her. To my surprise she said, 'I don't know how you could have known at the time, but I had metastatic cancer and was told I was going to die. After your healing, I went back to my doctor who was astonished to find that the cancer had completely disappeared. I just want to thank you for healing me.' And with that, she was gone.

"*Wasn't that the darndest thing?* I thought. *There really is something to this laying-on-of-hands healing.* Of course it wasn't me who had done anything. The Holy Spirit had done the healing. I just had to learn to get out of the way. Since then, I've found this sort of thing happening again and again. I no longer have any doubts. It works, but not because of me.

"Is there anybody here who has a medical problem you would like to have healed?" A woman who looked like she was in her sixties raised her hand. "Come up here," Ron said. The woman walked slowly, as if in pain. When she eventually reached the stage, Ron asked her what her medical problem was.

"I have had terrible back pain for fifteen years. Nothing has helped. I've tried every kind of medical treatment, including back surgery. Chiropractic and acupuncture haven't helped either."

"Come, stand before me," Ron prompted. "Try to bend over." She bent forward no more than fifteen degrees.

"This is as far as I've been able to bend for years," she said as she stood up wincing.

He ran his hand up and down both sides of her back, pressing occasionally in one place or another. "There. Try bending over now." To her amazement and everyone else's, her fingers reached the floor. She straightened up without pain.

"I never thought I would ever be free of this pain," she said through tears of joy. Another data point took its place in my web of belief.

"Healing like this is available to each of you at every moment. You need only open to the power of the Divine. Sometimes it happens in an instant. Sometimes the healing takes time. Now I invite you all to come forward and receive healing from the Holy Spirit."

Row by row the participants filed before Ron. He laid his hand on their heads, or sometimes other parts of their bodies as he was moved. Fully a third of the people he touched instantly became unconscious. A team of catchers spontaneously formed behind each person he touched, helping ease to the floor those who fainted. There they lay for up to twenty minutes, reporting later that they found themselves physically unable to move for that time. When it came my turn, he paused and then placed the tips of his fingers into the right lower portion of my abdomen. It felt as if he were pressing lightly, but Virginia, who was standing next to me, said she saw his fingers push so deeply into my abdomen she caught her breath thinking he must be pushing all the way to my back. I neither knew what he saw in my abdomen nor what he thought he was treating.

As I returned to my seat, I pondered the miracle of the woman's healing. As a physician, I could conceive of a psychosomatic cause of her long-standing back pain that could then be cured in an instant. But this felt like making up an explanation after the fact without any real basis. Yet at least such an explanation would not violate the dominant medical paradigm. The cynic in me wondered if she had been planted in the audience and had faked the whole thing. But all my intuition dismissed this possibility. The stories I later heard from many other participants of spontaneous healings they and sometimes their children had experienced through Ron's laying on of hands told me my intuition was on target.

Was Ron lying about the woman who reported spontaneous healing of her cancer after his laying on of hands? I didn't think so, though that is not an adequate scientific basis for drawing a conclusion. If pressed, I could conceive of some conventional medical explanation for her cure involving an extraordinary triggering of the woman's immune system and its suddenly and unexpectedly becoming capable of attacking and destroying a cancer that previously had multiplied unchecked within her body. But this felt like another stretch to preserve a medical paradigm that could not adequately account for this data point. In the end, I was convinced that something extraordinary had occurred in the healing of the one woman's back pain and the other woman's cancer, and that my current web of belief could not adequately explain either.

Yet there had been just as many if not more who had hoped for a healing from Ron Roth but had not received one. Why did one person heal and another not? I'd heard numerous spiritual paradigms used to conjure an after-the-fact explanation. Karma. Past lives. Merit. Lack of faith. But none of these qualified as scientific or satisfying.

I recalled something taught by my ninth-grade English teacher when we had studied Greek mythology. He had said, "Magic always works." By this he had meant that belief in magic could not be disproven when a magical intervention had failed. Instead, an explanation would always be invented after the fact to explain the failure, such as that someone in the village had been impure, the sacrifice to the gods had not been good enough, someone had to be punished for unnamed sins, etc. This is not science. It's superstition.

Yet this after-the-fact explanation is exactly the same process physicians use when our medical interventions fail. We conjure a purported mechanism to explain the failure, using the trappings of our most current scientific theories. "Your father's immune system was not able to mount a strong enough response to his pneumonia." "Your wife's genetics made her less likely to respond well to this medication." "Your daughter's cancer developed resistance to the chemotherapy." When physicians do this, we ignore that we are applying incomplete theories that will certainly change over time as our scientific paradigm evolves. I have engaged in this exercise in my own practice with the intention of providing comfort to patients, too often failing to recognize I was also comforting myself. I now realized each time I had been fooling my patients and myself into believing that medical science understands more than we do.

The answer to why one person heals and another does not, whether from a medical or spiritual intervention, remains a mystery. Good science recognizes this as the enigma it is without trying to shoehorn it into an unsatisfactory answer.

* * *

"Today I wish to speak to you of forgiveness," Ron began the following morning. "For this I turn to Jesus, my teacher. His parable of the prodigal son remains one of my favorites.

"The story tells of a father with two sons. The elder son is dutiful, responsible, and follows in his father's footsteps. The younger son asks for his share of his father's wealth. Once in possession of it, he spends wastefully, travels far and wide, and eventually finds himself penniless in a faraway land. In a moment of desperation, he decides to return to his family home. When his father sees him coming from afar, the father is filled with compassion and rushes out to greet him with open arms. The prodigal son says to him, 'Father, I have sinned against heaven and against you. I am no longer worthy to be called your son.' Instead of berating him, the father calls for his son to be dressed in the finest robes and for a fatted calf to be killed for a feast. The father's heart is overjoyed because his son was dead and is now alive, was lost and is now found.

"What is Jesus, the great teacher of wisdom, compassion, and love, trying to show us in this parable? Is Jesus simply exhorting us to act like the father and forgive others, to turn the other cheek? Well, yes. But have you ever tried to do that? I have. And most of the time I fail. I say to myself, 'I'm going to forgive anybody who wrongs me.' Then somebody cuts me off on the road, perhaps with an offensive gesture, and my first impulse is to give them that gesture right back. I feel angry and I'm likely to hang onto that anger for a while. If I'm angry about being cut off on the road, that anger might last minutes. If I'm angry because I feel betrayed by a lover, that anger might last a lifetime."

Betrayal by a lover...or a wife. Yes, I felt betrayed by Marsha. Was I ready to forgive her? My gut tightened at the thought.

"If I feel wronged by somebody, I feel angry. I want to strike back. It's the most natural impulse, in spite of all my good intentions. But where does this impulse come from? It comes from the ego. And what motivates the ego? Fear. All anger has at its root fear. We cannot act otherwise unless we have something to replace this fear. That something is God. The essence of God, the essence of our connection to God, is love. And this is the choice we face in every moment. This is the choice that lies at the heart of the prodigal son story. In every moment you must choose. You can choose the ego or you can choose God. You can choose fear or you can choose love.

"What happens if you choose fear? You feel anger. Notice the sequence. You judge. You blame. Then you feel angry, which means you also feel unhappy. The key to ending this unhappiness lies inside you. The more you hold on to your anger, the more you are connected to this person and your perceived injury at their hands. You stay connected to your blame of them, your anger at them. And who suffers from this? You do.

"Caroline Myss, my friend and a gifted spiritual teacher, describes this way of staying attached to old wounds as woundology. Her prescription is for you to unplug, to sever the connection you have been maintaining with this wound and the person you have been blaming for it. The exit from your suffering is forgiveness. It is to make a different choice...To choose love...To choose God.

"This is what Jesus meant when he said, 'The Kingdom of Heaven lies within.' It is what you choose that either separates you from God or connects you to God and the Kingdom of Heaven. It is yours in every moment, but only if you choose love, if you choose forgiveness. This is the lesson of the prodigal son parable.

"Now think of someone in your life you feel has wronged you." I immediately thought of Marsha.

"The prodigal son had wronged his father, yet this father forgave his son. More than that, the father loved his returning son without judgment. God loves each of us. In God's eyes there is nothing to forgive, for God sees the Divine in each of us that has done no wrong. God judges us not. Can you do the same? Can you open your heart to forgive the one you feel has wronged you and judge them not? Try now. Open your heart with forgiveness for that person. Open your heart by opening to God. Hold them before you with God's love flowing through you and offer them forgiveness."

I saw Marsha clearly before me. *Unplug*, I thought. Unplug my energetic connection from her. Reclaim whatever power, whatever portion of my happiness I continued to give over to her.

I had been here in therapy. I had been here in yoga. Now I found myself here again with a spiritual teacher telling me the secret to releasing, to unplugging, is to choose love over fear, God over ego. For the first time I could see the promise of choosing this path, of choosing God. But what would I be choosing? What might the nature of this God be if not the bearded man on a cloud? I had no answer, no concept of God, no experience of God, and no connection strong enough to compete with the seduction of my ego. I could only stand in this place and look longingly down a path I could not follow. But perhaps catching a glimpse of this path was a first step to walking it.

* * *

The makeshift store, actually a few tables set up outside the room in which Ron Roth conducted the workshop, held many books. Just reading each of the titles was an experience in challenging and stretching my web of belief. But my eyes settled on one book in particular, *Power vs. Force*[3] by David Hawkins. I opened the book and began to read. Dr. Hawkins

---

[3] Hawkins, David. 1995. *Power vs. Force: The Hidden Determinants of Human Behavior.* Carlsbad, CA: Hay House, Inc. (now available from Veritas Publishing).

described human consciousness as existing along a spectrum. Negative consciousness states, such as shame, fear, and anger, are characterized by what he called a low calibration. Positive ones, such as reason, love, and joy, are characterized by higher calibrations. Everything, from a thought to an emotion to a book or a song, could be calibrated. Thinking there was something to this, I read on.

According to Dr. Hawkins, the state of one's consciousness correlated with one's emotions, one's life view, and even one's view of God. Something rang true about this insight. Experiencing life through the lower levels of consciousness, according to Dr. Hawkins, led one to view God as vengeful, punitive, and condemning, whereas experiencing the higher consciousness levels led to a view of God as merciful, wise, and loving.

I paused with a question. Could it be that the attributes of God did not necessarily reside in God but were created by the consciousness conceiving God at that moment? That would explain much about the history of religion and the endless disagreements, debates, and even wars fought over differing views of God.

So far Dr. Hawkins's analysis felt compelling. I was intrigued but less sure of the next piece as Hawkins went on to state that one or a few individuals holding a high calibration state carry much greater power than many individuals holding lower calibration states. He contrasted the capacity of such *power* to effect change in the world with the much weaker effects of *force* that result from the application of human will and resources (hence the title of the book *Power vs. Force*). This is how a Gandhi or a Martin Luther King could triumph over great numbers of individuals arrayed against them and their cause. Their very consciousness served as their source of power.

As I read further I became troubled. Hawkins was making an astonishing claim, not that his framework had the ring of truth, but that it was *the truth*. On what basis did he make this claim? Applied kinesiology. Upon reading this I groaned half out loud. What I knew of applied kinesiology was enough to make the scientist in me run in the opposite direction.

Applied kinesiology, at least what I knew of it, involved the practice of a tester placing a substance in the outstretched hand of a subject. The tester would push down on the subject's arm. An arm remaining straight out was considered a "strong" response. An arm collapsing under the pressure was considered a "weak" response. Hawkins had used this methodology to "test" if a specific consciousness state calibrated above or below a particular number on a logarithmic scale from one to a thousand. For example, the tester would hold the statement, "The consciousness state of courage exceeds one hundred." If the subject's arm stayed strong, the tester would increase the number until a weak response was obtained. That would "calibrate" the consciousness state of courage at a specific number.

This felt like the worst kind of pseudoscience. At a minimum there was no way to control for the consistency of the tester's pressure or the exertion of the subject. Blinding of both tester and subject was impossible. Other methodological concerns poured in.

Once again I paused, not wanting to commit the error of scientism. Dr. Hawkins claimed his methodology had achieved consistent results over millions of tests across thousands of subjects. Would I allow these findings to constitute data? The degree of consistency in this claim seemed worthy of consideration even if the methodology appeared troubling.

I wondered what had led Dr. Hawkins to assert the seemingly outlandish claim that his methodology somehow produced results worthy of being called truth. Reading on I realized he hypothesized that the subject unconsciously tapped into a universal source of knowing that directly produced the weak or strong response, something that clearly stretched my web of belief uncomfortably far. Then I thought of all the things I'd at one point firmly held to be untrue—palpable energy fields, reincarnation, time between lives—recognizing that each of these now fit somewhere in my web of belief, yes, even as a scientist and a skeptic. I wondered where Dr. Hawkins's extraordinary claims might one day come to settle.

***

The following year, Virginia and I attended another Ron Roth workshop. Again singing set the open-hearted tone for all that was to happen. This time Ron conveyed a different message.

"I'd like to speak to you today about living a *Spirit-directed* life," he started. "Many of you are familiar with the Prayer of Saint Francis. Let me read the opening portion of this prayer to you.

> *Lord, make me an instrument of your peace.*
> *Where there is hatred, let me sow love;*
> *where there is injury, pardon;*
> *where there is doubt, faith;*
> *where there is despair, hope;*
> *where there is darkness, light;*
> *and where there is sadness, joy."*

The familiar words resonated in my heart. I recognized this prayer expressed the intention that had motivated my decision to become a doctor, giving voice to the true nature of healing with an eloquence I never could have articulated myself. More than that, these words spoke to my deepest intentions. From the youngest age, I had felt called upon to serve others, to heal, beginning with a shivering little kitten. Wherever I had found darkness and despair, I had sought to bring light and hope. These opening words of the prayer gave voice to the possibility that love could be the true purpose for our lives on Earth.

"What do you think Saint Francis is really saying here?" Ron went on. "Do you think he is saying he will try to sow love? No. No. He is saying, 'I turn my life over to God so that through me, God will sow love.' This is what I am referring to when I speak of a Spirit-directed life."

I paused at these words. I had always assumed that my motivations were MY motivations, rooted in my personal experiences, my identity... and yes, my ego. Even when I'd sought words to express the intention to do loving acts motivated in the highest and best for something greater than myself, those acts were still based on my motivations. Could it be that what I had always experienced as personal to me could have had another source? Something in me resisted...but something else began to open.

"Let me ask you all a question. Who do you think is in charge of your life? On one hand, that is a simple question. You make many choices about your life: where you will live, what job you will take, whether you will ask someone out on a date, whether you'll say yes to a person asking you out on a date, and many more. Does this mean you're in charge of your life? Perhaps. But here is the question: When you make all those choices, how well do those choices turn out? It depends on which voice inside yourself you listen to. When I have to face a choice, I am very aware that there is a voice inside, a voice of 'little Ron,' who wants to choose based on my worldly desires...Oh yes, and my fears. Will I make enough money at that job? Is that person attractive to me? How can I avoid embarrassment and humiliation? How can I protect what I already have? How can I make sure I won't be hurt like I was the last time I let someone into my heart?

"But there is also a 'big Ron' available to me at all times. This is the Ron who recognizes that attempts to control what happens in my life usually end with me messing it up, especially when they are motivated by my desires and fears. I have learned over the years to let go of any attempt to control what is going to happen. Instead, I seek to listen...to be quiet enough to hear the voice of the Holy Spirit...to hollow out a space inside myself to make room for the Divine to come in and through me.

"This requires recognizing that my ego creates most of the problems. Now don't get me wrong. We each need a strong ego to make our way in the world. I'm all for that. But don't confuse making your way in the world with making wise choices. We need our ego to learn quickly that if we put our hand on a hot stove we get burned. We need our ego to drive a car safely. We need our ego to help us meet deadlines in our work. But when it comes to making life choices that really matter, our ego usually gets it wrong. The ego is so worried, so full of fear, so interested in protecting itself, that it crowds out the voice of guidance available to every one of us at every moment. If you open to that voice, if you hollow out a space inside you that allows something bigger to come through, you will live a Spirit-directed life."

Once again, Ron's words found their way in. Never before had I considered living a Spirit-directed life. Now I stood at a threshold I had not seen coming and felt...fear. What was I afraid of? Giving up control of my life? Had I not already learned that control was just an illusion? Was that not the lesson for which I'd paid so dearly through the breakup of my marriage and the suffering of my son?

"This is what makes the sacrament of baptism so important," Ron went on. "It is a sacred moment in which the individual being baptized consciously chooses to live a Spirit-directed life. Yes, we can baptize a baby or a child, but that act expresses our wishes for the child. It may bring God's blessings upon the child. But it does not establish within that child the inner commitment to live a Spirit-directed life. That commitment can only be made by someone who has come of age and then freely chooses to open themselves to be guided by Spirit—to at all times seek to do not their own will, but the will of the Divine.

"Baptism is not limited to being a purely Christian ritual. We do not need to baptize someone in the name of Jesus. I've explained to you all before that Jesus would never have taught that there was something special in his name. Oh no. Baptism is a universal ritual in which the spiritual seeker freely dedicates him or herself to living a Spirit-directed life."

In the early hours of the following morning, I sought out a quiet place at the retreat center for a private yoga session. I needed to let go of the words I'd heard from Ron and others and open to something...something...words no longer seemed adequate to describe what I now experienced during these yoga sessions. *Let your mind melt into sensation*, I repeated silently as I moved deeply into each posture. I could now feel the prana as I released a posture and moved spontaneously as the energy directed me.

That movement seemed now to take the form of pacing, which had never before happened. I moved with measured steps from one end of the small space to the other and back again, over and over. I sensed my feet tracing a path…the path of my life. Looking backward I could see the arch of my life leading to this very moment. Looking forward, the path was unclear…except for the next step. I took another step. Then another. Each step somehow felt right…felt like it naturally flowed from all that came before. All I could do was hope to know where to place my foot for the next step on the path.

Then I sensed a presence at my side with each step…loving…supporting…helping to guide my foot. I turned over control of the next step to this presence, and again the next. Slowly the thought formed as I took one step and then another that I was experiencing the very presence of Spirit…at my side, guiding me on a path leading I knew not where, but trusting in that loving presence to guide each next step. *This is the experience of a Spirit-directed life*, I thought. *It feels…wonderful.* I invited that loving presence to guide my next step, and my next. *So this is how a Spirit-directed life works*, I thought. I relaxed into the experience of opening my heart, my full self, to whatever the next step held for me and for all the others my life touched.

I took another step…this time not with my own will…instead I turned it over to the presence beside me…the words "not my will, but Thy will" became the intention of each step. I felt joy in releasing my will and allowing my next step to be guided by the loving presence that was not only beside me but all around me. I paused. *Was this God?* It was a…a consciousness…next to me while also permeating everything in the world… in the universe…a consciousness whose essence was love. *Yes*, I thought, *I could turn the direction of my life over to such a loving consciousness.* As I continued to pace, a conviction arose within me, a decision to commit my life to a Spirit-directed path. This felt immense…beyond words. I needed to be in silence with this decision before I could fully embrace it, to pause at a threshold I had not known existed. After whatever time was needed, if it truly felt like the next step on my path, I would ask the Reverend Ron Roth to baptize me into a Spirit-directed life.

* * *

I remained in silence for the next two days. Words felt inadequate to express all I was experiencing...No, it was more than that. Any attempt to put it into words pulled me outside of the experience. I walked slowly and with great solemnity, allowing the weight of the decision to settle deeply within. As the certainty grew, I submitted a brief note to the ministers asking if I could be considered for baptism on Sunday, the last day of the retreat. Martin, the eldest of the ministers, approached me. I trembled with the gravity of the moment. He beckoned to speak with me in private. As we huddled together, I leaned over, anxious to hear the important words he would share in response to my request. "I pulled you aside," he said, "to tell you your pants have a large split in them and your underwear is showing." My two days of self-imposed silence ended with a burst of laughter at the absurdity of the moment. *How appropriate*, I thought. *A Spirit-directed life not only includes humor, but a hefty dose of not taking yourself too seriously.*

* * *

When Sunday arrived, I found myself kneeling with two other initiates before Reverend Ron Roth. His powerful voice intoned, "You have freely chosen to open yourself to the guidance of Spirit, to hollow out a place for the indwelling of the Divine within you forevermore. All here bear witness to your courageous choice."

For an instant, the voice of doubt whispered in my ear, "Are you really sure? Are you prepared to release your personal will to a higher purpose?"

After a moment's hesitation, a wavering voice within answered, "Yes. I am." And then another word followed. "Hineni."

A sprinkle of water showered over me. Suddenly I felt Ron's hands on my head, and a powerful energy surged through me. The words that followed seemed to come from far away, hard to recall after the fact. Some-where inside I heard a message I would always remember: "I call upon the Holy Spirit to be your guide, to never forsake you, and to always be a light unto you. I baptize you into a Spirit-directed life."

In that moment I knew my life was about to change in ways I could not anticipate. I felt both excited and deeply uncertain. I had stepped over a new threshold. What would I find on the other side?

* * *

Back home, seated on my yoga mat, I lit a candle. As had become my custom, I began with a silent prayer. Now, after being baptized into a Spir-it-directed life, I watched as that prayer shifted in a subtle but important way yet again.

Dear Spirit, I open my heart—fully, willingly, complete-ly—to be vulnerable to love. I ask for your help to do not my will, but Thy will, to live a truly Spirit-directed life, in the highest and best for myself…for all those whom my life touches…and for Spirit itself. Amen.

CHAPTER VII: ONENESS

"Any experience of separateness is an illusion."

The next retreat with Ron Roth opened in a surprising way. Gary, one of the ministers, began with a story.

"We have been planning this retreat for months. Two weeks ago all that planning went out the window when I got a call from Ron one morning way too early for me to be awake. 'Who in the name of Sam Hill is Shree Bagwon?' he bellowed into the phone. 'I don't know. Why are you asking, especially at six in the morning?' I responded.

"He said, 'All night long I kept hearing a voice in my dreams saying, Shree Bagwon...Shree Bagwon...Shree Bagwon. I called you because of all the Celebrating Life ministers, you've had the most experience with Eastern religions, and I can only hope this has something to do with one of them.'

"'I'll look into it and get back to you,' was all I could say. An hour later I called Ron back. 'Here's the story I could piece together from some on-line research. A famous holy man in India, who is addressed as Sri Bhagavan, leads what he calls *the Oneness Movement*. Sri Bhagavan is considered to be an avatar, an extremely advanced spiritual being whose mission is to help all of humanity. My best guess is that he has been trying to contact you. He clearly has an unusual way of making a phone call, but I suggest you answer it. Would you like me to find out who is leading the Oneness Movement in America and see if we can get you connected in a more conventional way?'"

So began a new phase in Ron Roth's eclectic spiritual journey, and eventually mine as well. Sri Bhagavan had indeed been sending out a message that Ron had apparently picked up. The original schedule for the workshop was thrown out, and instead we were all introduced to a representative of the Oneness Movement. Several months later, Ron led a group of his ministers on a trip to Oneness University in India for what was known at the time as the 21-day process. At the next Celebrating Life Ministries workshop, he and the ministers shared their stories—each a profound journey in itself. I wondered if a trip to India was the next step on my now Spirit-directed path.

This sense of being pulled to India persisted, even after Virginia went with Ron and over a hundred other members of Celebrating Life Ministries to Brazil to see a man known as John of God. "You have to go there," Virginia had gushed upon returning. "It's extraordinary. I know you'll love it."

"Perhaps," I had responded noncommittally. "But something tells me the next step on my path is not Brazil but India."

That path took an unexpected turn when our beloved teacher, Ron Roth, suffered a devastating stroke. The remaining leaders of Celebrating Life Ministries considered canceling the next already-scheduled four-day workshop, but instead rallied together knowing Ron would want the work to go on. A considerably smaller group gathered in a hotel in California for this workshop, unsure of what to expect with Ron no longer leading it. We sang and clapped to the same songs, but each of us felt a hollowness knowing that Ron was not sharing them with us, at least not with his physical presence.

As the singing drew to a close, Emily of the wonderful smile began, "Many years ago, in a small Japanese town, there lived a Zen master renowned for his wisdom. A young woman who resided next door to the master found herself pregnant from a clandestine relationship with her young lover. Rather than betray the secret of their affair, she falsely named the Zen master as the father of her child. When confronted with this shameful accusation, the Zen master did not deny it but instead replied, 'Is zat so?' When the child was born, the young woman's father arrived at the door of the master, bearing the infant and demanded, 'Since you have shamed my family and defiled my daughter, it must be you who raises this child.' The master again responded, 'Is zat so?' as he accepted the child into his arms. For the next year, the master raised the child as his own, with love and affection. But eventually the child's mother, burdened with guilt, admitted the affair and named the real father. With profound apologies, the woman's father again came to the master's door, this time to take the child back to be raised by the true parents. The master responded, 'Is zat so?' and promptly laid the child he had cared for so lovingly over the past year in the man's arms.

"What is it that life has brought you to which the appropriate response is, 'Is zat so?'" Michael's image rose before me. He was now in high school. His outbreaks of rage had lessened in frequency but not intensity. Tension had grown between us fueled by the complex dynamics of our reconstituted family. When Michael was fifteen, Virginia and I had bought a vacation home, hoping it would be the place to which we would one day retire. With the goal of creating a new space that did not carry the history and negative energy we'd lived with for so long, I informed Michael we would not accept any of his outbursts in our vacation home. I had not realized how much pain Michael was still living with inside, that at the time he was struggling to even stay alive. My decision proved a final straw for him. A rupture occurred in our relationship. Michael shut me out of his life.

I got a sense of Michael's inner pain when, in the midst of this, Marsha discovered a short story he'd written for an English class. It described a

young man contemplating suicide, eventually cutting his wrists, painstak-
ingly watching the ebbing of his life, drop by drop of blood. The final line
of the poem spoke of his regret for having taken his own life when, with
his last breath, he caught a glimpse of the nature of death.

This story provided a window into Michael's own suicidal state. He
admitted the only thing keeping him from killing himself was his fear of
what death would be like, and even this he experienced as barely a tenuous reason to cling to life. My heart ached with the thought that Michael
might kill himself. Yet cut off from him by his own choice, there was nothing more I could do…except pray. I prayed with all my heart once again
for Michael's healing, for him to feel enough love and hope in this life to
not want to leave it. I prayed for healing of his soul. In the face of my son's
suffering I could not adopt "Is zat so?"

I approached Emily and poured out my son's story to her. I told her
I could not find it within me to embrace a detached stance in the face of
my son's torment.

She looked at me with compassionate eyes and responded softly, "The
message of the Zen-master story is not that we should not care. We should
care very much, just as you do for your son. Pray for him and his healing.
And may your prayers be answered. But the challenge is to accept the
truth that the outcome is not in your hands. This, too, is part of a Spirit-directed life. In the end, you have no choice but to accept that his fate
will be decided by forces greater than you. Do all that you can for him.
That is what you are called to do as his father. But you will inevitably be
called to release him to his own fate. What he does with this life is ultimately between him and God."

I thought of Ryan, the small, six-month-old boy who had died of a
meningococcal infection. I thought of the relative ease with which I had
told his father that the most loving thing he could do was to release his
son. Now I found myself confronted with a moment in which I was called
to release my own son. When Emily left me, I fell to my knees, and tears
flowed, as did a torrent of words. "Dear, dear God," I prayed, "please pro-

tect Michael. Please keep him safe. Please heal him. Please touch his heart with love, with hope that this life is worth living." Sobs broke through. "Please help him to know how much I love him." I do not know how long I stayed in this state of prayer. Eventually, feeling hollow and spent, I stood up. For a moment the thought arose that I had not prayed for detachment from Michael's ultimate fate. I could not.

* * *

"Close your eyes while I play a song for you," Martin instructed us. "Take this song deep into your heart. Let it heal the places within that it touches." This loving man, who at one time had called me aside to tell me my pants were split and that my underwear was showing, began to touch my heart. The music started, and a warm, deep voice sang out the words to a song by Alaskan singer/songwriter Libby Roderick:

> *How could anyone ever tell you*
> *You were anything less than beautiful?*
> *How could anyone ever tell you*
> *You were less than whole?*
> *How could anyone fail to notice*
> *That your loving is a miracle?*
> *How deeply you're connected to my soul.*[4]

The music continued as Martin's voice rose above it, "Whom do you want to sing this song to?" An image of Michael appeared. The voice began to sing again.

> *How could anyone ever tell you...*

---

[4] Lyrics to "How Could Anyone" reprinted with permission.

As the words flowed over me, I thought of all the times I had lost my temper when another of Michael's tantrums had destroyed an evening, a vacation, or just my plans for a Saturday at home. I realized I, too, had contributed to how badly Michael felt about himself when my all-too-human side had become exasperated and had added my injury to his own. From thousands of miles away, I sang the words to my son.

...How deeply you're connected to my soul.

As the last line lingered, I knew Michael was and always would be deeply connected to my soul.

Martin's voice rose over the music again. "Now think of all those any-where in the world who need to hear this song...souls in pain...souls who suffer...souls you can touch with your love. Sing this song to them from your heart."

I sang the song again, love from my heart pouring out to all those living and suffering in countless corners of the world. I sang this song to all those brave souls who every day recreated the miracle of continuing to love in the face of so much pain.

Yes. You are all connected to my soul. We are all brothers and sisters who share this planet...Each of you is connected to my soul, and I love you all.

The music finally came to a close. Again Michael's image rose before me. *I love you, Michael...I pray that someday I will be able to sing this song to you as you stand before me...I pray that you come to know its truth in your heart.*

* * *

The next time Virginia and I attended a Celebrating Life Ministries work-shop was three days after her dog had died. I say "her" dog, because they truly were soulmates. For anyone who has not deeply loved and lost a pet, it is hard to explain the heartache a pet's death brings. Virginia was in grief while I was seeking the next step on my path. During that workshop, we each separately wondered if India was where we were being guided. This was late June, and the first available Oneness University program ran for three weeks in August. I checked my calendar. I never had three weeks without multiple professional commitments, but those exact three weeks were open. We took advantage of this "coincidence" and booked our flights to India. As I anticipated flying halfway around the world to turn myself over to a man who called across continents through dreams, I sensed a loving presence pointing the way.

* * *

After the long flight and two-hour taxi ride north from Chennai, we arrived at Oneness University. We drove into a walled compound actively under construction with countless workers, both men and women, scurrying about in the oppressive heat, manually laying beam upon beam and brick upon brick. Underfed and ill-treated dogs roamed everywhere. This partially finished campus served as the training center for the Oneness Movement, the inspiration of Sri Bhagavan and his wife, a beatific woman also recognized as an avatar and called lovingly *Amma*, which means *mother* in multiple languages.

The 21-day process involved morning, afternoon, and often evening sessions led by dasas, the instructors of Oneness University. These cherubic-faced young men and women, all appearing to be less than thirty years old, seemed to hold the wisdom of the world in their eyes and their loving smiles.

"The Oneness process," explained one of the dasas during the opening session, "is comprised of three phases. The first is healing the heart. Next is awakening from the dream that is our illusion of the world into the reality of what is. The final phase is awakening to the Divine. The goal of this process is to help each of you experience oneness, the deep connection that already exists between you and all that is. A life lived in oneness is a life of joy."

A life of joy. Could I truly live a life of joy given the pain I had experienced and the pain I continued to see in countless others? My wondering was interrupted by the dasa's next announcement.

"To help you take this process in as deeply as possible, we ask that you remain in silence when not in a session in this hall or an individual meeting with one of the dasas. This means eating all meals in silence and maintaining silence in the dormitories. Please take care of whatever arrangements you need to address and be back here at one o'clock prepared to commence three weeks of silence."

* * *

After we had reassembled, with just a few hushed whispers among the almost 150 participants from more than a dozen countries, one of the dasas stepped forward and asked, "What is it in your past that has caused you pain?" I thought of Marsha's affair, our divorce, and the pain Sam and Michael continued to live with as a result of our failure to keep our marriage together. "For the next seven days we will each review our own lives, stopping to examine the moments that still cause us pain today."

Not again, I thought. I had done this work in therapy. I had done this work on my yoga mat. I had heard these words from Ron Roth. Did I really have to fly halfway around the world to hear it again? I did the math in my head, figuring out how many therapy sessions the airfare and program fee could have bought, and in a lot more comfortable surroundings than an all-male dorm with a narrow cot in a three-hundred-yard by three-hundred-yard walled compound populated with countless mangy dogs.

That evening we held the first small group meeting with our personal dasa, one of the teachers assigned to work specifically with me and a few of the other program participants. Our dasa opened this initial meeting with our group by asking each of us to set our individual intention for the Oneness process. As I reflected on what I would choose, I readily went to the intention I'd set when I had asked to be baptized: to live a Spirit-directed life. But somehow this answer came too easily. It was an old answer, much like my old answers to examining the moments that still caused me pain. It did not take me to my growing edge, and our dasa recognized this.

"What do you want for yourself?" he prodded.

What could I set as my intention now that would be genuinely transformative for me? I wondered. I thought of the previous dasa's description of a life lived in oneness as a life of joy. All my aspirations up to this moment, I realized, had been about struggle—struggle to change what is, to make the world better in whatever way I had defined *better*. My calling to heal others, to love all who suffer, to right injustice wherever it might arise—these had been my motivations for as long as I could remember. What if, instead of seeking to change the world, I could change myself? That would be a transformation of immense proportion. So that would be it. "My intention for this Oneness process," I announced, "is to live life in joy."

After saying these words, I paused. Did living a life in joy mean accepting what is and giving up working for the changes our world so desperately needed? Could I do both? I did not know. I only knew the coming three weeks in India would be the next step on the path unfolding before me.

* * *

"Today we will explore the four truths," an angelic-looking, female dasa began one morning.

So all of the Truth with a capital "T" I've been seeking for the past thirty years can be summarized in four truths? Not likely, I thought.

"The first of the four truths is that ninety percent of all suffering is self-created. By this we do not mean that life doesn't bring hardships. One need only look around, especially here in India, to recognize that hardships surround us. But these hardships—illness, poverty, death—only cause a small portion of the pain and suffering experienced by all of us. How we hold these inside, what we feel and do in the face of hardships, all we do in the often misdirected effort to avoid suffering, these create by far the greatest portion of human suffering.

"The second of the four truths is that the outer world is a reflection of the inner world. The third truth flows from the second. If the inner world changes, the external world will change as well. The fourth and final truth is that as you feel, so shall it happen."

Was each of these true? How would we know? What would constitute proof of these truths? I wondered. The questions poured in. But I had not come to India only to answer questions about truth. I had come, in the words I had recently adopted, seeking to live in joy.

The dasa's sweet voice continued, "Human experience includes count-less moments in which we feel disappointed, rejected, or otherwise hurt by the actions of others. See how many of the following thoughts occupy a prominent place in your thinking today. If only such and such hadn't happened, I would be happy now." I thought of my divorce, which had created so much unhappiness for my children and me. "If that person hadn't done that to me, I wouldn't be so unhappy now." I thought of the deep violation of trust I'd experienced through Marsha's affair and her leaving me for Nancy. "If my spouse/mother/father/child/etc. would only do so and so, I would be happy." I thought of the ways I hoped Virginia would change so our relationship would work better for me. Looking around I noted many heads nodding in recognition along with mine. With a wry smile I was forced to acknowledge that years of thera-py hadn't eliminated these thoughts. "If you are holding on to whatever happened in the past as a justification for not being happy today, you are likely to remain unhappy. If you are spending your precious energy hoping someone else will change so you can be happy, you are likely to remain unhappy."

I had to admit, I'd spent too much energy trying to get others to change for me to be happy.

"The key is to accept that whatever is, is." I paused at this way of putting it. "There is a certain 'isness' to existence that neither you nor anyone else can change." Again, an odd turn of phrase, but one that put this ancient problem in a new light for me. "Your challenge, the challenge that confronts every individual seeking happiness, is to accept the isness of existence—to accept that absolutely nothing that *is* needs to change for you to be happy." I recognized the voice of the Buddha here, that desire is the source of all suffering. The Zen master's "Is zat so?" grew out of this tradition. The Oneness Movement, with its roots in Hinduism, embraced this key Buddhist principle. I heard Ron Roth's words: "There is only one religion, the religion of love." Was it true that at their core all great spiritual traditions share a common wisdom?

* * *

That evening we returned to the meeting room for a meditation. We would be joined by three individuals referred to as *enlightened ones*, men and women who lived a life of almost constant meditation and prayer, the type of people who in days past would have lived a hermetic life of spiritual devotion in a cave somewhere. Oneness University had invited them to live within the Oneness community. Their role was helping others attune to their exceptional consciousness.

When the double doors at the back of the meeting room opened, two women and a man entered. Although appearing no more than thirty years of age, they moved with slow, almost painstaking steps that reflected what seemed to be a great effort to maintain the connection between their high meditative state and the need to make their earthbound bodies move against gravity. They finally settled into chairs at the head of the room, a hint of a smile intermittently passing across their otherwise peaceful faces. One occasionally let out a soft chuckle.

I closed my eyes, beginning to focus on my breathing. Since I continued to find sitting meditation difficult due to restless thoughts that bounced from one to the next, I concentrated on opening the chakras as I had done so often in my favorite yoga session. With the next breath, I brought my attention to the first chakra, silently expressing the words, "All is one." I felt a gentle opening at the base of my spine. For the following breath I brought my attention to the second chakra with the words, "I honor the other as other," feeling an opening in my lower abdomen. During each successive breath, I focused on opening the third, fourth, fifth, and sixth chakras. Finally, with another breath, I brought my attention to the seventh chakra at the crown of my head, focusing on the words, "I open to the Divine." At first those words surprised me, as I had not until that moment felt comfortable even using the word Divine. But it seemed to flow naturally, so I set my surprise aside and let the thought just be.

I remained physically in the same place but experienced my awareness moving upward in something I could best describe as vibrational frequency. Could this be the rising calibrations Dr. Hawkins had described? Soon my rising slowed; I had the sensation of compression developing above me as I rose, a barrier building up much like a plane approaching the sound barrier when waves of sound become compressed before it. As my intention focused on this continued upward movement, the barrier melted away. For a moment I wondered if somehow the presence of the enlightened ones had helped me transcend a previously unsurpassable limit. The sensation of moving upward resumed until again I encountered a buildup and slowdown. Again I felt myself pass through this barrier, rising still higher.

With each breath I felt myself moving upward, feeling an ever greater sense of lightness. I lost count of how many barriers I passed through. Eventually I became aware of a stirring around me. I cracked my eyes open enough to realize that everyone around me was standing. I, too, rose, noting that the enlightened ones had made their way almost to the double doors where I watched them disappear into the night.

One of the dasas instructed us to lie on the floor and allow ourselves to integrate the experience. As I lay there, I earnestly sought to hold on to the experience but instead found myself drifting off into a sleep-like state. Sometime later I again sensed movement around me and realized others were getting up. After a few deep breaths I opened my eyes. Standing up with some difficulty, I began the slow, silent walk back to the dormitory. It was not lost upon me that I found it almost arduous to put one foot in front of the other.

* * *

"Each of us, all of the dasas, we have been blessed." The lilting beauty of this young woman's voice and her open, guileless face made me want to take her into my heart. "We are here as your teachers because all of us came as children to the school Bhagavan and Amma ran. We did not know at that young age that we were graced to be with two avatars, only that Bhagavan told wonderful stories and that Amma's heart felt bigger than anyone's we'd ever met. One day one of the boys was sitting in Bhagavan's office when Bhagavan offered to give him a blessing. The boy readily accepted, and Bhagavan placed his hands on the boy's head. Within moments, the boy felt a huge ball of golden light descend, coming first through the crown of his head and soon permeating him completely. The boy's eyes filled with wonderment. 'This is a blessing you can in turn give to others,' Bhagavan had said with great kindness. The boy rushed out to tell his friends. Each of us eagerly asked him to 'do it to me.' Each of us experienced the golden ball of light descending. Soon we were all doing this for each other, unaware that anything unusual was happening, just that it felt so wonderful. Only later did we learn that Bhagavan had performed an ancient ritual, the transfer of Divine energy known as *deeksha*, or what we now call the Oneness Blessing. The blessing comes from God; the one performing the blessing is only the vehicle. Those who received this blessing, whether they saw the golden ball or not, very often experienced transformations in their lives. Whole villages have been rejuvenated after a critical mass of residents received the Oneness Blessing. Each of you today will receive the Oneness Blessing. We hope you will accept this blessing as a spark of Divine energy to awaken the enlightenment process within you."

In silence we lined up to await our turn to receive our Oneness Blessing from one of four dasas at the front of the room. I found myself in a line leading to one of the male dasas. When my turn approached, I knelt in front of him, and he placed both hands on the crown and outer portions of my head. I waited, not knowing what to anticipate. After about a minute, the dasa lifted his hands, placed his arms around me in a hug, and then released me. Our instructions were to lie quietly on the floor after receiving the Oneness Blessing. *Let go of any preconceived ideas of what it should feel like*, I told myself. No golden ball. No epiphanies. Perhaps a sense of a shift, a flattening and widening of the inner space in which my awareness and thoughts rested. Upon returning to the dormitory, though it was only mid-afternoon, I fell into a deep sleep. Had anything changed? No answers came.

* * *

The thin rice mat covering the floor had been pushed together by the other chairs around me, creating a wrinkle in the mat as it ran under my bare foot. I attempted to move my chair, but there was little room on either side. I tried to smooth out the mat, but the chairs and people crowded together prevented any shift or stretch. Efforts to move my foot to another position left my body twisted. There was little I could do but accept that for the next few hours there would be a wrinkle under my foot. It felt somewhat uncomfortable, but I had no choice but to simply let it be.

After a lengthy introduction and meditation during which I kept being distracted by mild discomfort where the wrinkle pressed into the bottom of my foot, a new young dasa began, "Today we will explore the four keys." *If the world could be understood with four truths, I suppose I could get by with just four keys*, I thought wryly. "The four keys are self-acceptance, setting right your relationships, prayer, and a deep relationship with the Divine." The first two keys repeated topics I'd gone over endlessly in therapy. The third I'd begun to explore through my journey with Ron Roth.

But a deep relationship with the Divine? While the word *Divine* had spontaneously come to me during that first meditation with the enlightened ones, I still struggled to say the word *God*. Why? In this moment I got a clear answer. I did not experience a personal relationship with anything I could call God or the Divine.

The dasa's soft but penetrating voice pulled my thoughts back. "To begin our work with the four keys, we will start by opening the first three chakras." This was familiar territory, or so I thought. We began with yoga postures I had done many times but never as intensely or as long. The breath work, *pranyam* as it is called, and meditation seemed to go on forever. As we finished what felt like more than an hour of preparation, our dasa said, "Now lie down with your eyes closed. To move into complete self-acceptance, let your life up until now come to you. Let each moment, important and otherwise, arise in your mind. Hold it dispassionately. Let it just be." Childhood images arose. Moments of happiness. Moments of sadness, fear, guilt. Each seemed to surface and then be left behind. A searing moment arose, the moment when my first love, Sarah, had looked deeply into my eyes and called me by another man's name. I knew then that I'd lost her to someone else. My heart had broken, shattering my innocence with the newfound knowledge that all love must end with pain. I grieved for years afterward, holding this as a defining moment in the depths of who I knew myself to be. Yet now, as this scene passed before me, something shifted. I felt a deep peace, accepting what had happened. I surprised myself by experiencing the isness of that moment much as I had experienced the wrinkle of the mat under my foot…somewhat uncomfortable, but knowing there was nothing I could do to change it. It simply was.

This image receded and others took its place. Michael's night terrors, Marsha's affair, Michael's tantrums. With each breath, I inhaled greater lightness, a sense of ease filling the places in my body where I had held painful memories and difficult relationships. Years of therapy had not accomplished what the past few hours had. Was this self-acceptance, the first of the four keys? Yes. Was this setting right my relationships, the second key? In part, for I found within me acceptance of others. Not yet forgiveness, I noted, but acceptance. Without forgiveness, I knew, I could not fully set right my relationships. Perhaps forgiveness would come someday.

* * *

"Achieving a life of peace, a life of joy, requires three elements," our dasa for the morning had begun. "You can provide two of these: your intent and your effort. Intention is the wellspring within you from which flows all else. Be clear and loving in your intention and the same will flow into your life. Remember that the outer world is a reflection of the inner world. But intention is not enough. Your effort, in whatever form it takes, is required. The third element does not come from you. It comes from the Divine, for I am speaking of grace. There is just so much we as human beings can do to achieve a life of peace, a life of joy. At some point each of us must acknowledge that we cannot be our highest selves, achieve our highest purpose, without grace from the Divine."

This statement, more than any other, flew in the face of all I was brought up to believe. By my father I was taught from the very earliest age that all things, good and bad, flowed from my personal efforts. From my mother I was taught that the values I chose to live by, to express through my actions, came from within me and were a personal choice. To accept that I might need anything from outside myself to live the life I so fervently sought, a life of highest ethics, deepest love, and joy, felt like cutting some entrenched cord tying me to my family.

I am a scientist, a seeker of truth. How would I ever find an answer to the question of whether a force beyond the physical and personal—call it Spiritual or Divine or God—is an essential element of a life lived well? I had had personal experiences of energy that could not be measured or reproduced in a laboratory (at least not yet). I had witnessed incontrovertible yet inexplicable phenomena, such as Marsha's awakening the moment

Susan had gone into labor. I had come to know and trust intimately a woman, now my wife, who had had a personal experience of life after death at the age of nine. I had had my own experiences through hypnotic regression that seemed to best be explained as recollections of past lives and time between lives. Did these add up to proof that humans can only achieve our highest goals through the intervention of grace from a Supreme Being? How would this question ever be answered other than through that most unscientific of acts, an act of faith?

Suddenly a memory arose from the retreat we'd attended with Ron Roth before his stroke. "Today I want to talk to you about discernment," he had started. "You wouldn't be here today if you weren't seeking a spiritual path. That's wonderful. But if you stay on this path, you will inevitably be exposed to many things someone will claim to be true. If your experience is anything like mine, I'm afraid you'll find much of this to be pure poppycock." A few chuckles had broken out in the audience. "No, really, you'd be amazed at what nonsense passes for spiritual teaching. I'd like to say that's only true today, but it's always been true. Lots of people have spiritual experiences, but that doesn't mean they understand them rightly. If they think a few spiritual experiences make them qualified to be a spiritual teacher, watch out.

"The world has always been filled with false prophets, with individuals and institutions that distort spiritual truth, either because they do not authentically know this truth or to fulfill their own ends." He had paused for emphasis. "You who wish to travel an authentic spiritual path must always carry with you an indispensable tool: discernment."

Yes, I had thought, *discernment is the right word for telling truth from falsehood. But what is the basis for discernment?*

It was as if Ron had heard my question. "Discernment has its basis in the human capacity for intuition. We have no idea what constitutes intuition. Perhaps it is your spirit guide whispering to you. Perhaps you've linked into a collective consciousness. Perhaps God is tapping you on the shoulder. Whatever the source of this knowing, if it is authentic, you will recognize its validity through your capacity for discernment. Listen to and develop your capacity for discernment. Use this capacity every moment as a critical barometer of authentic truth."

Now, eight thousand miles from home, listening to words of spiritual teaching from a seeming innocent who had lived all his adulthood in the cloisters of a monastic life, I felt Ron's challenging words hang in the air, words made all the more poignant because I had not realized at the time they would be the last lesson Ron would teach me before the final stroke that silenced him…at least on this physical plane.

The dasa's voice interrupted my thoughts. "While grace from the Divine may be bestowed at any time, as human beings we can enhance the opportunities for grace through prayer, the third of the key steps." I had already welcomed prayer into my life, so I decided to exercise discernment by allowing my questions about grace to coexist with my willingness to engage in prayer.

"Effective prayer requires the following four elements: pray with specificity, love what you pray for, ask and release, and be in gratitude regardless of what happens." I should have known there would be four elements. "Praying with specificity means that you should not hesitate to ask in your prayers for specific things you would like to receive." I raised my hand, no longer able to contain myself. "You have a question?" the dasa asked with seemingly infinite patience.

"Yes, I do. You are suggesting that our prayers be filled with details. Shouldn't I only be praying for the big things? It feels somehow wrong to waste a prayer on a parking space."

"Ah, I see," came the reply. "You are assuming that God will only answer some limited number of prayers, so it is best not to waste a prayer on something as trivial as a parking space."

"Precisely," I responded.

"Then we must take a moment on yet another important truth." There was that word again. "As you envision God, so shall God appear to you. If you envision God as a vengeful God, you will experience God as exacting vengeance. If you envision a God of infinite forgiveness and compassion, that is how God will appear to you. If you experience God as what we call *the Presence*, interpenetrating all that is with God's loving essence, that is how you will experience God. In your case, you've told all of us that you envision a God that fulfills only a limited number of prayers, so that is how God will appear to you."

I sat stunned. "You mean if I envision a God of abundance that answers all prayers, I will experience God as abundant?"

"Exactly so."

Must I take responsibility for the qualities of God as I envision them, for that is how God will manifest in my life? I suddenly remembered David Hawkins. He, too, had come to the same conclusion that as one envisions God, in his case based upon one's own level of consciousness, so God will appear. Bhagavan and Hawkins. Two thinkers, two systems of thought developed on opposite sides of the world, had arrived at the same conclusion.

"Let us practice prayer," our dasa continued. "Select what you will pray for. Be specific. Love what you pray for. Ask and release attachment to the outcome. And be in gratitude regardless of what happens."

After a few deep breaths my thoughts cleared, and I prepared to pray. I felt almost giddy that I could pray for anything I wanted. Finally I settled on three prayers.

> "Dear God," I began, envisioning not a being but the consciousness of infinite love, compassion, and generosity I'd somehow already sensed as a presence both next to me and permeating all that is, "I pray for healing for my son Michael." A rising fear gripped my throat as I suddenly despaired that my prayers might not be enough to hold him back the next time he contemplated suicide. With some effort I continued. "I pray for healing for Michael's depression and phobias, healing for his emotional instability. I pray that he comes to feel loved, to love

himself, to live a life filled with an abundance of love. And I pray for healing for his soul.

"I pray for a deep, loving, mutually satisfying, mutually fulfilling marriage between Virginia and me." I then thought of the need for specificity, and that given what I'd already experienced, I'd better make clear I was talking about this lifetime and not just a short period of time. "I pray for a deep, loving, mutually satisfying, mutually fulfilling marriage between Virginia and me for a long, long time in this lifetime.

"Finally, I pray that I live a life of joy." *No qualifiers on this one*, I thought.

"Hold everything you have prayed for lovingly, with great intention," the dasa instructed. After a pause he went on, "Now release attachment to the outcome of your prayer. Go in silence with a sense of gratitude."

* * *

"Relationships are always hard," I said during my next one-on-one meeting with my personal dasa, thinking I had stated an obvious truth. I was speaking my own truth, including that the deep personal and cultural differences between Virginia and me had continued to create difficulties in our marriage.

"Actually, relating to another person is the easiest, most natural thing for a human being to do," he retorted immediately. "Perhaps you learned as a young child that nothing comes to you unless you work at it."

Bingo! That was exactly the message I'd learned from both my parents.

"Relationship is simply the act of being with the other person," he went on. "There is no need for them to change or for you to change. Each need only accept the isness of the other's being. The result is joy."

I sat stunned. Could this man-child, no older than twenty-five, who had lived almost his entire life in a sheltered spiritual community and perhaps never had his heart broken in love, possibly hold the key to happiness in my marriage with Virginia, indeed happiness in every relationship in my life?

I wondered if my dasa had just handed me a formulaic answer he'd used many times. "Have you given this same advice before?"

"Never."

"Then how do you know what you've told me is true."

"It just came to me. Sitting here with you, I somehow knew you were going to talk about your marriage, and whatever it was you needed to hear simply came to me."

I thought of all the messages I'd received over the years about the importance of getting my needs met in relationships. I had always believed (or been taught) the best way to do this was to put my needs out there cleanly and clearly with the other person and talk through all relationship conflicts to resolution. What had been the result? Endless processing of issues in my relationships, which often had done more to stir up conflicts than resolve them. Approaching Virginia in this manner had done nothing but push her away and escalate conflicts between us. Was it possible for me to simply accept her, even accept myself, as just what is? Nothing would need to change for me to be happy in my marriage. Virginia would not need to change. I would not need to change. We would simply *be* in relationship with each other. If we each accepted the other with open-hearted love, would the result be joy? Perhaps.

Then one more thought formed. Were my dasa's words an answer to two of the three prayers I'd made just hours before? I felt a quiet yet stunning affirmation. I did not know at the time that my prayer for Michael's healing would one day be answered as well, but that miraculous moment would have to wait.

* * *

"Today we will meditate on the highest three chakras," a dark-haired young woman began. "Come into a seated position with legs crossed and close your eyes. Breathe slowly, drawing each breath deep into your belly. As you let it flow out, release any thoughts that arise." The usual thoughts came flooding in, but after ten days of this Oneness process, I was surprised how quickly those thoughts melted away. The dasa went on, "Bring your attention to the fifth chakra, the chakra centered in your throat. With each in breath, imagine energy of a deep blue frequency growing more and more powerful in your throat. With each out breath we will chant the mantra for this chakra, the sound that resonates with the vibration of this energy center, opening, expanding, and attuning it. For the fifth chakra the sound is hammmmm….." She struck the opening of this sound with an intensity that surprised me and then held the chant on the "m" sound, drawing it out. "Please join me."

I drew a breath deep into my belly. "Hammmmm…" We repeated it again. I noticed she held her breath out after each chant, holding it longer than felt comfortable to me. I had done this type of chanting in yoga sessions over the years but never with the breath held out as long. As I matched her timing, all efforting fell away, and I found myself simply enjoying the meditation. I smiled from spontaneous joy. That thought, too, fell away with the next breath.

"Now shift your focus to the sixth chakra, the dasa said. "With each in breath, experience the vibrational frequency of royal purple filling the space in the center of your head. On the out breath we will chant the mantra for this chakra, om, the original vibration of all creation. Ommmmm…." Again she held the sound for a long time. Again she held the breath out at the end of each chant. Again the chanting went on for a very long time.

From somewhere far away I heard her voice say, "Now bring your attention to the seventh chakra. Picture a thousand-petaled white lotus at the crown of your head. While there is no mantra for the seventh chakra, we will chant 'om satyam om,' with *satyam* being the Sanskrit word for *truth*." *Ah yes*, I thought, *truth*…"Ommmmm satyammm ommmmm…," she began.

As I joined in the chant to open the crown chakra, I felt transported upward. My body began rocking in fine movements, the rhythmic rocking becoming a dance as I felt myself rise to meet an energy…dancing with me as we rose together…I was dancing with…dancing with…the Divine. A broad smile broke out. Yes. I was dancing with the Divine. It felt…exquisite…intoxicating. I stayed in this state, dancing in a realm I had never known existed, wanting to drink in this experience, wanting it to never end. Even when the dasa instructed us to lie down, to integrate the experience, I lingered in the dance, saddened to feel it coming to an end. Reluctantly I lay down and quickly drifted into a state of inexpressible peace. Sometime later I became aware of others stirring around me. Lingering yet again, I eventually began to move my hands, then my feet, feeling myself return to consciousness of having a body. Or was the sensation one of being back in a body after having been outside of it? With some effort I stood up slowly, still unable to walk. I don't remember the walk back to the dormitory. But I do remember the feeling of joy.

* * *

"Your mind is not your mind. Your thoughts are not your thoughts. Your body is not your body. The self is just a concept."

The dasa paused. What did she mean *my mind is not my mind?* "When we were young schoolchildren, Bhagavan would sometimes come into our classroom to teach us. He would begin by asking, 'Whose shirt are you wearing?' We would eagerly answer, 'It is my shirt, teacher.' He would smile and ask us, 'Why do you say it is your shirt?' We would answer, 'Because my parents gave it to me.' He would then ask, 'And where did your parents get this shirt to give to you?' 'They bought it in a shop,' we would answer. 'And how did the shop come to have this shirt?' he would ask. 'They bought it from the seamstress who made it,' came our happy reply, because we thought we were playing a game with Bhagavan. 'And what did the seamstress make this shirt from?' he would next ask. 'From cloth and thread,' we would call out. 'And where did the cotton for the cloth and thread come from?' he would again ask. 'From the cotton plant,' we would reply. 'From what did the plant make this cotton?' 'From sunlight, water, and soil,' we would answer. 'Ah, so your shirt originally came from sunlight, water and soil. And are those yours, too?' he would ask with a twinkle in his eye.

"When we grew older, Bhagavan would come into our classroom and ask a different question. 'You each have a body, do you not?' he would begin. 'Yes, teacher,' we would eagerly reply. 'And what is your body made of?' he would ask. 'Muscles, flesh, and bones,' we would answer. 'From what did your body make these muscles, flesh, and bones?' 'From the food we eat,' came our response. 'And where did this food come from?' 'The earth, rain, and sunlight,' we answered. 'And are these yours, too?' he would ask with the same twinkle in his eye.

"Over time we came to see that Bhagavan was not playing a game. Instead, he was teaching us an important truth: that each of us is connected to the earth, the sunlight, and the rain. And each of these is in turn interconnected with each of the others, and in fact with all that is. Any separation—of my shirt from your shirt, my body from your body, or my self from your self—is a concept in the mind of the person thinking it. Such separation is not a reality because in truth, everything is connected to everything else. We are all one. All that is is one. Any experience of separateness is an illusion created in the mind."

Was this true? Of course there are boundaries between one person and another, such as my skin and the skin of another. But how is that boundary any different than the boundary between *my* liver and *my* intestines, both of which are part of the oneness that makes up me? My skin is a semipermeable membrane around my...or should I say *this* body, just in case it's actually not *mine*? The skin lets in some things but keeps out others. The same is true for the membranous capsule surrounding my liver...I mean *the* liver. Physics teaches us that all matter is composed of molecules, which are in turn composed of atoms, which are composed of protons, neutrons and electrons, which are composed of fundamental particles, whatever we consider those to be at any given time. Is it any more meaningful to ask what is the boundary between one atom and another than to ask what is the boundary between one person and another? On the levels of social and cognitive convention, that boundary exists. But on another level everything is part of a matter-energy continuum that encompasses all that is. *I* am part of that matter-energy continuum. It suddenly became clear to me that any experience I have of being separated from any other part of that matter-energy continuum depends upon the perspective I choose to take to that experience, and I can choose which perspective to take because perspective is created by my mind.

Could the "self" truly just be a concept? I paused at this threshold, not wanting to let go of a part of my web of belief that, until now, had been so central to all I had thought I knew, a filter through which I had made meaning of all I experienced. I anticipated that giving up the self would not be an easy transition...but suddenly it seemed easy. More than easy, it felt relieving...even healing.

If I am part of everything around me, then I am not alone. My experience of aloneness, any sense of alienation from people or objects around me, is just a creation of my mind. Any experience of separation I feel from Virginia is created by my mind. And even the thoughts that create this experience are derived from thoughts that are not completely mine. *My* thoughts include those learned from my parents, from books I have read, or words from a friend or teacher. Perhaps *my* mind (whatever that is) could rearrange these thoughts in a creative way, but does that truly make them mine?

And what is the relationship between "my" thoughts and "my" body? Philosophers since Descartes have wrestled with what they call the mind-body problem, the idea that our thoughts are separate from our physical body. I now wondered if my very thoughts could be part of this matter-energy continuum, making it a matter-energy-thought-consciousness continuum. As I sat with this idea, I felt a palpable shift in my web of belief. Yes... all *is* one. Something within me expanded with this thought. Peace filled my entire being.

* * *

The next day, as I wrestled with a new architecture for my web of belief, I found myself for the first time listening to Bhagavan speaking. Our dasa had introduced the session saying, "We will now hear Bhagavan's teaching in his own words." With great anticipation, I expected Bhagavan to enter our hall, but then the dasa bent down to turn on a DVD. A video screen filled with a radiant face holding unfathomable eyes greeted us with love.

"Dear friends," Bhagavan's slow, resonant voice flowed over us. I felt I could melt into that voice, healed just by the vibrational quality emanating from his very being. "We are about to enter a golden age for all mankind on our planet. This coming age will be ushered in by a shift in consciousness for humanity, a recognition that all is one. This oneness consciousness will dissolve all duality. Mankind will finally live in peace." Yes. Since allowing the thought *all is one* to occupy a central place within my web of belief, I had certainly felt great peace. But now, hearing these words from Bhagavan, I felt a twinge of disappointment. Was he just another well-intentioned charismatic leader selling mankind an impractical utopia? If so, he would take his place in a long line of false prophets stretching back thousands of years.

His next words pulled me back. "I am sorry to say that the current order will not give way easily to this new consciousness. We are entering a period of great unrest." This I agreed with. "Those attached to old ways of thinking, to old fears, will rise up to defend the only reality they know, a reality based upon fear, perceived isolation, and violence. The time to act is now. That is why we have founded Oneness University. We seek to create worldwide consciousness of our oneness with each other and with all that is. If we can achieve this shift in consciousness for a critical mass of individuals throughout the globe, the result will be a shift in consciousness for all humanity."

A swirl of thoughts flooded in on me. Bhagavan's words merged with those of David Hawkins. Bhagavan's intention to achieve some critical mass of people with oneness consciousness as the means for causing a shift in consciousness for everyone aligned perfectly with Hawkins's finding that a few individuals holding a high consciousness state carry more power than many individuals holding lower consciousness states. Bhagavan had established Oneness University and the Oneness Movement with the mission to help as many individuals as possible make this transition to a higher state of consciousness. I sensed urgency in his mission, an urgency I shared. Could it be possible that shifting the consciousness of those open to such a change could have an impact on the forces of negativism and destruction? If so, I wanted to be part of that change, wanted it with all my heart.

Another thought gnawed somewhere within me. Was this the stuff of which cults are made? Bhagavan appeared to have the qualities of an authentic spiritual leader. But how could one distinguish an authentic spiritual leader from the leader of a cult, a false prophet professing false consciousness and untruths? Hawkins would say the answer could be obtained from applied kinesiology testing. But I was far from having enough evidence to trust applied kinesiology to provide a distinction between truth and falsehood.

Just then I could hear Ron Roth's voice saying one word: discernment. I went over the data points I had accumulated on my search for truth. Marsha's waking up knowing Susan was in labor. My personal experience of bumping into energy. Virginia's dying at age nine. My personal hypnotic regression into past lives and life between lives. Photographic evidence of orbs I could not explain. Feeling my own energy rise out of my body to dance with the Divine. I felt clear within myself I was not simply following a cult. Instead, I was on a search to learn what is true. I did not leave discernment at the start of this search and was not abandoning it now.

My thoughts came into focus. *If there is a chance that by dedicating myself to raising the level of my own consciousness I can have a positive effect on others, and by so doing contribute to raising the consciousness of all humanity on the planet, I freely choose to do so.* I could see no downside to this effort.

But much more than just being a rational choice, I yearned for this—yearned to do everything possible to bring healing and peace to as many as I could. Was this not why I'd felt so called to a career in medicine? And was this perhaps an invitation to some unforeseen next step on my path? No, I was not blindly following a cult or even a single spiritual teacher. Neither was I flitting from one guru to the next. Instead, I was continuing my lifelong pursuit of a foundation for the truth and for making ethical choices about how we should live. Yes, discernment, exercised thoughtfully and consistently, had led me to this moment.

As the session drew to a close, I found myself uttering a prayer.

> "Dear God, help me to be of service. Help me live a truly Spirit-directed life. Please help me do all I can to open to ever higher levels of consciousness, to have the greatest impact on all those whom my life touches, to help heal and bring peace. Lord, make me an instrument of Your peace. Amen."

* * *

"It is time for you to prepare to become givers of the Oneness Blessing so you can bring this act of service to your homes and communities," the dasa began. Not until this moment did I understand that one of the intentions of the Oneness process was to train participants to provide Oneness Blessings to others. It suddenly became clear that training wave after wave of students to give Oneness Blessings and sending them back to their communities was one of the strategies Bhagavan was using to raise human consciousness across the planet. *I can support this intent*, I thought, even though I felt no ego investment in becoming a Oneness Blessing giver.

"Over the past few weeks you have each received multiple Oneness Blessings, or deeksha, which is the transfer of Divine energy to the receiver. The source of this energy is not the person giving the blessing. It is the Divine. So to serve as a Oneness Blessing giver, each of you must seek and develop your own personal relationship with the Divine. This relationship and your capacity to allow the Divine to flow through you provide the potency of the Oneness Blessing.

"We shared with you previously that as you conceive God, so shall God appear to you. It is time to take this lesson deeper if you want to achieve the relationship with the Divine that you seek. The secret to this relationship lies within you: as you treat others in the world, so shall you experience God treating you."

The dasa was giving us a restatement of the Golden Rule: do unto others as you would have them do unto you. Only now it was God who would do unto me as I would do unto others, or at least I would experience God in this manner.

Did this have the ring of truth? I reflected back on my initial sense that God parses out granting some prayers and not others. Was this how I had responded to others? Reluctantly I had to admit that I had. What would it look like for me to more consistently respond to others with spontaneous generosity, to be completely open-hearted to others?

I suddenly felt fear…fear of rejection…of loss…and that lowest vibrating of all human emotions, shame. Yes, I had lost love and suffered Marsha's betrayal. I could see now how this experience had created a dark underbelly to some of my motivations, created a desire to control or manipulate others so I would protect myself from pain. But I now held each of these memories in a new way, as a wrinkle under my foot. With this newfound perspective, could I love more open-heartedly? Could I love without fear, without any attempt to control or manipulate others? Could I love without jealousy? It would take courage to make this shift, courage to open my heart in the face of fears.

The dasa made clear this was my work to do. If I wanted to experience the overflowing abundance of God's love, a life of joy, I would have to treat all others in my life with an overflowing abundance of love. Was I prepared to love with this much courage? I realized I could not answer this question just for today. I would have to answer this question anew every day.

* * *

"Tonight we will not only meditate in the presence of the awakened ones," the dasa instructed us, "you will each come up and be embraced by one of them."

As the meditation with the awakened ones began, I felt the now familiar experience of an opening, an almost visceral sensation of the Divine, in the crown chakra at the top of my head. As time went on I felt this opening descend in succession to each chakra, finally reaching my first chakra at the base of the perineum.

Somebody tapped me on the shoulder, indicating I should open my eyes and come to the front of the room. I waited my turn as a round-faced man sitting with eyes closed, smiling broadly, gave deeksha to the people in front of me. Every few minutes he broke into a quiet laugh, seemingly unable to contain the joy of his current state. When my turn approached, I knelt before him. He took my face tenderly in his hands, and I felt myself melt. He then pulled me towards him, hugging me as he shook intermittently with soft laughter. I smiled, feeling what could best be described as joy at being embraced by the Divine. He then held me away for a moment, and again pulled me towards him on the other side as we shook together with laughter. After what seemed like a long time, he finally released me.

I walked slowly to the back of the room and lay down. The experience of each chakra opening…opening ever further created an increasingly intense sensation of intimacy with the Divine. I felt myself growing younger and younger, more and more vulnerable, and felt the love of the Divine entering ever more powerfully into each of my chakras. I was now a helpless infant being filled by a golden light, caressed and infused by love from the Divine. As the experience came to a close, from somewhere inside I heard the words "rebirthed in the arms of the Divine."

* * *

"Today you will be the first group ever allowed to enter the Oneness Temple," our dasa announced. "The temple is still under construction, but you are all being invited to bring your beautiful energy to bless the main meditation hall."

Many times over the past three weeks I had climbed to the roof of our building and gazed down the road to the majesty and beauty of the Oneness Temple. Its vast, white roof punctuated by multiple spires and peaks, its outer balustrades supported by row upon row of symmetric marble columns, the Oneness Temple had seemed more a mystic vision than a building one could enter.

We wound our way through the outer passageways of the Oneness Temple, climbing flight after flight of white marble stairs, until we emerged into an immense open space that was the temple's top floor. Built without columns to enhance the collective energy of the up to eight thousand individuals who could meditate together in this single room, the main hall inspired awe. In one corner of the room stood a huge, empty marble throne. It would forever remain empty, we were told, so that all who would come here would be able to see on that throne God as they envision God. It would also remain empty so that those who believed there is no God would feel welcome.

Our group sang and chanted, filling the not-yet-finished space with love and laughter, doing our part to begin building the energy that would soon emanate from this exhilarating place of universal worship. As the chanting came to a close, Virginia and I found ourselves standing on the western edge of the massive room, along the outermost balustrade, gazing out at the mountains. Somewhere beyond those mountains Michael still suffered. I wanted to offer a Oneness Blessing to him, wanted him to experience the healing and love I knew he so desperately needed. If all is one, might Michael be able to be reached from where we stood? My dasa had said that if I wanted to do all I could to help Michael's healing, I could perform a Oneness Blessing from a distance for him each day for forty-five consecutive days. I immediately committed to do so. Now, standing at the edge of this soon-to-be-consecrated place, Virginia and I offered the first of these Oneness Blessings to reach Michael, to infuse him with the loving energy we had each come to know intimately over the past three weeks. My whole being ached with the hope it would reach him.

* * *

A few months later, Marsha informed me that Michael, who had great talent in acting and singing, had landed a role in a school production of *Children of Eden*,[5] a musical that told the stories of Adam and Eve and Noah. As we'd done for countless school shows before, Virginia and I dutifully bought tickets and planned to attend in spite of the distance Michael still kept from me. As the first act opened, God, depicted as Father, lovingly created Adam and Eve. I could feel that love and re-membered the experience of being birthed in the arms of the Divine. I smiled. In the next few scenes, God/Father spoke often with Adam and Eve, with the love and intimacy of a caring parent. *Yes*, I thought, *this is God as I have come to know God, loving, intimate, ever present.* But then, after Adam and Eve had eaten of the Tree of Knowledge, God/Father became angry with them, banished them from Eden, and cursed them to toil endlessly and birth in pain. *No!* I wanted to call out. *No! God has not cursed man with pain. Pain is our teacher. Pain is how we learn to open our hearts.* I suddenly yearned for everybody to understand that if we chose to see God as judging and punishing, this was how we would experience God. We had a choice to experience God differently, and I wished everyone to be blessed with this knowledge.

---

[5] Music and lyrics by Stephen Schwartz. Book by John Caird. Book © 1996 by John Caird. Music and Lyrics © 1996 by Stephen Schwartz. All rights reserved. Content and excerpts used by permission.

God/Father disappeared from the stage. The story of Cain and Abel was told with all the intensity of the first fratricide. Eve grieved for the death of one son and the banishment of the other. She never again saw Cain. We next saw Eve as an old woman. She recounted the journey of her life with tears for the loss of her sons and the death of her husband, but also with smiles as she described the goodness of her son Seth and the abundance of her other children and grandchildren. Now, in the twilight of her life, she called to God, but he did not answer. He had not answered her since the banishment from Eden. God/Father appeared on stage, back turned to Eve in silence. *No!* I wanted to shout again. *No! God does answer us. God is there for us to reach out to at any moment. It is we who have turned away from God, not God from us. I should know. I spent most of my life unwilling and unable to reach out to God. But when I finally did, I was met with more love from the Divine than I ever knew possible.* Mercifully, God finally answered Eve.

"Father, is Cain alive?" she asked with fear and hope.

"Cain is alive," he answered.

"And did he find some happiness?" she asked with the heart of a mother who had never stopped loving her son.

"He found some happiness," God answered, giving Eve's old and aching heart a modicum of peace.

"Thank you, Father."

"No thanks to me," God answered. Once more I wanted to shout, *No! God does not withhold happiness from us. We do so with our own actions, our own choices.*

"Father," Eve said.

"Yes, my daughter?"

"I've missed you!" She started to cry. With a mixture of compassion and sadness, I realized there is never a reason to miss God. God is always here.

After the show, before Michael rushed off to the cast party, I tried to share with him what had so moved me during the performance. He responded flippantly, "Still working out your unresolved father shit, aren't you?"

"No, Michael, it's something more, much more. I wish I could share it with you." But that was not to be, at least not that evening.

Chapter VIII: John of God, the Brazilian Healer

Miracles Happen. The Question Is, What Do These Words Mean?

My trip to the central highlands of Brazil to see the healer known as John of God really began twelve years earlier on a mountaintop in Utah. There, the pulls and tensions of our newly forming stepfamily played out when Virginia, seeking to keep up with Sam, Michael, and me, all fanatical skiers, tore the cartilage in her knee on a mogul field she should never have been on.

For six months she lived with pain in her knee. Finally, after hearing so many stories from friends about their miraculous results from arthroscopic surgery, she had the procedure. The orthopedist came out beaming as he proclaimed he'd been able to perform a complete repair, placing two screws in her cartilage, bringing the edges of her tear into perfect alignment. "I know I promised she would be walking within a few days," he said, "but because we were able to repair her cartilage rather than only cut out the damaged part, she needs to be on crutches and non-weight-bearing for six weeks. She should still be pain-free within a few days."

Despite his prediction, the pain not only persisted, it escalated. Her leg became intermittently mottled, cool, and disturbingly dark purple. Four weeks into her recovery, that same orthopedist diagnosed reflex sympathetic dystrophy, or RSD, a rare, disabling, neurological condition marked by increasing chronic pain, loss of limb function, and disability that threatened to consume her life. Upon being sent to one of the top RSD specialists in the country, she looked directly at him and said, "Tell me the truth. What do you honestly think my prognosis is?"

From behind his desk, he met her gaze and said, "Personally, I give you no hope."

With a strength and determination I hadn't fully appreciated in her before, Virginia set out to do all she could to reclaim her life from the devastating sentence that had been pronounced over it. After months of painful deep tissue massage and physical therapy, agonizing nerve injections into her back, hundreds of hours applying all she knew of energy healing to her own leg, and countless other unconventional and alternative therapies, her symptoms slowly began to reverse. Two years later they'd stabilized, allowing her to live close to a normal life, but with intermittent recurrences that threatened to progress into the devastating nightmare so many others with RSD live with every day.

Throughout the whole ordeal, she prayed for healing.

* * *

In the midst of a particularly distressing flare-up of her symptoms, Virginia shared, "Ron Roth is taking a group from Celebrating Life Ministries to Brazil to see a spiritual healer known as John of God who performs miracles in a little Brazilian town called Abadiania. After my friend Shirley badly injured her neck in a car accident, she went there and experienced amazing healing. And it was more than physical healing. She experienced healing of body, mind, and spirit. I think that's what it will take for me to heal from RSD. I want to go, but the trip is already full. I'm number eleven on the waiting list, and the trip leaves in just a few weeks."

"Brazil?" I said somewhat incredulously. This was years before we'd ever considered going to India, and the thought of traveling that far in the hope of receiving some spiritual cure seemed farfetched to me at best. I had not yet had the life-changing experiences that lay ahead for me at Oneness University, and my skepticism, always lying close to the surface, now came to the fore. Plus the seeming self-importance of his name, John of God, didn't sit well with me.

"Something tells me I'm supposed to go," Virginia responded. "It just feels right." I'd learned early in our relationship that when Virginia got an intuitive hit like this, there was no sense in arguing, as most often she was right.

"Well, do what you have to do about a visa, and let's hope a miracle happens so you can get on this trip."

Only days before the group was to leave, that miracle happened. "The trip coordinator at Celebrating Life Ministries just called," Virginia exclaimed. "I'm in. I'm going to see John of God!"

"What happened to the other people ahead of you on the waiting list?" I asked, more than a little surprised.

"Somehow every one of them, all ten, said they couldn't go. So my name is now at the top of the list."

"Somehow?" I said, my eyebrows raised. "Let's chalk this up to another data point. I'm sure you'll come back with a few more to shake my world."

* * *

"Abadiania is precious," Virginia gushed when she got home, "and I'm healed! My RSD symptoms are completely gone! The experience was amazing. Rick, you have to go there!"

RSD symptoms completely gone? A lifelong sentence of chronic pain lifted? With that surprising, very welcome, and unexplainable data point, I knew a trip to Brazil was on my path...just not yet. I did not feel pulled to Brazil...but when we heard John of God was coming to Atlanta, we made plans to see him there.

A close friend's death at the last minute kept Virginia from coming. Without her by my side, I went to see John of God, not knowing what to expect. Instead of seeing him in his home environment, the place which had touched Virginia so, I was to see him at the convention center of a downtown Atlanta hotel. Already I sensed something missing. In spite of this, on the morning of the first day, I dutifully followed Virginia's instructions, which were to show up wearing all white and wait in a line, a "first-time line," with hundreds of similarly white-clad individuals of all ages. Others were waiting in a "second-time line," a "revision line," and some other lines, but I had no idea what the names for those lines meant. I also had no idea how one man could see, and supposedly treat, the sea of people surrounding me, numbering perhaps a thousand, in just one day.

Along with others in the first-time line, I slowly wended through rooms with row upon row of people seated with eyes closed. These were current rooms, we'd been told. People sat in current, performing a kind of meditation, focusing on positive, healing thoughts, or as one person described, focusing on love in whatever way they conceived it. The combined consciousnesses of these people somehow created the energetic environment John of God needed to do "the work," whatever that meant.

After perhaps two hours shuffling forward in the line, I finally entered the room in which John of God sat. As we turned the corner and headed towards him, I caught glimpses of a burly yet kind-faced man, also dressed in white and sitting on a large chair, quietly saying something to each person who stepped before him. Oddly, he didn't even seem to be looking at the person in front of him. Virginia had explained that he looked four or five people down the line, making his so-called diagnosis by looking at each individual before they came before him. I've since learned it is understood that in a glance, he takes in the individual's aura as a full-color hologram, including physical, mental, spiritual, and karmic information, making a diagnosis and prescribing treatment of the individual's whole being. As I moved closer, I held in my mind a list of the things for which I wanted healing. My eyes briefly met his when I was about six people away, a moment in which he seemed to look through me more than at me. When I came before him, he was indeed looking down the line behind me and quietly intoned some Portuguese words that were translated as "Spiritual intervention at two o'clock."

"What? What does that mean?" I asked.

"It means the Entity, which is how we refer to John of God when he is incorporated and doing the healing work, will provide a spiritual intervention to treat you," the translator explained. "In Brazil, they refer to it as a spiritual surgery, but here in the United States we are not allowed to refer to it as 'surgery,' because this might be perceived as crossing the line into practicing medicine without a license." I didn't know what "incorporated" meant, but spiritual surgery was what Virginia had had when she had gone to Brazil, so I knew I was in for…for something.

That afternoon I felt somewhat bewildered sitting with thirty other people in the "surgery room," a section of the convention hall cordoned off with hanging sheets. "Close your eyes and place your hand over whichever part of your body feels most in need of healing," one of the volunteers instructed us. "If you have multiple requests for healing, place your hand over your heart," he went on. Since I had quite a list of things I hoped to have healed, I closed my eyes and placed my hand over my heart. About ten minutes later, I heard John of God's resonant, baritone voice say something. The translator announced, "The spiritual intervention is complete. You are to go back to your rooms, go to bed, and stay in bed for the next twenty-four hours. Ask others to bring you food or order room service. Don't do any strenuous physical activity for at least one week. Seven days from now, when you go to sleep, wear white and place a glass of water next to your bed. During the night your stitches will be removed."

Stitches? What stitches? I almost asked out loud.

"Please follow these instructions carefully. They are very important."

I rose but felt uncomfortable standing fully erect. Something in my upper abdomen felt...felt...not quite normal. I made my way back to my room walking a little hunched over. "Go to bed," he'd instructed. I climbed into bed and almost immediately fell asleep, even though it was only a quarter to three in the afternoon. Dinner somehow arrived. I ate some and fell back to sleep almost immediately. Any time I got up to go to the bathroom, I felt a pulling in my upper abdomen. *What happened to me in those ten minutes?* I wondered each time I emerged from that odd sleep state long enough to have a conscious thought. Then almost immediately I would fall back asleep. The following morning I still did not want to get out of bed. I tossed in a fitful sleep off and on until the afternoon when I finally felt ready to get up and could do so without violating my instructions.

On the third and last morning of John of God's visit, I made my way back to the main area. *What do I do now?* I wondered. There was no reason to go before John of God since I'd already supposedly been treated, so I asked if I could sit in the current room. The organizers were letting in the last few people, so I took a seat to do...I didn't know what. *Think about love* had been one of the instructions. Also we were told it was very important to keep our eyes closed and not cross any parts of our bodies, like our legs, as doing so would somehow disrupt the energy of the current. So I closed my eyes, took a few deep breaths, and focused on opening my heart. With each in breath I imagined drawing loving energy into my heart, and with each out breath I imagined breathing love out to everyone around me.

After some time had passed, I had the urge to check my watch but remembered the admonition to keep my eyes closed. When my buttocks began to feel sore, I shifted my position and tried again to focus on breathing in and out love. Then my back began to hurt, so I shifted again, and again returned to breathing in and out love. *How long would this last?* I kept wondering, and then returned to my breathing. Finally, I heard a person in our room begin a closing prayer. When it was over, we were instructed to open our eyes. Checking my watch told me more than three hours had passed. Three hours sitting still in meditation! I'd never successfully pulled off more than twenty minutes of sitting meditation. How did I manage to do it for three hours? All I did was think about love. Not a bad way to spend time…as long as I didn't mind the butt discomfort and back pain. So I decided to line up to sit in current again for the last afternoon of John of God's visit.

After another long session, which went much like the morning's, I heard an announcement that anybody in the current room wanting to see John of God before leaving could open their eyes and get in line. With no particular intention other than to express gratitude, I joined the line. When my moment to pass before John of God came, I was shocked at the transformation in him. He slumped in his chair, his eyes almost bulging out of his head, a limp hand taking mine for a brief second before the next person in line moved forward. This was a picture of exhaustion beyond any I had ever seen. Only later did I learn that during this visit, we in the United States had not been able to create and hold the quality of current that was accomplished regularly in Brazil, and that doing this work without the strength of current to which he was accustomed took a terrible toll on the man.

If it weren't for Virginia's reminder, I might have forgotten seven days later to dress for sleep in white and leave a glass of water next to my bed. Somehow the thought of having stitches out didn't seem absurd after the sensations I'd experienced in my abdomen following the "surgery."

As my first encounter with John of God came to a close, no miraculous cures happened, at least none of which I was aware. I had experienced odd sensations in my abdomen. I had been knocked out for almost twenty-four hours of what felt like drug-induced sleep. And I'd spent more than six hours in a single day meditating on love. I had no idea where to place this experience in my web of belief, so it took up residence somewhere on the periphery. Four months later we went to Oneness University in India. Experiences there created new space in my web of belief for this encounter with John of God. But having space did not equal understanding or even acceptance. For that, and so much more, I would have to wait.

* * *

Several months after we returned from Oneness University, a minor fall caused Virginia's RSD symptoms to recur (a known risk for anyone with this condition). She immediately scheduled a second visit to Brazil, and again came home in complete remission. Thankfully, she has not had an RSD recurrence since. For myself, following my experiences at Oneness University, I began to sense Brazil had become the next step on my path, so we planned a joint trip to Abadiania for the following summer.

Virginia had been telling a number of people, many of them practitioners from diverse healing modalities, of her experiences with John of God, and one individual after another decided to join us on a trip to Brazil. Eventually a group of almost thirty formed, many from the medical field, including two other physicians, a number of nurses, acupuncturists, and energy healers.

Unlike the experience in Atlanta, which I had done on my own, we chose to go on a guided trip organized by Bob Dinga and Diana Rose, the couple who had led Virginia's trip to Brazil with Celebrating Life and who at that time had been to see John of God more than thirty times. The evening before our first session with John of God, they insisted we attend an orientation to the Casa (as everyone there referred to the site of John of God's work) with Diego, a loving and generous man who volunteered his services to support the work of John of God.

Entering through an open gate, we passed a room filled halfway from floor to ceiling with old wheelchairs, canes, and walkers. "These have all been left by people who came to the Casa needing them and departed no longer needing them because they'd been healed," Diana explained. "Miraculous healings happen here all the time."

Miraculous healings? Gazing at the mountain of discarded medical equipment, I wondered if healings of this magnitude were possible.

As we took our seats in one of the Casa rooms, a man I took to be Diego began, "Welcome to the Casa." His genuine smile and warm voice made him instantly likeable. "*Casa*, which means *house* in Portuguese, is short for Casa de Dom Ignacio de Loyola." He went on, "The spirit of Dom Ignacio, founder of the Jesuit order, provides overall direction to all the work performed here." It was not lost upon me that Saint Ignatius, as he is known in English, died sometime in the 1500s. "Some of you may be wondering how a man who's been dead for more than four hundred years can provide guidance to our work today." I was definitely curious. "This is possible because all the work done here at the Casa is carried out in the context of Spiritism, a belief system indigenous to Brazil, though versions of Spiritism are practiced in countries throughout the world. It's probably not proper to say Spiritism is practiced, because it is not a religion in the sense most of you use that term. Spiritism is a set of beliefs that has been around for hundreds if not thousands of years and was codified by Allan Kardec, a Frenchman who wrote a series of books based upon his research into Spiritism. Spiritism can be summarized as a belief in the existence of spirits, meaning nonphysical beings that live in an invisible or spirit world, and the possibility of communication between these spirits and living people through what is called mediumship.

"Mediumship can take many forms," he continued. "Some mediums write, or put more properly, they allow a disembodied spirit of a no-longer-living being to write through them. One of the most striking examples of writing mediums was Chico Xavier, a Brazilian who wrote 412 books in his lifetime. Anyone who has ever written a book knows how much time and effort goes into that process. Writing ten or twenty books might be considered a great lifetime accomplishment for any author. Completing fifty books, an intimidating goal. But writing over four hundred books in a person's life does not seem possible…that is if it's the person doing the writing. If a spirit is doing the writing…" He let the thought hang in the air.

"Some mediums paint images provided to them by spirits. Others allow spirits to communicate through them. Perhaps some of you have attended a channeling in which this has occurred." An image arose in my mind of the person I'd witnessed speaking in a strange accent, channeling information about a man's battle to the death in a past life with someone now incarnated as his son in this life. Was it possible I already shared the beliefs of Spiritism?

"We are all here at the Casa because João Teixeira de Faria—João as he is affectionately referred to—is a full trance incorporation medium. This means he gives up his body and mind completely to a disembodied spirit. During the time the spirit occupies his body, or is incorporated as we say here, João is literally not present. When it's over, he remembers nothing of what happened during the incorporation.

"This first occurred to him spontaneously at the age of fourteen (though some accounts report him to have been sixteen) when, while walking along a road, he saw a vision of Saint Rita who told him he was to be a great healer. The vision directed him to a church in the next town. He remembers nothing of what happened there, but four hours later awoke, for lack of a better term, to hear from members of the congregation that King Solomon had incorporated in him and performed healing miracles for many people present. Only aware of feeling tired and hungry, he did not believe what he had heard. But after the same experience recurred multiple times, including different spirits incorporating into him and performing unexplainable healings, he finally accepted his mission to serve others, to serve all humanity through selflessly offering himself as a medium for the healing of others. Now, more than fifty years later, millions of people have experienced miraculous healings through this extraordinary man, one of the greatest trance mediums alive today. We have been told João has prepared seven lifetimes for the mission he has generously taken on in this lifetime. Chico Xavier, the writing medium I mentioned earlier who served as one of João's teachers, gave him the name by which he is best known today, John of God. Despite this title, João is a deeply humble man who clearly states, 'It is not I who heals, but God.'

"Now I must make an important point. The *Entity*, which is the word we use when João has incorporated any one of the healing spirits, is very clear on this. The healing offered by John of God is not to be thought of as replacing whatever conventional medical treatment you are currently receiving. It is in addition to that treatment. So always, always follow the treatment prescribed by your physicians. Do not stop any medical treatments until told to do so by your physicians. The work of healing here at the Casa is intended to be combined with conventional medical treatments, not to replace them.

"Since settling in Abadiania thirty years ago, João has been offering healing at the Casa to all who wish to come, from anywhere in the world, and he charges nothing for this. You have come to a spiritual hospital that is free to anyone who seeks healing."

How different from America's hospitals, I thought.

Diego continued. "All that is asked of you is that you follow the rules of the Casa…and yes, one more thing…that you open your heart. For the true work of healing begins with opening your own heart to love…to love others, to receive love from others, and to love yourself." *A hospital deriving its healing services from the realm of the spiritual, requiring all who enter to open their hearts to love, and providing all services for free—such a hospital*, I thought, *has much to teach us all.*

"Sometimes when you come before the Entity, he may say, 'Sit in my current and do your work.' Your work is to open your heart. The more you open your heart, the more healing you will receive from the Entity." The instruction I'd received in Atlanta for sitting in current, to open my heart to love, now made much more sense.

"The Casa has two current rooms," Diego went on. "The first current room, also referred to as the mediums' room, is a place anyone who chooses to serve in current is able to sit. You must be in your seat in that room at least fifteen minutes before the session starts and be willing to sit in meditation with your eyes closed until the session ends. This may be two hours, and it may be six hours. We never know how long a current session will be. However long it lasts, your role is to help create and hold what is best described as an energetic space, a field of loving energy necessary for the Entity to do the healing work here. It may be helpful to know that the Casa is built upon a mountain of almost pure quartz that extends deep into the ground. This crystalline quartz appears to play some role in creating and sustaining the current energy.

"I said before that the entity may say to you, 'Sit in *my* current.' This refers to the second or Entity's current room. The Entity sits in a special chair at the head of this room, and you may sit in this area only if you have been instructed to do so by the Entity.

"The Entity usually holds two current sessions, one in the morning and one in the afternoon, on Wednesdays, Thursdays, and Fridays, unless João is traveling out of the country. Beyond these designated sessions, the Casa grounds are open and available to you seven days a week, and you are welcome to spend as much time as you like at the Casa. You are only asked to treat these grounds with respect, as the sacred space this is. And recognize the spirit beings are always here. They don't have the same experience of time as we do. Healings have spontaneously occurred at all times of the day and night, both on the grounds of the Casa and for people back in their pousadas.

"Part of the treatment all receive here is the blessed soup, a delicious soup prepared with love and prayers. Everyone who comes to the Casa during the morning session is to have a bowl of soup after going before John of God. We do this as part of the healing, and also because many Brazilians who make the pilgrimage to the Casa, sometimes traveling for days, might have this soup as their only meal of the entire day.

"You will find two large wooden triangles on the Casa grounds, one hanging on the wall at the back of the raised stage in the main meeting room and one on the outer wall of the main Casa building. Each of these, known as prayer triangles, is considered a portal, an opening to the spiritual dimensions, a portal that delivers to the Entity any prayers prayed while resting your head inside the triangle or written on a piece of paper and tucked into the triangle. Outside the main meeting hall you will also find a prayer basket in which anyone may leave a written prayer for assistance from the Entity, and such prayers will be responded to in the same way. Some of the most amazing healing miracles, both for those who have come to the Casa and for those not here but who are prayed for by someone visiting the Casa, have happened in response to prayers left in either of the prayer triangles or the prayer basket."

Could prayers here at the Casa truly be answered by the Entity? I thought of our dasa's teaching in India that the way we each perceive God is the way God will appear to us. Was I prepared to perceive God as answering prayers in this manner?

Diego's voice interrupted my thoughts as he went on, "One day here at the Casa, a woman put a letter to the Entity in the prayer basket listing many things she was requesting healing for. Three days later she took a copy of this list to the translator saying that she wanted him to read it to the Entity to make sure he knew what she was asking. When the translator started reading it to the Entity, he interrupted saying, 'We just got this list three days ago, and we are still working on it,' and waved his hand for her to move along."

Prayers answered. I paused to take in this thought. Prayers passing through a portal directly to spirit beings on the other side, spirit beings collectively known as the Entity, beings capable of fulfilling prayers for healing. I had come this far for...for what? The Casa, John of God, had simply appeared as the next step on my spiritual path. Was I prepared now to allow myself to pray for help from this Entity, help for what mattered most? Suddenly a prayer arose in me, a one-word prayer. Michael. Could such beings heal my son? Was this too much to pray for, too much to hope for? My heart ached with a sudden, fervent prayer for Michael's healing...healing for his emotions...healing for his soul. Healing so that he could live a life filled with love, a life in which he fulfilled all he came into this lifetime to do. I knew as soon as Diego completed his instructions, I would make my way to this triangle and pray with all my heart for Michael's healing.

Diego went on to explain the various names of the lines I'd heard in Atlanta: the first-time line for those who had never been in front of the Entity, the second-time line for anyone who had been in front of the Entity at least once or had had their picture taken before the Entity, and other lines. Eventually he described the revision line for those who had had a spiritual surgery and had had their stitches out but had not been before the Entity since that time. This described my situation, so I planned to join the revision line in the morning.

* * *

That evening, Bob and Diana suggested we each write a list of all the things we wanted healed for ourselves, including any physical conditions, healing for our emotions, and spiritual healing or healing for our souls. They said the Entity sees and responds to everything we put on our list, even if we would only have seconds in front of him.

Sitting with pen suspended over paper, I wondered what I truly wanted to have healed. I had not come to John of God explicitly for healing of a particular condition, as had so many others. Instead I had come because it had felt like the next step on my spiritual path. Yet I had learned enough on that path to recognize that much of it had to do with healing. So being age fifty-four and watching my body begin to decline, I began by listing a dozen physical conditions in need of healing.

Next I thought of the many emotional feelings or situations I could ask to be healed. I thought of the wound still remaining from Marsha's affair, a wound that had been helped in India but not fully healed. Then Michael's face arose before me. Tears began to fill my eyes. We had been instructed to ask for our own healing during the first week of our stay in Abadiania and healing for others during the second week. I had not known of this guidance when I'd spontaneously bowed my head with ardent hope at the prayer triangle earlier in the evening. With reluctance, I set aside further prayers for Michael's healing, at least for the moment. But I could ask to heal the ache in my heart for Michael's suffering, the pain I felt for the broken relationship between us, and all the fears for him I held in my heart.

Reflecting on these and other thoughts, I realized all the emotional healing I desired distilled down to one: to open my heart to love. So I wrote on the paper, "To love others fully, completely, without fear, without jealousy, and without any desire to control or manipulate another." After a pause I realized something was missing for my heart to be truly open. It was not just about my loving others, so I added, "To open my heart to receive love."

Then I wondered what healing to request for my soul. As I opened to the question, a cascade of thoughts flooded in, and I did my best to capture them in words. Eventually the list included:

> To open to the next step on my spiritual path
> To serve God and be an instrument of God's peace in the highest and best for myself, for all those my life touches, and for Spirit itself
> To fulfill what I incarnated to do
> To heal past life traumas that are impacting this life
> To release ego attachments so they do not have power within me to drive emotions and actions
> To heal unresolved karma
> To live in joy at all times
> To experience oneness with God and all that is at all times

After reviewing the now substantial list of my physical, emotional, and spiritual healing desires, I uttered one word: "Amen."

* * *

The following morning, wearing a white cotton shirt and pants, I joined a parade of similarly clad individuals and small groups filling the tiny streets of this small Brazilian town, streaming toward the Casa in the early morning sun. Snippets of conversations in German, French, Spanish, Italian, and English could be heard buzzing through the crowd. Some were here for return trips. Many were here for the first time, filled with anxious questions and wondering if they had made the right decision in traveling across oceans in hope of a miracle. Despite assurances from Virginia and my initial experiences in Atlanta, I identified with this latter group.

Following the instructions we'd received, I went to the Casa bookstore and picked up a small piece of paper laminated in plastic with the word "Revisio" on it, meaning I was to get in the revision line. Virginia's read, "2nd," which meant the second-time line. After placing our healing request lists in the prayer basket, we made our way to the main hall, a partially open-air room with a small, raised stage at the front and seats for several hundred. Already almost filled with people wearing white clothing, it teemed with activity. Amid this throng I found a seat in the far left corner of the last row. Chaos seemed to reign around me as hundreds of individuals swarmed about, the air mixing with ever more anxious questions from first-timers and hearty, vocal greetings among the returning.

As I settled in to wait, I reminded myself that I was still a scientist and a skeptic. How did a scientist and skeptic find himself in a small Brazilian town, dressed all in white, awaiting what could only be described as a miracle to be delivered through a man who embodied the spirit of dead healers? As I reflected on the steps along the path that had led me to this moment, at no point did I feel I'd abandoned the tenets of science or skepticism. Radically applied, science and skepticism, mixed with insatiable curiosity and a commitment to pursue truth wherever it might lead, were the very drivers that had impelled me on this journey.

Seeking to quiet my restless mind, it occurred to me that the time spent awaiting the revision line could best be passed acting as if I were in current. Beyond the main hall were the current rooms where I had glimpsed people already sitting in meditation, as I had done in Atlanta. They were in current no more than a hundred feet from where I sat. If they were there to build and hold some matrix of energy, it didn't make sense for that matrix to end at the door to the first current room.

So I closed my eyes, took a few deep breaths, and began to...*to what?* I wondered. I'd done my best in Atlanta to meditate on love, but now, having experienced the Oneness process in India, that approach seemed far too limited. As I began to envision what a different meditation could be like, a procession of those who had served as my teachers on this spiritual journey arose. All I had learned from the yoga instructors at Kripalu, Ron Roth, David Hawkins, the dasas at Oneness University, Bhagavan and Amma, and others seemed to coalesce as I sought in the highest and most powerful way to open my heart, my full self, to love.

With eyes closed and after several slow, deep breaths, I sought to clear my mind and just attend to my breathing. Having learned long ago that sitting meditation, simply watching my breath, rarely quieted my thoughts, I moved on to visualize opening my chakras. Starting with the first chakra at the base of the perineum and slowly progressing to the seventh chakra at the top of my head, I created intentions with each breath. I felt my first chakra open as I breathed in the intention, *I am one with all that is.* With the next breath, this became *I am one with all humanity* as I visualized connecting with the consciousness of all people around the world. I shifted to the individual level with the phrase, *I am one with Virginia, and she is one with me.* With those words I imagined all the barriers between my wife and me dissolving, pictured us as already a single, shared energy, I completely open to her and she to me. Nothing needed to change for this to be, I realized. We already were one in energy, the boundaries between us being just thoughts in our mind when viewed from the perspective of the matter-energy-thought-consciousness continuum. Continuing, I breathed in the thought, *Virginia and I are one with all humanity and with all that is.* As I heard these words, I felt the energy of this connection to all human beings everywhere. Next it seemed appropriate to connect with those in the specific region in which I found myself. So with the following breath I breathed in the thought, *I am one with all the people of Abadiania…all the people of Brazil, and together we are one with each other, with all humanity, and with all that is.* Again, these words connected to an intention, a sending out of the energy of this intention to all the people of Abadiania, all the people of Brazil, and then all the people in the world. Successive breaths became *I am one with all the people of South America, and we are one with each other, with all humanity, and with all that is…I am one with all the people of North America, and we are one with each other, with all humanity, and with all that is.* I continued this with one breath each for Africa, Europe, Asia, and finally Australia, New Zealand, and the Pacific islands. With the next breath I breathed in the thought, *I am one with all humanity,* picturing a sea of human consciousness surrounding the entire earth, *and together we are one with each other and with all that is.*

It seemed right to expand beyond just connecting with people. So I breathed in, *I am one with all animals on the earth, and we are one with each other and with all that is,* feeling my consciousness reach out to and connect with the energetic web of all animals around the world.

I am one with all plants on the earth, and we are one with each other and with all that is. Then, *I am one with the entire biosphere, and we are all one with each other,* visualizing all life on earth, from the highest mountain to the deepest ocean, as an interconnected, singular energetic web. With the next breath this expanded to *I am one with all the earth, and the earth is one with me and with all that is.*

With each successive breath, my thought, my intention, expanded ever farther. *I am one with the moon and all the planets.*

I am one with the sun, viscerally experiencing myself as one with the almost unfathomable power and energy of the continuous nuclear explosions of that orb. But even this was not big enough, as the next breath became *I am one with all the stars, matter, and energy in our galaxy,* sensing my consciousness expand out to the vastness of the galaxy. But knowing this was only one among countless other galaxies, this next became *I am one with all the stars, matter, and energy of the entire universe,* feeling my consciousness stretch beyond any capacity I'd ever experienced, taking in the whole sweep of the known universe and feeling at one with it all. Finally I thought of that which created and potentially stood outside this vast expanse of universe. I thought of God. Keeping with my evolving image of God, instead of some single being or deity who made the universe as an act of will, I envisioned a consciousness so large as to encompass all the universe, a universe countless billions of light years across, a consciousness permeating every tiny corner of this vast universe, a consciousness the essence of which is love. With this thought I breathed, *I am one...with...God,* experiencing an opening into oneness with all that is, into oneness with a loving consciousness filling the universe, an opening into oneness with God.

I then breathed the energy from the first chakra up into the second and visualized it opening with the phrase, *I honor the other as other.*

With the next breath this became *I honor Virginia as other,* envisioning not our oneness, but accepting and honoring her separateness from me.

I honor my mother as other.

I honor my father as other.

I honor Sam as other.

I honor Michael as other. I had to pause at this, accepting that Michael was not me and his journey was not mine. This felt like an important shift to make.

I honor Marsha as other, releasing her to live her life separate from me, releasing any attachment to her.

Then I breathed the energy from my first chakra, through the second chakra, and into the third chakra with the phrase, *I honor myself.* I paused, wondering if this was truly "my" self or simply "this" self. In response, the next breath became *I honor this body.* Next, *I honor the passions of this self.*

I honor the personal history of this self. And finally, *I honor the karma of this self.*

I breathed the energy to open the fourth chakra with the words *I open my heart to love.*

This shifted to *I open my heart to receive love.* With the next breath I visualized my heart opening to receive love from Virginia, the love of my wife, complete, lacking nothing, filling my heart. I felt peace and joy. Next, I opened my heart to receive love from my mother, a woman with whom I'd struggled on and off all my life. I visualized love flowing from her heart into mine, the essence of mother-love, sensed the true intent in her heart even if she had trouble expressing it, feeling it completely, lacking nothing. In that moment, I knew nothing needed to change for me to experience love and completeness in my relationship with my mother. A deep sigh released something I'd held inside for longer than I could remember, and again I felt peace and joy. Next I did the same with my father, a loving but highly judgmental man whose approval I'd sought all my life. I felt the essence of his father-love flowing from him into my heart, filling it, lacking nothing. A lifelong wound seemed somehow to dissolve. I extended the image to receiving love from other family members, friends, co-workers, and from all humanity

I shifted to giving love with the phrase, *I open my heart to love fully, willingly, courageously, without any desire to control or manipulate another, without any jealousy.* With each breath I brought into my mind a role model for how to love well. I thought, *I open my heart to love as Bhagavan and Amma love, with the power of ten thousand lives of enlightenment,* and felt my heart open even more. The next breath brought *I open to love as Ron Roth loves, with the power of the Holy Spirit flowing through me, out to all others,* feeling a loving energy fill my heart and then flow outward in all directions.

I open to love as the highest Christed beings love, opening my heart yet more with the image of loving as Jesus loved, as the Buddha loved, to love as all of the most highly enlightened beings who have ever lived. Finally the phrase *I open my heart to love as God loves.* With this, my heart almost exploded, feeling it could not be contained inside my chest. *I love with complete forgiveness...beyond forgiveness...there is nothing to forgive for you...you have done no wrong.* With this I extended forgiveness to Marsha and to all whom I'd ever felt had wronged me. They had done no wrong.

They were simply living out their lives as best they could. If God did not judge them, neither would I.

I now shifted, breathing in energy to open the fifth chakra. *I open to do not my will, but Thy will.*

*I open to speak only the truth…to use the gift of communication that has been given to me in this lifetime in the service of the Divine…to live a truly Spirit-directed life…*and finally, *Lord, make me an instrument of Your peace.*

Next I breathed the energy up through all the chakras and into the sixth chakra with *I open to the peace that surpasseth all understanding.* Though I'd used these words before, never had they produced such a profound opening within my consciousness as at that moment, an opening that seemed to go outward and upward without end, accompanied with the deepest sense of peace.

I open to the wisdom of all masters, feeling an opening in the center of my head into which unnamed teachings from countless enlightened beings seemed to pour.

I am one with all that is, feeling my consciousness extend outward to the entire universe once again…*With all that ever was,* feeling my consciousness open backward into the beginnings of time…*And with all that ever will be,* experiencing my consciousness released from all constraints of time.

Finally I breathed the energy from my first chakra up through the others one at a time, culminating in opening the seventh chakra at the top of my head. *I open to the Divine.* I felt my energy continue upward…upward as it had when meditating in the presence of the enlightened ones in India…the rise slowing at times as it had then…I breathed my intention, my will, into elevating the vibrational frequency of my consciousness, feeling the rise resume its hesitating but progressive journey upward. When it seemed to reach as far as it would go, I simply remained in this state, unaware of the passage of time.

The noise level around me rose. I felt some stirring of people about me, but I had not heard the revision line called, so I resumed sitting in current.

Following this slight disturbance, I shifted my intention to bringing in as much love as I could. With an in breath, I imagined drawing the energy of the Divine down through the crown of my head and drawing the energy of Mother Earth up through my first chakra, the two energies meeting in my heart…filling my heart…healing my heart…With the out breath, this energy healed every cell in my body…then flowed further outward to all who were at the Casa, bathing them in love.

At some point I became aware that the room had again become quiet… too quiet. Had I missed my line? Was everyone already inside the current rooms? With a sudden panic I opened my eyes, violating the instructions to keep my eyes closed during current. As my vision cleared, I realized the hall was empty. A few people meandered somewhere behind me. I stood up unsteadily, bewildered, now sure I'd missed my line. Staggering out of the meeting hall, I saw Virginia coming toward me. The words stammered out, "What…What happened? Did I miss my line?"

* * *

Virginia had looked over in my direction and seen me sitting with eyes closed at the back of the room. *He seems pretty well settled for a first day at the Casa*, she thought with some relief. She took a seat a few rows away and waited for the usual welcome and opening comments before the lines would be called.

Just then she heard an announcement: "All mediums of the Casa must go into current now. The Entity says they are needed in current right now." A medium of the Casa is someone appointed by John of God to be of special service to the Casa and the work performed there, and Bob and Diana were among the mediums. Virginia noticed them looking around with concern, as they had promised that they would help shepherd all members of their group through their first-day experience. The call came out again, "All mediums of the Casa must go into current now. They are needed in the current room immediately." When the Entity gives an instruction, there is always a good reason, though it may not be apparent to our level of understanding, so Bob and Diana asked members of their group to pass the word to other members. Our guides then took their places in the current room, trusting the right thing would happen for each member of their group.

Looking back at me, Virginia noticed my peaceful expression had not changed despite the small commotion the announcement had created.

"Bom gia!" Sebastian, a short, round man who served as one of the Casa managers called out from the stage, signaling the beginning of the session. "Bienvenue! Welcome! Willkommen! Buenas dias! Buongiorno!" The crowd settled down, but despite numerous calls for silence, a steady buzz of talking continued. A succession of announcements was translated into English, German, and French. Then, as if everyone knew what to expect, all in the meeting hall stood up in unison and began reciting the Lord's Prayer in their native tongues. "Our Father, who art in heaven..." Virginia joined in. As soon as this ended, the crowd began, "Hail Mary, full of grace...," and Virginia again joined. As the prayer ended, Virginia noted that I had remained seated quietly, a serene look on my face.

After instructions in multiple languages about all the lines, the call, "Operação!" and the translation, "Surgery!" rang out. "All those told to come for a spiritual surgery, please get in line now." More than fifty people rose from their seats and made their way to a line forming at the entrance to the current rooms and extending almost all the way out of the meeting hall. Conversations grew louder.

After twenty minutes of speeches about the work of the Casa and praise for John of God, the crowd stirred again as João came out on stage. He addressed the throng in Portuguese, his quiet but powerful demeanor coming through words Virginia did not understand. Heather Cumming and Norberto Kist, two of his primary translators, translated into English, French, and German what he said, noting his insistence on emphasizing, "It is God who heals, not I." Then João led the crowd again in the Lord's Prayer, but soon after it began, he stopped speaking, briefly stiffened while leaning on one of the men next to him, and assumed a more erect posture. From her previous visit, Virginia knew this was the moment João was incorporating one of the spirits that would do the healing. His demeanor changed and a new intensity overtook his face as his dark eyes slowly scanned the audience. He then quietly left the stage, entering the current room.

The crowd resumed buzzing until the next announcement rang out. "Primeira vez, por favor! Primeira vez." And then the translation into multiple languages, "First-time line." Suddenly several hundred people started jostling toward the front of the meeting hall. The noise level rose again as first-time visitors anxiously asked in every language, "Is this my line?"

Over the next hour, several speakers came to the stage, each telling their stories of miraculous healings by John of God, each of the stories being translated into German, English, and French. Finally the call for the next line came, "Segunda vez!...Second-time line." Virginia stood up to take her place along with hundreds of others as the line overflowed well beyond the meeting hall. Looking over at me and noticing that I still sat so serenely, she wondered if I would hear the call for the revision line. She stepped out of line to give me a heads-up that Bob and Diana had been called into the current room and that I had to listen for the revision-line call myself. But as she approached me from more than six feet away, with multiple people between us, she sensed my energy field. Years of training as an energy healer had made this a common experience for her, but never had she sensed my field to be so big. It seemed right not to disturb me. More than that, she felt great trust in the Entity and in God and knew she need do nothing to intervene.

Returning to the end of the second-time line, Virginia slowly made her way to the Entity, where she was told, "Operação, surgery at two o'clock." Emerging an hour after having left me, she found me still sitting quietly in meditation. I'd been there for almost three hours and had clearly missed the call for the revision line, as the meeting hall was now completely empty. This time as she approached me, she sensed my energy field from fifteen feet away. Again, she trusted it was best to leave me alone.

She got in line for the soup, ate it, and returned to the meeting hall a half hour later. Still I sat in meditation, my energy field unchanged. Again she thought it better not to disturb me, so she and several friends made their way to the Casa bookstore. She was looking at some crystals when she suddenly turned to her friend and said, "Rick's waking up. I've got to go." She immediately left the bookstore. Just as she came around the corner, she saw me stumbling out of the meeting hall, looking around wide-eyed and bewildered. "What…What happened? Did I miss my line?" I stammered.

She answered, "Sweetie, I don't think you missed a thing."

* * *

After a quick lunch, we returned to the Casa for the afternoon session in time to get seats only three rows from the stage. Like the morning session, the afternoon began with the welcome, announcements, and prayers. Again the call came, "Operação!" and the translation, "Surgery!" This time I kept my eyes open and was rewarded when João came on stage, leading a woman and a man by the hand. I witnessed the moment of incorporation, recognizing the change in João's posture and visage.

"His energy field becomes so much bigger after he incorporates," Virginia whispered to me. "Can you feel it?"

"No," came my one-word reply. But this had always been my answer whenever Virginia had asked me about feeling energy. I had always followed this with a comment like, "I'm too dense. I don't sense the things you and your friends experience."

I had had my moments of bumping into and manipulating energy. I had had visceral, subjective experiences of the energy of each of my chakras, the experiences in India, and that morning's profound meditation. Was it time to stop describing myself as too dense to sense energy? Perhaps.

But what of those who have never had the experience of sensing energy, at least the kind of energy Virginia and I were talking about? It seemed arrogant to assert that since they personally could not sense this energy, and our current technology couldn't measure it, such energy did not exist. It also seemed like bad science. Good science would identify the experiences of individuals like Virginia and João and would seek the truth about them. That, I realized, was one of my goals in making the trip to Brazil.

The two individuals following João stood with closed eyes and their backs against the wall at the rear of the stage while João addressed the crowd briefly. An assistant held out a tray with a container of clear liquid (blessed water, I learned later) and surgical instruments. I realized I was about to witness the Entity, as I was learning to call João when he was incorporated, doing physical surgeries, something I'd seen on a DVD about João that Virginia had insisted I watch before our trip. The physician in me came to the fore, intensely focusing on his every move.

The Entity lifted up the woman's blouse and ran his hand over her belly. Taking a scalpel from the tray, he pinched the skin together near the lower left portion of her abdomen and cut a three-inch incision in her skin. Despite receiving no local anesthetic that I could see, the woman remained completely calm and did not flinch when the scalpel cut into her. I watched as the Entity extended the incision down into the subcutaneous fat. Only a small amount of blood oozed from the wound, dripping onto the upper edge of her white pants. He then probed the wound deeply with his bare fingers, pulling and pushing on the tissues. Eventually his fingers pulled out a small piece of fat and tossed it onto the tray. He then took a straight surgical needle attached to what looked like cotton thread, poking it through her skin in two places and pulling the wound together before tying a knot. With the thread cut, the Entity placed another stitch, closing the three-inch incision with only two sutures, several fewer than most surgeons would have used. All the while the woman's face remained placid.

A rolling chair appeared, the woman's blouse was lowered over her abdomen without any dressing being placed, and one of the assistants rolled her offstage to recover in the infirmary.

Next the Entity ran his hands over the abdomen, chest, and face of the man standing against the wall. He turned and lifted a straight Kelly clamp, a surgical instrument that has a scissors-like handle, extending from which is a pair of five-inch arms that come together firmly when the handle is squeezed.

The Entity placed a small, folded cotton gauze pad in the jaws of the clamp, squeezed the handle together to hold the gauze, dipped it in the blessed water, and in one swift motion thrust the entire clamp up the man's nose to the hilt. Sitting just three rows back, I gasped as I heard a distinct crack. I pictured with a shudder the anatomy the clamp had just traversed, calculating that the tip of the clamp must have caused the cracking sound when it broke through the cribriform plate, the fragile bony portion of the skull just above the nose through which delicate nerve fibers travel. Yet the man had only flinched slightly with the initial thrust and remained standing against the wall with serenely closed eyes.

To my further horror, the Entity twisted the clamp, pulled it partially out, and pushed it all the way back up several times. Given the angle of entry for the clamp, the only place it could be was in the frontal lobes of this poor man's brain. The Entity's motions with the clamp reminded me of the coarsest technique for a frontal lobotomy, a procedure that scrambles the highest-functioning portion of the victim's brain. Finally the Entity pulled the bloodied clamp out. Another rolling chair appeared, and the man slumped into it, his head bending forward as a few thick strands of blood oozed from his nose onto his white shirt. An assistant whisked him off to the infirmary.

No prior description, no DVD, could have prepared me for the experience of watching such a physical surgery from fifteen feet away. The incision surgery, while intriguing, held little of the power and puzzlement of the up-the-nose surgery. A five-inch metal instrument thrust up the nose had to have traumatized all kinds of critical anatomy, yet the man had seemed remarkably unperturbed.

The scientist in me longed to interview this man, assuming he would still be able to speak following such a mangling of his brain. That wish was granted one week later when, while seated on the observation deck at the Casa overlooking a breathtaking view of the valley below, I turned and recognized the man only a few seats away. Hesitantly I approached him and asked, "Are you the man who underwent the up-the-nose surgery last week?"

In a broad Australian accent he replied, "That's me, mate."

"I hate to disturb you, but I'm a physician, and I'd love to ask you some questions about what happened to you."

"Sure. Go right ahead."

"What did it feel like when that instrument went up your nose?" I asked, picturing the metal clamp lacerating the delicate tissues of his nose, breaking multiple bones within, and ending up who knew where.

"It felt like someone pressing a little on the side of my nose, like this," he said, laying his forefinger alongside his nose and pressing a little firmly.

"What about the recovery period? What did you feel then?" I asked, picturing the days of painful healing required for lacerated tissues of the nasal lining to mend.

"It didn't hurt at all," came the surprising answer. "I had a few small blood clots come out when I blew my nose for the next day or two, but it never hurt, and it didn't stop me from doing anything else."

"What did they do for you in the infirmary?"

"They made me lie down on a cot, which is what I felt like doing anyway. After drinking some of the blessed water, I fell asleep for a while. A few hours later, they told me I could return to my pousada, and to follow the instructions they give everyone after spiritual surgeries, stay in bed for twenty-four hours and all that."

"How did you end up getting a physical surgery? Did you ask for it?"

"Yeah, you might say so. They explained that everything can be healed through the spiritual surgery, herbs, and other stuff done here, that nobody needs a physical surgery to be healed. But something in me thought it was what I was supposed to do."

"Is there a specific physical condition you came here to have healed?"

I asked, wondering what would move someone to volunteer for such a physical surgery.

"No, not really. I have a list of physical things I'd like healed, and some emotional ones, but when I heard about the Casa and John of God, I somehow knew I would come to this place, just like something in me knew to raise my hand to volunteer for that physical surgery. It seems to be working out OK."

As I walked away from this unusual exchange, I knew I'd been gifted a glimpse into a phenomenon, a data point, I could not explain.

I have since visited the Casa on seven more trips and seen John of God at New York's Omega Institute six times and in Toronto once. I have learned that the Entity is particularly partial to physicians who are open to the data points occurring around and through John of God, data points I now understand the Entity hopes will serve as triggers for our seeking a new medical paradigm for illness, health, and healing. Sometimes when João is incorporated, the call goes out, "Médicos! Doctors!" Then all physicians present are invited to come forward to see, as closely as they choose, the inexplicable physical surgeries and other miracles of the Casa. I have held the tray for and been only inches away from multiple incision surgeries, up-the-nose procedures, and a third type of physical surgery, eye scraping. In the eye-scraping procedure, the Entity uses a kitchen paring knife to repeatedly scrape the cornea of the person undergoing the procedure. Again, no anesthetic, local or general, is given. I have been close enough to see small mounds of soft, translucent material accumulating on the leading edge of the knife as it scrapes across the cornea, the Entity then casually wiping the knife blade on the subject's shirt before returning to more scraping. I have spoken to a urologist who, upon his first visit to the Casa, was handed the paring knife and personally performed an eye scraping, his hand allegedly controlled invisibly by the Entity. These truly were data points for which I had no explanation, data points calling out for us all to be open to a new paradigm of what is possible.

Early in these experiences I thought of the individuals who identify themselves as quack busters, those whose goal is to debunk unscientific claims of miraculous healing. They recommend that magicians, not physicians, watch so-called miraculous procedures to discover the fraud behind them. Such investigations have demonstrated that some practitioners claiming to perform miraculous healings are indeed frauds, performing a sleight-of-hand maneuver to give the appearance of performing the impossible. Could such a sleight of hand be responsible for these otherwise inexplicable procedures?

That question was definitively answered one day during my second trip to the Casa when a woman approached me and asked, "You are a doctor, yes?"

"I am," I responded hesitantly, wondering what would come next.

"I am so worried about my husband. He had one of those eye surgeries five days ago, and now his eye is terribly red."

Aha, I thought to myself. I had repeatedly been told these procedures produced no complications. That seemed unlikely given the unsanitary conditions under which the incision, up-the-nose, and eye-scraping procedures were performed. This woman presented my chance to prove that claims of no adverse effects from the Entity's physical surgeries were false.

As we walked to their pousada, I went over in my mind what to look for in case of serious complications. Infection would be the most likely condition. While most eye infections involve the conjunctiva, the thin covering over the white of the eyes and inside the eyelids, applying an unsterilized knife directly to the cornea and scraping off layers of cells could lead to serious infection of the cornea itself and possibly the region between the cornea and the iris. If either of these serious complications had developed, or if the cornea had been punctured, the redness in the eye would be concentrated along the edge of the iris rather than around the white of the eye. The anterior chamber between the iris and the cornea might be cloudy, another ominous sign. The man's vision could be severely reduced in the affected eye.

While reviewing what I might find, I remembered one of the explicit rules of the Casa: nobody who has been treated by the Entity should be treated by anybody else visiting the Casa. Many people coming to the Casa are healing practitioners, including massage therapists, herbalists, and energy healers. Because many visitors arrive with severe symptoms or develop them in the course of reacting to the healing they receive, all too often a visiting practitioner would have the impulse to help a fellow visitor by using their particular healing modality. The admonition was very clear: do not interfere with the healing provided by the Entity. What would I do if I found the man to be in need of medical help to prevent losing his eyesight?

Unsure of how I would answer this question, I followed the woman into their room at one of the pousadas. Her husband, a heavyset man in his late forties, lay propped up in bed, seeming quite upset. As I approached his bedside, I noticed his right eye was somewhat reddened, though not alarmingly so.

"How does your eye feel?" I asked, wanting the man to describe his symptoms rather than basing my assessment on his wife's fears.

"My eye is fine!" he blurted out.

"Then what is the problem?" I asked a little puzzled.

"My favorite football team, what you call soccer, has a major match against Italy right now, and I must watch it. But that man, whoever he is, said I can't watch TV for an entire week after having the eye scraping. I think he's wrong, and my wife is telling me I can't watch the match. She doesn't understand what's at stake in this game."

"Does your eye hurt?" I pushed, trying to get back to why I thought I'd been asked to examine him.

"No, not at all."

"Is there any discharge coming out of your eye?"

"None. Can I watch TV?"

"Let me examine your eye before I answer," I replied, buying time to sort out how I might be most helpful.

His eye was indeed a little reddened, but all the redness was around the edges of the eye, not near the iris, I noted with some relief. "Look over to the left," I instructed, so I could look at the cornea from the side. Typically, when the cornea is even a little scratched, the pain is excruciating. Often a scratch causing severe pain is so tiny it can only be identified by instilling a drop of fluorescent dye into the eye and shining an ultraviolet lamp on it. Any small defect in the cornea accumulates a puddle of dye and glows. In the case of the man before me, no such sophisticated diagnostic tools were necessary. Looking at the silhouette of his cornea on edge, I could readily make out deep irregularities, even gouges, taken out of his cornea. "Does your eye hurt?" I again asked, incredulous that the physical picture before me was not producing intolerable pain.

"No. Not at all. Can I watch my game?"

"Cover your right eye. Can you see your wife's face across the room?"

"Yes, yes perfectly well."

"Now cover your left eye. Can you still see your wife's face well?"

"It's a little less clear, but only a little. Now can I watch the game?"

I paused, not knowing what to do. I had been called here ostensibly to help a worried wife determine if her husband was suffering complications from his eye scraping. The only complication I could find was a marital one. I also knew the rules of the Casa.

"I'm pleased to tell you that your eye looks remarkably healthy. You clearly show signs of having had your eye scraped, but there are no complications that I can find."

"Oh, thank you! Thank you so much!" his wife burst out. "I was so worried."

"Now can I just watch my game?" he pleaded.

"I'm afraid that will be your own decision. What I can tell you is that the Entity is quite clear that following any eye procedure, the instructions are not to use your eyes for reading, using a computer, or watching TV for seven days until the stitches are removed. You could choose not to follow the Entity's instructions, but since you've come this far for the Entity's help, my advice is to follow the instructions you've been given."

With that, I left them to work out their marital moment without me.

But as I walked back to the Casa, I reviewed what I'd witnessed. Gouges in a cornea that should have left this man shrieking in pain provided clear evidence that the cornea scraping had not been a sleight of hand and that no infection had occurred despite the most unsanitary of conditions. Together these produced a data point in my web of belief. Was this a miracle? It certainly was not explainable through any medical science I'd been taught.

I had experienced precisely what the physical surgeries are intended to do. They push us to recognize that our own mental models, medical and otherwise, are too limited to encompass the fullness of truth. I've heard repeatedly that no physical surgery at the Casa is needed to treat any condition. Spiritual surgery, herbs, and the many other known and unknown interventions occurring at the Casa are enough. Yet physical surgeries are what John of God is most known for, or in some circles, most notorious. He has been accused of practicing medicine without a license and has suffered beatings and jailings as a result. Those who seek to either sensationalize what he is doing or demonize it point most to the physical surgeries. Yet of the thousand or more people who come to the Casa on any given day, typically no more than five and often fewer receive a physical surgery, and only when they personally ask for one. The physical surgeries represent just a tiny portion of the healing work at the Casa, but they constitute some of the most potent data points, calling upon all who would open their eyes to see them to in turn open their web of belief. In my case, they helped shatter it.

* * *

Later that first week, having finally gone through the revision line (a time when whatever was worked on the first time I'd seen John of God in Atlanta got tweaked with some final touches), I had the opportunity to go before the Entity with the full list of all I wished to have healed. To be more accurate, I'd shortened that list, as Diego had instructed, and the translator had reduced it further to a few scribbled words on a small piece of paper. After a long wait in the second-time line, I came in front of the Entity, and before the translator had even finished reading those few written words, the Entity said, "Spiritual operation at two o'clock." *Well, I'd asked for healing, so let's see what might come out of this surgery,* I thought.

The surgery room turned out to just be another bench-filled room beyond the two current rooms. Sitting down with the others, I settled in for another spiritual surgery, taking off my sneakers and watch to remove any distractions. As I did, one of the Casa volunteers gave the familiar instructions to close our eyes and place one hand over whichever part of our body felt most in need of healing. If we had multiple requests for healing, we were to place our hand over our heart.

I've since heard descriptions of the spiritual surgeries by those with the vision to see what is happening. They describe a blizzard of spirit beings descending upon the surgery room. An entire team of these spirit beings is assigned to each individual undergoing surgery, a team capable of conducting up to nine distinct procedures during a single surgery. I've even learned of cases in which doctors have found medical imaging evidence of internal stitches following spiritual surgeries in patients who had never undergone a conventional surgical procedure. I've personally seen post-spiritual surgery scars on an individual who never had a prior medical surgery, scars that healed and completely disappeared only days later.

But at the time, I knew none of this, so having created a long list of anticipated physical, emotional, and spiritual healings, I leaned back into the bench, placed my hand over my heart, and prepared for as profound a healing of body, mind, and spirit as I could imagine. As I did, John of God entered the room and in a deep voice announced words immediately translated as, "In the name of God, I pronounce this spiritual intervention complete." Complete? I hadn't been sitting there more than thirty seconds. How could it be complete? I'd come six thousand miles for treatment by a...a disembodied spirit alleged to be a master healer working through the body of a man reputed to be one of the greatest trance mediums ever to live, and the whole experience had lasted less than a minute.

I couldn't help but wonder what kind of sham I'd allowed myself to be drawn into and at what expense. Putting my watch and sneakers back on, I dutifully joined the others in the area in which we received post-surgery instructions.

One of those instructions, to take a taxi back to our pousada because we were not to do any extensive walking after the surgery, seemed silly after such a short procedure. Yet as I walked to the taxi stand, I noticed a little difficulty standing fully upright, much as I had after my spiritual surgery in Atlanta. A pulling sensation in my upper abdomen made me move slowly as I took my seat in the taxi. The five-minute ride to our pousada became increasingly uncomfortable each time the taxi went over a bump. Getting out of the taxi, I could do no more than hunch over and stagger the handful of steps to my room, crawling gratefully into bed, and falling immediately into a deep sleep.

The next twenty-four hours passed both slowly and quickly. Endless dreams filled my sleep, punctuated by a meal brought lovingly by Virginia and devoured voraciously by me. I again fell back asleep only to be awakened for another meal followed by another bout of unnatural sleep. I remember thinking in the haze of it all that something had definitely happened in those thirty seconds.

* * *

The extraordinary experience I'd had during the very first session at the Casa had given me a taste of the power of simply sitting in current without going before the Entity. So as often as possible over the two weeks in Abadiania, I sat in current. Each session, I went through the same meditation process as the first day, slowly taking the time to open the chakras, reaching out with my personal consciousness to embrace the whole world and beyond. Some sessions lasted two hours, some up to five.

In each current session, sitting with eyes closed, I heard the scrape of crutches, the rolling of a wheelchair, and all too often the cry of a child, knowing a desperate mother or father clutched that ill, perhaps disabled child near to their own heart. Each carried with them pain, fear, and hope for their personal miracle. And in response to each, I felt my heart open to offer love, wanting to do all I could to be of service to everyone who had made this pilgrimage and to the extraordinary work of this amazing place.

Sitting in current provided glimpses into the immense burden John of God had accepted in faithfully serving his lifelong healing mission. Day after day for more than fifty years he had welcomed and done all he could to help heal an unfathomable well of human suffering. My heart went out in gratitude to this man and all he had done in love and service.

In the middle of one morning session, I heard a woman's voice coming from somewhere in the line. It began as quiet whimpering, escalating rapidly to shouts in Portuguese. With my eyes closed, I could not tell if they were shouts of pain or joy. Sobbing followed, and I was left to wonder what had happened.

At lunch, I asked Bob and Diana if they'd heard anything about the woman who'd been so profoundly affected during her time in the line. With a broad smile Bob responded, "We were also sitting in current and heard the same thing. So I checked with Heather who explained that the woman is a nun in her forties who'd been blind since childhood. While in line, as she turned the corner from the first current room into the second current room, she began to see vague lights and colors. The closer she came to the Entity in his chair, the more she saw. As she approached the Entity, she could see clearly for the first time in more than forty years. What you heard were her shouts of joy and gratitude. A true miracle."

A true miracle? Most certainly according to any current medical science. I paused, beginning to conjure an after-the-fact explanation that perhaps her blindness had been hysterically caused, and that through her belief system, this moment of engaging with John of God had triggered resolution of more than forty years of hysterical blindness. To say this explanation felt like a stretch was an understatement. Then the skeptic in me became cynical, having the same thought I'd had years earlier with

Ron Roth, wondering if this woman had been a plant or a shill, pretending to undergo a miraculous healing. While possible, this, too, felt like quite a stretch. I was left to wonder what mechanism, scientific or otherwise, could heal sight in such a sudden, stunning manner. Yes, *miraculous* seemed the apt word.

* * *

Having been encouraged during our second week at the Casa to request help from the Entity on behalf of others, day after day I visited the prayer triangle and prayer basket. One fervent prayer after another poured from my heart for friends and family members in need of healing, but none came with the torrent of tears and hopes as my prayers for Michael. I thought I had learned how to pray for him from Ron Roth and again in India. Yet now the experience of being in Brazil, at the Casa, a sacred space filled with inexplicable wonders and healings all around me, induced a new level of desire mixed with hope. On my knees, I prayed with all my heart for Michael's healing. At the same time, I recalled the admonition to release attachment to whatever one is praying for, a step I had not yet been able to take.

With a final session sitting in current Friday afternoon, our two weeks at the Casa came to a close. I had experienced that first remarkable meditation. I'd had a spiritual operação that had knocked me out and done who knew what else to me. I had witnessed physical surgeries I could not explain, surgeries that had shattered my old web of belief. I had listened while a woman who'd been blind for forty years miraculously regained her sight. Yet the most miraculous experience of my first trip to John of God occurred in the Rio de Janeiro airport on the way home. My cell phone rang. On the other end, Marsha's voice raced with a torrent of words. Michael had gone into crisis. He had stopped all his medications on his own and had spun into uncontrollable panic, depression, and suicidality. He was unsafe to leave alone.

From the southernmost reaches of Brazil I felt powerless to help Michael. "We're on our way home," I responded. "Do what you can to keep our son safe. I will do what I can from here…I'll pray for him."

With a rising sense of panic, I sought a corner of this busy airport for a moment of solitude. The rapid-fire patter of Portuguese conversations on all sides faded into the background as I began, "Dear God…" Tears flowed and would not stop. "Please, please do all you can to keep Michael safe…" Another impulse led me to shift my prayer. "Dearest Entity, I have asked for your help for Michael, and now I am on my knees asking again with all my heart. Please do whatever you can to heal my son…" Then a thought arose, a thought that brought a smile through my tears. Somehow I knew that Michael's crisis was already an answer to the prayers I had poured out at the Casa for the past two weeks. I did not know how, but I had a sure sense that this moment marked the beginning of Michael's healing. In deepest gratitude the words escaped my lips softly: "Thank you."

Five tumultuous days later, a plan emerged to send Michael to a wilderness program for troubled young adults. At ten o'clock on a Thursday morning, he got on a call with the intake coordinator at the program. Twenty minutes later he had been accepted into the program and had agreed to go. "Have him at the Las Vegas airport at noon tomorrow, and we will take care of the rest," were the final instructions to us. Michael, now nineteen and no longer a minor, had agreed to go voluntarily. Marsha and I saw him off on a flight to Las Vegas the following morning, grateful for his willingness to go and hopeful for whatever outcome lay ahead.

Marsha and I were asked to write Michael a letter each week. I poured my heart into those letters. They gave me the chance to share what I felt most deeply for my son with whom I had not had a civil conversation in almost four years. Somewhere, seated on a rock high in the wilderness, he would read them. He could not turn away. He could not refuse to listen. He would have to take in my words, so I did all I could to make every one count.

One of these letters concluded with words I had for years longed to share with my son:

> I have found a song that speaks what is in my heart. I have sung it to you countless times, though you have never heard me do so. I have not always spoken and act-ed from the place this song expresses. For that I am sorry. Please know that I will continue to sing it to you. I hope someday you will be able to hear this song directly from me. Perhaps in the end, you will be able to sing it to yourself from a place of deep acceptance, acceptance of yourself just as you are.

> *How could anyone ever tell you*
> *You are anything less than beautiful?*
> *How could anyone ever tell you*
> *You are less than whole?*
> *How could anyone fail to notice*
> *That your loving is a miracle?*
> *How deeply you're connected to my soul.*[6]

That I would share these words with my son was itself a miracle.

Five weeks into his wilderness program, knapsack on my back, I made my way up the hill leading to the wilderness program's campsite in the Utah high desert. There Michael stood, darkened with the false tan of dirt that comes from living outdoors, smiling as he hugged me. For the next two days, with guidance from his counselor, we spoke from our hearts and found our way back to each other. Our final instruction was to conduct a ritual that expressed our relationship. After some fumbling with this assignment, we settled on creating a physical embodiment of the journey Michael and I had traveled, his birth and early childhood, the trauma of

---

[6] Adapted words printed by permission.

divorce, his tantrums, the rupture in our relationship, and coming finally to this moment together. As our ritual came to a close, there, in a small clearing among the trees, surrounded by the other program participants and counselors as witnesses, I turned to my son and sang the words I'd carried for so many years in my heart.

How could anyone ever tell you...

As the last words echoed across the wilderness, Michael and I embraced. I knew my son's healing had begun. My prayers had been answered. This scientist and skeptic stood in awe. Gratitude to the Entity and to God poured from my heart. A miracle had happened. Yes, a miracle.

* * *

Over the years since that day in the Utah desert, I have often wondered if the timing of Michael's unraveling and entering the wilderness program could have only been a coincidence, having nothing to do with my trip to John of God. Of course this is a possibility. Nothing about the sequence of events could prove cause and effect from my prayers to the Entity's intervention to Michael's healing. Each of us will always have a choice regarding how these facts fit into our personal web of belief. Michael, for one, does not believe John of God or the Entity had anything to do with the timing of his breakdown and eventual recovery. In years past I would have wholeheartedly agreed with him, adopting the coincidence explanation with great but unfounded conviction, and not a small amount of self-righteousness. Today I find this not to be an explanation, but only a defense of a particular worldview. As a scientist and skeptic, this is no more satisfying an explanation than blind, unquestioning faith.

Regardless of how others make meaning of these events, I am left with a feeling of gratitude every day for Michael's healing and for the rekindled father-son relationship we enjoy today. These hold a special place, a sacred place, near the core of my personal web of belief.

* * *

At the start of a return trip to Brazil, I prepared, as had become my custom, a list of all I wanted healed physically, emotionally, and spiritually. Again I had no problem coming up with a substantial list in each category. Reviewing the list, I noted several items I had previously asked to be healed hadn't made my current list. This caused me to pull out the original list I'd created during my first visit to Brazil. To my surprise, none of the items on that first list could be found on the current one. Each was completely resolved or much better. I took note of another data point, one that warranted a now familiar single-word response. Wow!

* * *

Another far more heartrending data point occurred when Robert, a friend whose acupuncture practice I had supervised many years earlier, developed stomach cancer. His had already been a life filled with heartbreak and challenge. His second son had been born with a genetic abnormality, giving him a dire prognosis of severe mental retardation, no language capacity, and early death, likely by the age of ten. Not accepting this as his son's certain future, Robert and his wife had dedicated their lives to achieving different expectations, endlessly searching for complementary and alternative treatments. Time and again their son surpassed milestones the physicians' prognostications had labeled impossible until, though still challenged, he had learned to communicate, love, and live a meaningful life, going strong well after the age of twenty.

But his son's genetic disorder was not to be the only heartbreak for Robert. When their son was only five, Robert's wife developed breast cancer. Again Robert devoted himself to finding untapped complementary and alternative treatments. Year after year his wife confounded her physicians by living a full life in spite of their morbid predictions for her early death. But her capacity to overcome each new obstacle had its limits. Fifteen years after her diagnosis, she died, leaving Robert to care for their two sons.

Only months after losing his wife, Robert received the devastating news of his own cancer. When it spread to other organs, Robert's prognosis became grave. Though we had drifted apart after my divorce, I had continued to care deeply for Robert and his family. Saddened to hear of yet another devastating blow, I included them all, especially Robert, in my prayers.

As I prepared for one of our trips to the Casa, I heard that Robert's condition had worsened and that talk of hospice had begun. Robert wanted nothing to do with hospice, feeling it his duty to remain alive for his handicapped son who, having already lost his mother, depended on Robert for everything. Though it had been years since I'd last seen Robert, I knew it was time for me to visit him.

Entering his home, a home in which I had spent so many happy family times before Marsha and I had separated, I found my old friend much the same but much changed. While still mentally sharp, his frame, always tall and thin, now hung on his protruding bones with the gaunt, sallow look I'd seen so often in advanced cancer. We sat on his couch. He moved little, as movement caused his stoic face to wince in pain. The years that had passed had done nothing to diminish the love we felt for each other.

It was from this love that I began, "Robert, you know I have been to see John of God in Brazil." He nodded. "I have seen miracles of healing there."

"I have heard of his healing work," Robert responded in his measured way that belied the intensity burning inside him.

"I have had spiritual surgery from this healer, interventions on both a physical and energetic plane. I am going back to Brazil next week. Should it be your wish, when I am at the Casa, I will do a surrogate surgery for you."

"A surrogate surgery?" Robert asked, his fatherly heart seeking to find hope in this unusual offer more for his son than for himself.

"In surrogate surgery, I stand in for you. I will be in Brazil and will present your photograph to the Entity, asking for healing on your behalf. If the Entity agrees, I will go into the surgery room at the appointed time. You will be here, dressed in white just as I will be. I will serve as an energetic link between the spirit beings performing the healing and you. On the spiritual plane, distance has no meaning, so you can undergo the spiritual surgery with me as the conduit." As I said these words, I wondered if they were true. I did not know. But if there was any chance of success, I felt it my responsibility to try.

Two weeks later I presented Robert's photograph to the Entity along with my offer to serve as a surrogate for my friend's surgery. The Entity agreed. I informed Robert of the scheduled time. The next morning I took my seat in the surgery room and formed the intention to serve as a direct link to Robert, visualizing him dressed in white, lying in his bed four thousand miles away, reminding myself distance, space itself, has no meaning on a spiritual plane. I also knew this was not just for Robert; I wanted a data point so incontrovertible the world and all its skeptics would have to take notice. I wanted confirmation for myself that my dizzying journey of opening to web-shattering experiences was grounded in truth. But most of all, I wanted with all my heart for my friend to be healed, healed so that he would not be forced to abandon his sons, who had already lost so much, to a lifetime as orphans.

Upon returning from Brazil, I went to Robert's home, hoping for a miracle. Robert greeted me with a smile. After just a few moments, I could contain myself no longer.

"What happened for you during the surrogate surgery?" I blurted out.

"I didn't know what to expect," Robert began. "So I just lay down in bed at the time you told me and waited. After a while an angel came to me. I recognized her as an angel I'd seen often as a child but had forgotten about and not seen since I was seven years old."

This was not what I had expected. I had hoped my friend would have felt physical changes that would have meant his cancer was being fixed in some way. I had hoped for relief from his pain. I had hoped for a miracle cure for his terminal condition. He received none of these, at least that I could tell. But he had received an angel.

Two months later Robert died. I learned that his visit with the angel had brought him new peace. He still did not want to die and leave his sons, but by the time of his death, he had an angel in his life who comforted him, who let him know there is more to life than what we see on earth.

I had entered into surrogate surgery with the intention of my friend going into remission and hopefully being cured. Did his death mean the surrogate surgery didn't work? Or did it accomplish exactly what it was supposed to do? Perhaps reuniting with this angel provided Robert with reassurance that when he died he would not be alone, or that he had so much more to look forward to after death. Were these musings another attempt to conjure an after-the-fact explanation that would allow me to deposit this apparent failure into a comfortable place in my current web of belief, as conventional physicians so often do?

I could no longer engage in such an exercise, either for failures of medical treatment or failures of spiritual treatment. Many people come to the Casa, to John of God, and the medical conditions for which they seek help improve or completely resolve. But for others, this is not the case. Why is the outcome different from one to another? Perhaps there is such a thing as too late in an illness for a miraculous cure. Is there something for the soul of the ill individual to learn through their sickness and death that has a higher purpose? Could the same be said for their loved ones who suffer with them up to their death and beyond? Does this line of thinking constitute an explanation, or merely a way of incorporating a painful data point into one's web of belief without having to change it? As a scientist, it is most intellectually honest to simply admit that I do not know. But it is equally intellectually honest to admit the same applies to failures of conventional medical treatment.

In my grief over Robert's death, a question remained unanswered. Was my friend healed? What does it mean to be healed if we all must die eventually of something? What does it mean to be healed if we are all on a cycle of almost endless death and rebirth, each lifetime a series of lessons in opening our hearts? Is the goal to heal our bodies? Our emotions? Our thoughts? Our soul? Our shared consciousness? Today, the answer to these questions, an answer that holds a cherished place near the center of my personal web of belief, is yes to them all. So when an angel comes, what is being healed?

* * *

When John of God travels outside Brazil, he does his amazing work without the Casa's crystal mountain, staff, volunteers, and the usual multitude of individuals experienced in sitting in current who regularly create and sustain the energetic matrix needed for the Entity's work. Beginning in 2007 for Virginia and 2008 for me, we have had the honor of serving as volunteers assigned to fulfill this role at each John of God event in the United States and Canada. Every morning and afternoon, we and the other volunteers assemble, take our assigned seats in one of the current rooms, and do all we can to establish a strong, loving current of energy to support John of God and the Entity's healing work. Each time I begin with the same opening-the-chakras meditation I had spontaneously fallen into during my first day at the Casa, though it has morphed over the years as my spiritual path has continued to evolve.

At the end of each current session, after more than a thousand individuals have come before the Entity and received blessings and healings, one of the senior volunteers leads a shared visualization and prayer for all those sitting in the current rooms. The closing prayers, I eventually learned, are needed to clear the environment of any negative energies that have been released during that session's healings.

One afternoon, the closing prayer included a visualization that all the negative energies be taken down into the earth, where they would be transmuted, healed, and returned to the never-ending cycle of energy that constitutes existence. Until then, my opening-the-chakras meditation had followed the process of visualizing drawing down energy from the Divine through my seventh chakra and pulling up energy from Mother Earth through my first chakra. I suddenly realized this meant I had been pulling energy up from the very place into which we were visualizing countless negative energies being drawn down. It seemed wrong to be pulling energy up from the very entry point of such negativity. I did not realize at the time that many spiritual traditions recognize the virtually limitless capacity of Mother Earth to transmute negative energies. My human's eye view of this process led me to perceive it as limited, a "misperception" that was soon to have extraordinary consequences.

The following morning, while seated in my current meditation, instead of drawing energy up from the earth, I visualized drawing the energy of the Divine down through the seventh chakra at the crown of my head. As I sought to draw more energy through my crown, I had the distinct sense of trying to pull this energy down through a narrow straw. I shifted the visualization to opening fully to the same energy simply pouring through my entire being. Suddenly it felt as if someone had turned on a fire hose. What had moments before felt like a trickle became a torrent of almost intolerable intensity. My arms, legs, and trunk began trembling from the energy gushing through the core of my being. In an effort to work with this newfound energy stream, my visualization shifted to experiencing myself as a channel for this energy. This shifted further into an intention to open myself to serve as a clear, powerful, effective channel for the Divine to manifest on earth. With this, the torrential energy flow persisted, as did the trembling of my entire body, for the remaining hours of the session.

As the session ended, I had difficulty standing. Stumbling more than walking, I could not find words to describe what had just happened. That afternoon we returned for the next current session. Again I went through the opening-the-chakras meditation. Again I opened to the torrent of energy flowing through my crown chakra. Again my entire body began to tremble. This time I recognized that I had been trying to control and direct the energy and that this effort had created resistance that in turn generated the trembling. My visualization shifted to asking to serve as not just a clear and powerful channel for the Divine to manifest on earth, but to do so as a superconductor, with zero resistance to this overwhelming energy flowing through me. Instantly the trembling stopped, replaced by an inner sense of the energy flow shifting from turbulent to smooth. The remaining hours of the session passed in silent ecstasy as this powerful energy streamed through me while I asked that it pour out into the world to be of greatest possible service to all.

As the session neared its close, I heard a call from one of the leaders that any volunteers serving in current who wanted to come before the Entity should do so now. With some reluctance, I pulled myself out of the meditation and rose to my feet. Feeling only slightly steadier than after the morning session, I took my place in line. As I passed before the Entity, his quiet words to me were "Sit in my current." Sensing I had been doing just what I was supposed to by sitting in current, I headed back to my seat. After I'd taken only a few steps, John of God's voice rang out. The translator announced to the entire room, "The Entity says that if everyone prepared for current as this man does, the work done here could be so much greater." With a jolt I realized those words referred to me. I had come before him numerous times, and never had he said anything like this. Could the Entity see what had transpired for me during the prior two current sessions, the shift in my intention, the torrential flow of Divine energy? Whether he was referring to this or to the opening-the-chakras meditation I'd consistently used to prepare for sitting in current, I did not know. I staggered back to my seat filled with gratitude that my efforts to be of service to the Divine were seen, acknowledged, and apparently more effective than I'd thought possible.

When the session was almost over, I felt a hand take mine, pulling me upward. Opening my eyes, I saw one of the leaders who whispered in my ear, "The Entity wants you and me together to provide the closing prayers." Once again the Entity singled me out for some unseen purpose. In further shock, I stood before hundreds of seated individuals. The leader began with a visualization she had used to close a previous session. She then turned to me with, "Our brother, Rick, will now add his closing words."

I stepped forward thinking that if the Entity had singled out my meditation that day, I should share the intent that lay behind it. "My brothers and sisters," I began, my voice tentative and uncertain, "we are here to be of service." I went on, slowly feeling a strength returning to my voice. "We are here to be of service to the Divine. Let us ask to be shown how we each may best serve the Divine. And let us do so with all our hearts, giving over our full selves to this intention." Then with words I'd first whispered before a candle on my yoga mat so many years earlier, I added, "And that this intention be for the highest and best for ourselves, for all those our lives touch, and for Spirit itself."

As I said these final words with closed eyes, I raised my hands on either side in front of me, palms opened upwards in a gesture of offering. To my astonishment, a large, warm hand took my left hand in his, raising it slightly upwards. I say "his" because I suddenly sensed a male figure standing to my left, rising to a height of what felt like fifteen feet. As I tried to take in this awareness, another large hand took my right hand in hers. Again I say "hers" because I sensed a female figure standing to my right, rising to a height of twelve feet. Breathless, I simply stood between these two invisible beings sensing more love, compassion, and peace than I'd ever thought possible. The session ended. People began making their way outside. I remained transfixed, not wanting to release these angelic hands.

With a smile I said to myself, "What do I do now? Moments like this don't come with an instruction manual." So I simply remained standing, hands raised, in complete bewilderment at the experience unfolding, not wanting to do anything to disrupt the connection I was having with the beings on either side of me. Eventually an individual came up to me and said something about my closing words, though I kept my eyes shut. Then another. Then another came and raised her hands, seeking to engage my hands in some type of energy exchange. At that moment Heather touched my arm firmly saying, "The session has ended. Open your eyes. It is not proper for people to seek to engage you in this way here." With some reluctance, I obeyed, and with an act of will, broke the connection with the beings on either side of me.

Only later did one of the leaders explain to me that for beings on the other side of the veil, there is no experience of time. Those spiritual beings would have stood by my side endlessly. It was up to me to break the connection with them in accordance with our experience of time on this plane. The leader also explained that the sessions are ended through formal prayer and an explicit pronouncement in order to bring closure to these connections with spirit beings. Before that afternoon, I would have had no idea what those words referred to and dismissed them as complete nonsense. Instead, I had a data point that made those words part of my web of belief, my reality, my truth.

* * *

During one of our visits to Brazil, Heather approached me because an Austrian movie director, David Unterberg, was making a movie about John of God entitled *Healing*. She wondered if I would agree to be interviewed for the movie to provide a scientific and medical perspective on all that transpires at the Casa. A slight hesitation arose in my mind as I recognized that for the most part, I had kept my spiritual path private, far from the growing national reputation I had been developing as a healthcare consultant, author, and educator. Doing this interview would out me to a potentially wide audience. If I spoke so publicly of what constituted the truth for me, would I be perceived as an untrustworthy consultant in the traditional medical establishment in which I earned a living? The hesitation lasted but a moment, as I knew my deeper commitment was to the truth.

That evening I spent some time anticipating questions that might arise in the interview. I grappled with how to explain to a potential movie audience likely to contain both skeptics and believers what I had observed and experienced at the Casa, with John of God, and with a collection of disembodied spirit beings I now so easily referred to as the Entity. I realized I had spent the previous thirty-five years preparing for this interview. With the passion of a young man, I had begun this journey by wrestling with classic philosophical texts while at Oxford, seeking an unshakeable foundation for truth and how we should live. Having recognized such answers could not be found through academia, I had embarked on a career in medicine, experiencing the joys and satisfactions of healing, but also engaging suffering, loss, and death, struggling daily to make meaning of these for myself and my patients. Over many years, I'd encountered data points that had first stretched and finally shattered the personal web of belief I'd originally woven, one I could now recognize had been so heavily biased by early family, academic, and cultural influences, but which could not withstand rigorous, scientific engagement with my experiences of how the world actually worked.

The following day, instead of interviewing me, the director asked me to speak extemporaneously into the camera. Using the outline I'd developed the night before, I spoke of Thomas Kuhn and scientific revolutions, of data points and webs of belief, of my personal experiences of physical surgeries I could not explain, but also of concern that the physical surgeries are too sensationalized and that all healing could be accomplished at the Casa without any physical surgeries at all. And I spoke from my heart of my almost inexpressible gratitude for Michael's miraculous healing.

I had spoken for more than an hour, carefully crafting as thoughtful, rational, and scientific of an approach as I could to the web-shattering experiences I'd encountered through John of God. In the final movie, my words were edited down to two segments totaling four minutes. Following my credentials, the first segment opened with, "I am a scientist and a skeptic…" and closed with my gratitude for my son's healing. The second segment challenged scientists not to fall into the trap of thinking a scientific paradigm will stand the test of time. Noting it had been only a century earlier that Einstein had shown us that time and space are not as we thought they were, the segment closed with the words, "What else is not as we think it is?"

After the filming ended, the director shared with me a brochure for the movie. Prominently displayed on the first page were the words of Saint Ignatius:

For one who believes, no proof is necessary.
For the nonbeliever, no amount of proof is sufficient.

I turned to him and added my own words, infused with the hope that a bridge between the two could be built.

Must it always be so?

Chapter IX: Medjugorje, A Course in Miracles,[7] the Qur'an, and Beyond

Each Religious Tradition Is Unique.
The Spiritual Journey Is Universal.

"We're going back to the Casa for the Rosary. Do you want to join us?" Diana asked one evening during my first trip to the Casa. Given my upbringing, I knew almost nothing about the Rosary. Diana quickly picked up on this, helped by my blank stare. "The Rosary is a beautiful series of prayers to honor Mother Mary," she explained. "An amazing group of women has dedicated themselves to reciting the Rosary every night at the Casa. They say the Rosary in Portuguese, but you can say the prayers in English along with them." This last suggestion was not particularly helpful, as I did not know which prayers make up the Rosary, whether in English or Portuguese.

---

[7] All references to and quotes from *A Course in Miracles* are from the Third Edition, © Foundation for Inner Peace, P.O. Box 598, Mill Valley, CA 94942-0598, 2007, www.acim.org and info@acim.org.

In spite of this, I responded, "Sure," with the same bemused willingness to try almost anything put before me on this spiritual path.

After a beautiful moonlit walk, I sat in the Casa's outer gathering room, the site of my first-day current meditation, as the soft chatter of multiple languages hummed around me. I closed my eyes, waiting quietly. Shortly a lone woman's voice began in Portuguese, intoning words I did not recognize. I let the rhythm of the words, their simple vibration, wash over me as a chorus of other voices joined in. Suddenly I heard words that seemed familiar, "Pai nosso..." I'd learned enough Portuguese to know "pai" meant *father*. I also heard Virginia reciting the Our Father prayer in English next to me, so I joined in with the words I'd learned at the Ron Roth retreats. Next I heard, "Avé Maria, cheia de grace..." As Virginia started reciting the Hail Mary prayer, I again joined in, stumbling over some of the words as I was not yet as familiar with this prayer, though the words gradually flowed more easily as the Hail Mary repeated multiple times throughout the Rosary. Finally the voices subsided, leaving a sweet, subtle vibration filling the hall around me. We walked back to our pousada in silence.

The next morning over breakfast with our group, I commented on how beautiful the Rosary had been the night before. Katharine, one of our friends, piped up, "Virginia, have you told them your Rosary story?"

"No. I mentioned something in passing to Rick when it happened, but I haven't told anybody else."

"You guys have got to hear this story," Katharine said, becoming excited. "Last year, during my first trip to the Casa, Virginia and I were roommates. One day I noticed an unusual little booklet on her bed. When I asked her what it was, she responded matter-of-factly, 'This is the booklet with the words of the Rosary the nun gave me.' The artwork on this thing was really unusual, and it looked pretty old. In fact, it didn't include the Luminous Mysteries Pope John Paul had added in 2002. So I was curious and asked, 'What nun?' That's when she told the most amazing story. Virginia, will you share it?"

"It started during my first trip to the Casa," Virginia began. "I was drawn to the Rosaries sold in the Casa bookstore and bought one. I wore it every day for several years even though I hadn't grown up with the Rosary and didn't know the words to the prayer. Then one day last year, while standing on a ladder, painting my office, I was thinking to myself, 'I wish I had the words to the Rosary.' Then *knock, knock,* I heard a gentle rapping on my office door. When I opened it, paintbrush in hand, I was instantly mesmerized by a young, radiantly beautiful nun dressed in a full, black habit from head to toe. This nun lovingly handed me a little booklet and said, 'I brought you your Rosary.' I looked into the woman's eyes and said, 'Thank you. I have been wanting one of these.' In the moment, it seemed the most natural thing in the world, though later, nobody else in the building recalled seeing a nun."

"Tell them what happened next," Katharine prodded, beginning to grin.

Virginia hesitated, looking a little sheepish. "Even though I've later held this as a sacred moment, at the time I just said, 'Thank you so much for coming, I have to get back to my painting now.' I closed the door on her and went back to painting, thinking nothing of it."

Exasperated and laughing, Katharine couldn't contain herself any more. "Didn't you think it was more than a little odd that this nun found her way to your second-floor office on a two-block-long street on an island in the middle of a bay and provided an almost instant answer to your silent request? Virginia," she concluded, "this was an apparition. You had an angel visit you and answer your prayer…And all you could do was politely thank her, say you had to get back to painting, and close the door in her face!" By this point Katharine's laughter had infected everyone else at our table. Point made. Another data point received.

* * *

So began Virginia's relationship with the Rosary. She would say her relationship with Mary had begun the first time she had sat in current at the Casa. She sought something to focus her mind upon that would be positive, loving, and healing. A painting of Mary hanging in the first current room drew her in. She did not know at the time she would spend years gazing through closed eyes at this painting, moving ever more into a truly devotional prayer practice dedicated to Mary. As her bond with Mary deepened, books about Mary found their way to her.

Her relationship with Mary and the Rosary took a profound turn when Bob and Diana joined a group trip to Medjugorje, a small town in Bosnia-Herzegovina in southeastern Europe, where a vision of the Virgin Mary had been reportedly appearing to six individuals every day beginning in 1981. On our next visit to the Casa following their Medjugorje trip, Bob and Diana gifted each member of our group a set of rosary beads they had purchased and had had blessed in Medjugorje. I received mine graciously but did not feel drawn to the item.

In contrast, the moment Diana placed Virginia's rosary in her hands, Virginia felt energy emanating from it, suffusing her with love. In that moment, Virginia knew she would be going to Medjugorje. She would later come to say she was being called by Mary.

Upon returning from this trip to Brazil, Virginia began voraciously reading everything she could about Medjugorje and the visionaries there as well as other well-known visions of Mary that had appeared in other parts of the world. Six months later, feeling overwhelmingly drawn to go, she learned of a group trip that would be leaving for Medjugorje in only a few weeks. Without hesitation, she signed up for that trip. Just as with John of God, upon returning she had a simple message. "Rick, you have to go there. It's profound."

Unlike going to Ron Roth, unlike going to India, unlike going to John of God, the thought of going to Medjugorje did not draw me at all. In fact, it put me off because it felt like taking a very deep dive into Catholicism, a dive I had no inclination to make. I had found Ron Roth's teachings about Jesus accessible because he had embedded them in a universal spirituality, seeing all authentic religions grounded in the same essence, the essence of love. Oneness University had not taught a uniquely Hindu theology, but instead a vision of the oneness of all without drawing distinctions. The Casa embodied somewhat of a Catholic feel but was deeply imbued with the beliefs of Spiritism, including mediumship, reincarnation, and trust in the universal journey of all souls to progress towards opening our hearts to love. Given my roots, my history, and most of all my web of belief, I wanted nothing to do with any religion that held its own beliefs to be uniquely true and its practices to provide the only path to enlightenment, the only path to God.

Yet I had learned to trust Virginia's guidance, whatever its source, and also to trust the unknown that lay ahead whenever I opened myself to the next step on my path. I would suspend disbelief enough to open to the possibility that Medjugorje might be that next step. But a different step was to occur first, another trip to John of God.

I had begun to feel I'd been placed in a unique position as a physician to help build a bridge between science and spirituality, especially the work of John of God. But I wrestled with how to fulfill that vision. During my next visit to the Casa, I poured out my concerns to Diego about how to do justice to the work of John of God. He interrupted me.

"Rick, I don't think you get it. The journey is about opening to the will of God." His words brought me up short. I had not expected them. The puzzled look on my face caused him to go on. "Have you ever done *A Course in Miracles?*"

"I've heard of the *Course* but not done it."

"You may want to."

Was this to be the next step on my path? I had no concept of what doing *A Course in Miracles* meant.

That evening during dinner at our pousada, I shared this story with people at our table, including Santi, one of our close friends who had joined us for several of our Casa trips. As soon as I finished, Santi piped up, "I'm an instructor for *A Course in Miracles.* I've been teaching the *Course* for twenty years."

Virginia and I had been friends with Santi for a long time but had not known this about her. She lived just one mile from our home. "Could it be this easy?" I said.

Everyone at the table responded in chorus, "Yes, it could be this easy."

All evening the words, "When the student is ready, the teacher will appear," played over and over in my mind. After all the shattering experiences on this journey, I couldn't help but wonder what I was ready for now.

* * *

The book arrived without fanfare. Opening the package, I found a paperback entitled *A Course in Miracles*. With a sense of anticipation, I settled into my favorite reading chair and opened the book.

In the preface I learned that all the material contained in the *Course* had been channeled by a woman named Helen Schucman, over seven years between 1965 and 1972. By this point I was no stranger to the phenomenon of channeling and found this fact intriguing. Schucman described herself as an atheist, which gave her some credibility with me given the shared originating point of our respective journeys. However, since my current web of belief included that *all* human beings experience cycles of reincarnation, simply because a being was not in a body did not automatically make that being enlightened. So I would wait to learn more about the source of the material and would suspend belief in the channeled content until I had experienced it more fully.

The introduction filled less than a page, beginning with, "This is a course in miracles. It is a required course. Only the time you take it is voluntary."(In-1:1-3).[8] A required course? *Ah, yes,* I thought, *all of life is a*

---

[8] *A Course in Miracles* utilizes this standardized annotation for identifying any particular quotation. It includes the major subdivision (In = Introduction, T = Text, W = Workbook, etc.), chapter number (not applicable to the Introduction), section number (not applicable to the Introduction), paragraph number, and sentence number. When a quotation is taken from the title of a Workbook exercise, it does not have a paragraph or sentence number.

required course, required for the evolution of our soul through multiple incarnations, our soul's journey to learn to love. Already I resonated with the *Course*...or so I thought. Then only one paragraph later, the introduction concluded with the words, "Nothing real can be threatened. Nothing unreal exists. Herein lies the peace of God."(In-2:2-4). I had a one-word response. Huh? I didn't get this. Having read plenty of dense philosophical texts at Cornell and Oxford, I did my best to puzzle over these words, but to no avail. They remained opaque and not particularly meaningful.

The first chapter listed fifty principles of miracles, each a pithy, equally impenetrable challenge to understand. My eyes began to droop and my concentration to fade as I pushed myself to read all fifty. Putting the book down and feeling no further enlightened, I had the sense I'd somehow "taken my medicine" but hadn't particularly enjoyed nor understood it.

Several hours later I came back to the book and found a workbook section, which provided 365 lessons, each a practical application of the material in the text. The number 365 obviously invited the format of doing one lesson each day for a year. I paused. My initial reading of the text had not been particularly pleasant or enlightening. Was I prepared to give a year to the *Course*? After a brief hesitation at this threshold, I crossed it, affirming that the *Course* had been provided as the next step on my path and that my role was to proceed.

So began my new daily ritual of starting each morning by reading that day's lesson, taking time to engage the content and the experience offered. I would end each day the same way just before bedtime. The instructions for some days included setting a brief moment aside each hour to pause and think about the day's lesson, but I found this difficult to accomplish with any consistency. Rather than criticize myself, I accepted that I was doing the *Course* to the best of my ability. Little did I know that I'd taken the first step on the path of forgiveness as defined by the *Course*, both of myself and of others.

* * *

Light streamed into my hotel room in Back Bay, Boston, as I opened the book to carry out lesson eleven. I had set my alarm half an hour early to ensure enough time to complete this exercise before having to spend the day in meetings for our company's annual retreat. "My meaningless thoughts are showing me a meaningless world,"(W-pI.11) I read. The first ten lessons had been building to this one, teaching me that none of my thoughts held any true meaning, that I personally gave meaning to each of my thoughts.

As a longtime student of philosophy, I certainly agreed that we each bring meaning to what we see. But the *Course* had taken this insight to a radical extreme, claiming not only that we create our own meaning, but that everything is, in its essence, meaningless. If this were true, I would have to abandon my lifelong pursuit of truth, as the very concept of truth requires some ultimate meaning that can be grasped by human consciousness. Perhaps even more troubling, if everything is meaningless, then all ethical choices are also meaningless, so there can be no defensible foundation for moral decision making and justice. I was not prepared to accept either of these tenets. Yet having committed to doing the *Course*, I reaffirmed I would suspend disbelief enough to work with each daily lesson. This did not mean I was convinced.

Periodically throughout the day I would remember the lesson and contemplate whatever I found before me—a building, a person, a fear—with the words, "My meaningless thoughts are showing me a meaningless world."(W-pI.11.0:0). The words would give me pause. *Release all meaning you imbue this thought with*, I almost whispered to myself.

That night our whole group went to dinner at the Union Oyster House, the oldest restaurant in Boston. As the meal ended, a fellow worker named Chuck approached me with an invitation. "Interested in walking back to the hotel rather than taking a taxi?"

I'd learned to regard these words with caution when coming from Chuck. He had been a world-class mountaineer, serving as the physician on a Mt. McKinley expedition as well as compulsively ascending multiple peaks throughout the world.

"I've checked," he responded to my skeptical look. "We're near the waterfront. It's just under three miles to our hotel in Back Bay. Should be a great walk on a beautiful night like this." I often enjoyed such walks with Chuck, and said yes.

We had just started to leave the restaurant when I stopped. Directly in front of us stood the New England Holocaust Memorial. I'd lived in the Boston area more than twenty years and had driven by this memorial countless times, but until that evening I had never visited it. A disturbing thought confronted me: *Was the Holocaust also completely meaningless?*

It was with this question that I approached the memorial, an outdoor space open at all times. I realized it had been built to be walked through, to be personally experienced from the inside. With a smile I had to admit it felt far beyond coincidence that after living more than two decades in the Boston area I found myself for the first time at the Holocaust Memorial on foot, wrestling with a challenging lesson on meaninglessness. A pause, a deep breath, and I began the slow walk through the memorial while Chuck waited for me at the other end. Six hollow glass columns rose from the walkway. As I entered the first column I looked up, seeing etched into the glass one million names of Jews who had died in the concentration camps. Looking down, I felt unnerved to see I was standing on a grate, below which glowed red coals, steam rising from them, winding up the glass chimney within which I now stood. The memorial's designer achieved his purpose, leaving me with a visceral sense of the burning fires of the crematorium ovens below me and a sickening sense of the death of a million human beings, each having a name worth remembering, a life lived, a life horrifically cut short.

Shaken, I stepped out of the first column and a few paces later entered the second. The sheer weight of another million names, another million fellow human beings who suffered and died, pressed in upon me. This experience repeated four more times before I emerged from the memorial. With a new urgency, the question confronted me. Was their suffering meaningless? Were the countless acts of inhumanity committed by the perpetrators of the Holocaust meaningless? A silent shout rose up within me: "No!" An entire generation before me had struggled with this question, had made uneasy peace with it, using the Holocaust as a touchstone for guiding moral behavior and proclaiming, "Never again!" Yet Cambodia's killing fields, the Rwandan genocide, and 9/11 stood with countless other atrocities to make a lie of such a proclamation. Was all human suffering, were all acts of violence by one human against another, ultimately meaningless? If this was the *Course's* teaching, something in me wanted to stop, to put it down, and walk away. Something stronger pulled me forward.

* * *

"Who is the 'I' that keeps being referenced in the *Course*," I asked Santi early in our first teaching session.

"Jesus," came her one-word answer.

Stunned, I could almost hear the clicking in my head as dot after dot connected. *This material is channeled. The source of the channel is none other than Jesus. This material is a direct link to the words and thoughts of a consciousness that has been interpreted and misinterpreted by countless others for two millennia. Our best sources for what Jesus actually said or meant, the Gospels, were not written until more than thirty years after the events they purport to report. The Course cuts through all the history, all the agendas of individuals and institutions down through the centuries that have clouded the true intentions of one of the greatest teachers in the history of the world. In my hands could I be holding words directly channeled from such an extraordinary consciousness?*

Santi understood all I was thinking and responded, "You understand the potential power of the material in the *Course* now. The text is unambiguous concerning the source. It is Jesus. How people hold this information is up to them."

I knew the quality of any channeled information depended heavily upon the clarity of the channeler, upon the level of their own consciousness. I decided to withhold judgment about the quality of this channeled material until experiencing more of the *Course.*

"Understood this way," I replied, "the *Course* must be perceived as a direct threat, if not outright heresy, by Christian religious institutions and leaders. I've already found in the text numerous quotes from the Bible, each followed by an explanation of how it has been misinterpreted by those claiming to establish religious orthodoxy. The misinterpretation is then followed by a 'correct' interpretation of what the quoted words were meant to express. If Jesus is truly the source of all this material, what a gift…and what a threat to so many."

How could the authorship claim of this allegedly channeled material be authenticated? No earthly proof could accomplish this. I paused with a smile, finding myself back in the midst of my personal web of belief. For me, the allegedly channeled interpretations of this biblical material rang more true than any I'd heard before, but its authenticity could never be proven. I would have to adopt an as-if attitude, approaching the material as if it were all true and all coming directly from a consciousness that appeared on earth in human form as Jesus two thousand years earlier. As the *Course* took up residence in my web of belief, I found myself eager to open the book each morning and take the next step on a path that now opened before me, beckoning I knew not where.

* * *

The "where" took on physical form as our plane touched down in Split, Croatia, just four weeks after I'd started the *Course.* A several-hour van ride punctuated by the chatter of a vivacious and perfectly cast tour guide brought us to Medjugorje. This trip, planned more than three months before Diego had asked, "Rick, have you ever done *A Course in Miracles?*" had already become a far different experience for me because of Diego's words. When Virginia had initially said, "You have to go to Medjugorje," I had worried about how deeply imbued with Catholic ritual and theology the whole experience would be. I'd heard descriptions of saying the Rosary and participating in Catholic Mass and Communion multiple times a day, as well as the extraordinary devotion to Mary that permeated the town and its people. None of these had drawn me. Instead I'd felt myself resisting them.

So why did I find Medjugorje the next step on my path? I asked this question again and again in the weeks leading up to our departure. Those same weeks coincided with my early work in the *Course.* A breakthrough had begun with my discovery that Jesus appeared to be the source of the *Course's* content. Shortly after this came lesson twenty-seven, "Above all else I want to see."(W-pI.27). *Yes,* I thought, *above all else I want to see the truth, to dispel all illusions.* Was an escape from my personal web of belief possible? The *Course* held this possibility. Lesson twenty-eight followed with "Above all else I want to see things differently."(W-pI.28). But in what way would I see differently if I were to see the truth? Asking this question led to a surprising answer for this scientist, this skeptic born into a culturally Jewish family and raised an atheist. I wanted to see as Jesus saw. But these words morphed into wanting to see as Jesus sees, in the present tense, because I now held in my web of belief that the consciousness that had animated the body we call Jesus of Nazareth still exists, is still seeing today. The desire to see as Jesus sees did not hinge on the truth or falsehood of any claims regarding Jesus's divinity. Instead, all I had come to understand, all I now believed to be true, had taught me I had much to learn from this immense spirit, this great teacher of the heart and master of compassion. My desire then morphed into wanting to love as Jesus loves. Another step seemed to follow naturally. I wanted to see as God sees and to love as God loves. Might this be what others refer to as Christ consciousness in a non-denominational sense? I began to catch a first glimpse of such a state and yearned to experience it. At the very moment in my journey through the *Course* when these became my goals, I arrived in Medjugorje.

* * *

"I hope we get to see the sun spin or maybe dance around the sky," I heard one member of our tour group say over supper shortly after we had arrived. "I hear this sometimes happens during the visionaries' apparitions of Mary." The sun spinning. The sun dancing about in the sky. Claims like this brought all my skepticism to the fore because the scientist in me knew they could not possibly be true.

So that first night, with my skeptical filter firmly in place, we joined an evening climb up Apparition Hill to the location where the six child visionaries supposedly first saw Mary in 1981. In the deepening darkness, Virginia and I ascended the rocky trail with hundreds of fellow pilgrims. As nighttime fell, we arrived at a statue of Mary on the site of the first apparition. A lone guitar could be heard as a handful of voices joined in quiet song. We waited.

A spirit of reverence moved me to close my eyes, to enter into the opening-the-chakras meditation that had now become a familiar ritual for me. I breathed into opening my first chakra holding the intention, "I am one with all that is." My established meditation process continued, with a new addition that the opening of each of my individual chakras expanded into the opening of a single chakra shared by all humanity around the world.

As I lingered in the sweetness of opening the seventh chakra, sharing a universal opening to the Divine, voices around me began to join in a multilingual rhythm I recognized as the Rosary. While still not familiar with all the prayers, I was able to join in the Our Father. As the words "Our Father, who art in heaven" flowed out, I experienced an exquisite energy, an energy of the Divine, descending on all of us on that mountaintop, descending on all humanity. Each time the Our Father recurred, I sensed this same, beautiful energy pouring down upon every person in the world. The Hail Mary prayers seemed to call forth energy of a different vibration, energy responding to the universal desire for healing. I heard the prayers of countless individuals around the world, prayers for their own healing; prayers mothers and fathers poured out for their suffering, ill children; prayers for peace where war and fear reigned.

Eventually the voices around me subsided. As if with a single mind, the crowd of pilgrims began to move down the mountain. I walked in silence. I would never again hear the Rosary prayed in the same way. This ritual held power. That thought expanded to recognize that all authentic rituals, from whatever religion, carried out with open heart and pure intent, held the same potential for power. As I drifted off to sleep half a world away from home, I did not doubt Medjugorje was the next step on my path.

* * *

"What are they doing?" I asked, looking at hundreds of people waiting in lines outside the main church.

"They're waiting for confession," Virginia answered. "Priests come to Medjugorje from all over the world for their own pilgrimage and while here, volunteer to hear confession from other visitors who speak their language. Medjugorje has become known as the number one place in the world for hearing confessions. So many people coming here find they are moved to unburden themselves of the weight they carry inside, unburdening themselves to God. I did confession during my first visit. Not having been raised Catholic, it was the first time I'd ever done confession. Before going, I took hours to reflect on my whole life, writing down all the times I'd done something I felt bad about, every person I thought I had ever hurt, praying for each of them."

"Being in this holy place," I responded, "I feel called to do the same for my life, for all those I have ever hurt. But something about confessing these as sins doesn't feel right. It smacks too much of guilt and shame, feelings that calibrate near the bottom of Hawkins's consciousness spectrum."

"I agree with you. Remember Ron Roth taught that the literal translation of *sin* is 'to miss the mark.' I've learned that Mary, in her messages to the visionaries here, referred to this as *karmic debt*. So I reflected on all the times I'd missed the mark, times I'd created karmic debt. I wrote each one down and brought the list to confession."

I'll have a long list, I thought to myself. But something about accepting responsibility for all the times I'd missed the mark, all the times I'd created karmic debt, and then releasing them seemed appealing. So that evening I made my list. The following day I waited in line in front of one of the confession rooms. When my turn finally came, I sat across a small white table from an affable man in his forties dressed in a priestly collar. "Welcome," he began with an English accent.

"I'm not sure how to start this," I opened. "This is my first confession." The priest's expression shifted, perhaps wondering how I had gotten to my mid-fifties without ever having gone to confession. That expression became troubled as I went on. "I grew up in a Jewish family and have been on an unusual spiritual path. I've come to Medjugorje as a spiritual pilgrim...seeking Christ consciousness." I expected this man of God to welcome such an intention. Instead his expression became more concerned. "I spent a long time last evening reflecting on my life, writing down all the times I felt I'd missed the mark." I pulled out the multiple handwritten pages I had poured my heart into, creating my honest account of the most important times I hadn't lived up to the standards to which I aspired. In my naiveté, I hadn't realized that the way I had opened our exchange created a problem for this priest in hearing my confession, not the least of which was characterizing myself as having been raised Jewish.

He responded with authentic concern, "I'm afraid I cannot take your confession unless you have been baptized."

In response I felt pleased to be able to say, "Actually, I have been baptized," thinking this would solve the problem so we could get on with the confession. Clearly I hadn't appreciated how far outside the mainstream my story must have sounded to this man who had taken vows to live and minister within the Catholic religion.

"Who baptized you?" he asked somewhat challengingly.

"Reverend Ron Roth," I responded proudly, "a former Catholic priest who had left the priesthood to start his own ministry. He baptized me into a Spirit-directed life."

Once again I hadn't recognized how my waving the red cape of having been baptized by a man who had chosen to step away from the same church institution into which this priest had been ordained would be problematic for him. He responded, with a slightly rising voice, "I cannot take your confession unless you were baptized with water, and the words, 'In the name of the Father, the Son, and the Holy Spirit.' Did he say those exact words and throw water on you?"

I was taken aback. I had thought that by going to confession I would be bringing my deepest misgivings about my all-too-human acts before a representative of God, of Christ consciousness. Sadly, I realized this well-meaning priest was not allowed, by the rules of his religion, to respond with the loving compassion I had hoped to receive from someone himself seeking to manifest Christ consciousness unless a handful of specified words had been said in a prescribed way at my baptism. This seemed so...so rigid...so petty...so missing the mark.

Addressing all that passed through my mind with this priest did not seem a good idea, so I turned to the effort of trying to reconstruct the exact words Ron had used at my baptism. I had no doubt Ron had baptized me with the intention, with the energy this priest sought. I knew that Medjugorje was Ron's favorite place on earth, that he had made eleven trips to this holy site. I could have simply said yes to the priest's question, and we could have moved on with my confession. But I did not want to falsify my answer to his question at this critical moment. Ron had been the first to help open me to God. He took Jesus to be his most profound teacher. He always called upon the Holy Spirit as part of his practice and faith…And he had sprinkled water on me. But did he say, "Father, Son, and Holy Spirit," at the moment of my baptism? During the ceremony, I'd been in such a profound state of giving over my will to live a Spirit-directed life that I hadn't paid clear attention to Ron's exact words. As the awkward moment with the priest stretched on, I did my best to reconstruct what Ron had said. I formed the impression that he likely had said, "Father, Son, and Holy Spirit."

"Yes…Yes…I believe those are the words he used," I finally answered.

"Good." The priest seemed satisfied now. "Then we may proceed."

"Here is my written account of everything I wanted to bring to my first confession," I said, holding up my multipage list.

"What year were you baptized?" the priest interrupted.

After a pause I responded, "I believe it was six years ago."

"In our tradition, the sacrament of baptism cleanses you of all sins prior to your baptism. So you need only confess sins since that time."

I paused, not having anticipated this response. When I had reflected upon my life until that time, the sins, the times of missing the mark I'd felt most called to confess, had happened prior to my being baptized. A bit disoriented, I responded, "Then I guess I'll only mention the ones that occurred after my baptism."

When I had finished, the priest seemed content and said, "Go in peace. You are forgiven all your sins."

As I walked out, I initially felt relieved at the priest's words that Ron's baptizing me had washed away all the sins of my life prior to being baptized. But upon further reflection, something felt amiss. During the previous evening I'd done the personal work of naming, feeling remorse for, and accepting responsibility for each of my most significant actions over a lifetime that had missed the mark. Coming to confession, I had anticipated an encounter with the Divine, an encounter that would have helped cleanse my soul with God's acceptance, forgiveness, and infinite love. To be told this had already happened through the prior act of baptism without my awareness at the time seemed to make the technique of the ritual more important than if I had come before God, engaged my deepest intentions, and opened myself to God's forgiveness.

I walked away from my first confession somewhat uneasy. The priest's apparent rigidity about the exact words that needed to have been said during my baptism and his ready acceptance that all my sins had already been forgiven when I hadn't known this to be part of the baptismal rite reminded me how easily we can place too much value on the mechanics of ritual rather than the energy and meaning a ritual is intended to achieve. I did not know that within hours I would encounter the awe-inspiring transformative power of genuine ritual.

* * *

The long line moved slowly, leaving much time to think. I wasn't quite sure why I'd taken a place in this procession of people, all waiting to touch the Statue of the Risen Jesus. Somewhere in front of me, at the head of this winding line, a huge cross covered the ground. A thirty-foot-high figure of Jesus arose from the cross.

Not having been raised Christian, I had always found the image of Jesus on the cross to echo the suffering of the countless unnamed victims who had endured torture and death at the hands of their fellow human beings throughout history. Here in Medjugorje, statues and paintings of Jesus's agony on the cross confronted me everywhere. The Risen Jesus had been created to connote a different message, a message of the resurrection and eternal life of the soul that follows death. That others believed Jesus to have been God incarnate did not take away from my experience of beholding in the huge, gaunt figure that rose before me the suffering and death of a tortured man.

That morning I had read lesson thirty-three in *A Course in Miracles*, "There is another way of looking at the world." (W-pI.33). Now, with perhaps hours ahead of me wending through this line, I had time to reflect on how far I could take this message. My studies of philosophy had taught me that we make meaning of our experiences far more than we find meaning in them. But the *Course* taught an even more radical formulation, that we create everything we see, that nothing we see is real. I wanted to argue against such a seemingly irrational view of our capacity to grasp the reality of the world through science and careful study. Santi had smiled when I'd raised this argument. Apparently every student of the *Course* does. She had invited me to open to a different possibility, to open to see differently. Only days earlier I had found new words to express this intent, an intent that now became a prayer. "I pray to see as Jesus sees... to love as Jesus loves," the words escaped half out loud. I looked up again at the larger-than-life, gaunt bronze figure rising before me and in a whisper repeated my prayer, "I pray to see as Jesus sees, to love as Jesus loves."

For more than an hour, as we crept forward, I repeated this prayer inwardly again and again. At one point, the line came close to the statue before bending away from it, allowing me to notice that each person approaching the statue stepped up on something I could not see to stand at the figure's right knee. Some pulled out what appeared to be a stack of small papers, rubbing them one at a time on the outside of the knee, coming away clutching them as if protecting a precious treasure. I recalled hearing that the statue "wept" a liquid but had not thought how pilgrims to Medjugorje might interpret it. I became aware of conversation snippets around me, with enough of them in English for me to piece together the story.

"The statue started weeping liquid from the right knee soon after it was erected."

"I heard the liquid's been tested and shown to be just like human tears."

"Scientists have tried to explain the liquid as condensation or the result of rain water. But sometimes the statue stops weeping for days. One time it stopped during a particularly rainy period, so the rainwater theory can't explain it."

And each concluded with "It's a miracle."

Was it a miracle, or simply a physical process with a rational, scientific explanation? I realized I did not have enough data to answer this question, so I returned to my prayer. With each repetition, something deep within me opened a little more.

Eventually I made the final bend with the line. Approaching the statue, my prayer became more fervent. Finally my turn came, and I stepped onto a small rise that brought my eyes level with the statue's knee. A trickle of water spontaneously appeared, coming from a small crack in the bronze. With fascination, I watched it wend its way down the well-rubbed outer portion of the knee. I reached out and wiped the fluid with my finger and, with an impulse, spread the mysterious moisture on my closed eyelids whispering the words, "I pray to see as Jesus sees, to see all with the consciousness of Christ." Opening my eyes, I noted a new trickle of liquid had formed. Wiping it again, I spread it over my heart with the words, "I pray to love as Jesus loves, to open to the Divine as Christ did." Pausing one more time, taking in the massiveness of the bronze figure rising above me, I stepped down.

Seeking to be alone, I wandered aimlessly in silence. Perhaps hours passed until the sun began to set. I made my way back to the sprawling outdoor worship area behind the main church, taking my place on one of countless benches as thousands of fellow pilgrims converged, awaiting the evening Adoration service. I had never attended an Adoration service and did not know what to expect. When I'd asked, I'd been told that during the Adoration service, the Host, the blessed wafers that Catholics believe become the body of Christ through the ritual mass and the process of transubstantiation, was displayed to be adored.

Waiting for the service to begin, I reflected on the long journey I'd undergone regarding the Eucharist. While married to Marsha, who came from a Catholic background, I'd attended Mass for family and holiday events but had always remained seated during Communion, feeling very much an outsider to this rite. Through the ministry of Ron Roth, who taught that everyone is welcome at the Lord's Supper, I'd taken Communion for the first time and many times thereafter, each marking a fledgling step in a growing relationship with this ritual. Here in Medjugorje, I'd attended Mass daily, embracing the act of taking in the Host as opening to and asking to be filled with Christ consciousness, an experience that deepened with every passing day. And now, as darkness settled, the haunting songs of the Adoration service began wafting over ten thousand pilgrims, each silently yearning in their own way for…for…I let the thought linger, releasing the need for words. Gazing at the Host, encased in a large, round, golden monstrance suspended high on the great stage, I opened my heart, my entire being, to the consciousness that animated this physical embodiment…that animated all that is. I felt the inner space of my own consciousness expand…rise up…break through all previous barriers…finding a deep rapture I'd never known possible. For the first time, I touched Christ consciousness.

* * *

"Did you see it?" one of our group members almost shouted as she approached.

"See what?" came our collective response.

"The sun. It was spinning! I went up Apparition Hill just now to be there for the time the visionaries see Mary. I looked up and saw the sun spinning!"

None of us had seen the sun spin. Part of me wanted to discount her report, but the scientist in me wanted to see for myself. So the following evening we made our way up Apparition Hill to be settled in before six forty, the visionaries' time to see Mary. Seated among the rocks, waiting with several dozen others who had made the climb, I glanced up at the sun several times, but despite wearing sunglasses, I was unable to look upon it for more than a few seconds.

"Look! It's happening!" I heard Virginia call out.

A quick glance at my watch revealed it was six forty. Looking back at the sun, I stared, trying to make sense of what I saw. The central disk of the orb appeared somewhat darkened, allowing me to continue looking directly at it for twenty to thirty seconds, while the sun's edge could be seen just outside the darkened disk. And yes, the bright outer edge appeared to be spinning! A pinkish hue emanated from the sun and expanded in concentric rings that filled the sky. All around I heard others exclaiming as they, too, saw the sun spin.

Ever the scientist, I did not believe the massive sun, ninety-three million miles away, had somehow started spinning. So after several minutes of taking in this extraordinary phenomenon, I set about to understand what I was perceiving. I covered first one eye and then the other while looking at the sun. I noted the slightly darkened disc covering most of the sun could be seen with each eye but without as strong a sensation of the sun spinning. When I looked with both eyes, the darkened disc seemed to dance about within the slightly larger sun. Could this be caused by my eye muscles subtly moving as I attempted to focus on the sun, with my brain merging the shifting images from each eye into a binocular vision that gave rise to the sensation of the brighter outer edge spinning? Perhaps. But why could I suddenly tolerate staring at the same sun for minutes that only moments before I could not tolerate for more than seconds? Had I burned out just enough of my retinas to cause the perception of a darkened disc in the center of my vision, which allowed me to keep staring at the sun? Again, perhaps. But this would not explain why dozens of others around me had experienced the same perception at the same moment. To conclude that we all must have separately experienced the precise cumulative impact each of our retinas needed to allow us to keep staring at the sun, and for this to have happened simultaneously for all of us, felt like far too much of a stretch to be taken seriously as a scientific explanation. Then again, the explanation I'd heard from others, that the darkened disc I had perceived suspended before the sun was the monstrance holding the Host, seemed anything but scientific. Had we all shared a common illusion triggered by our intense desire to perceive the spinning sun? I hadn't felt such a desire but merely a curiosity, so again this explanation failed to be convincing. Given the state of my web of belief, I could consider the possibility that our shared consciousnesses had been shifted in some way that in turn changed our perceptions. But "consider" was far from finding this explanation any more convincing than the others.

I sat for perhaps twenty minutes gazing at the spinning sun and then looking away, only to repeat the process and see the same, unchanging phenomenon. Eventually I made my way down the steep path, pausing periodically to look at the sun, noting the spinning continued. Sometime later I looked at the sun and noticed I no longer perceived it to be spinning. Baffled and moved, I concluded that I could conjure no satisfactory explanation for yet another challenging data point.

* * *

Upon my return from Medjugorje, I continued to carve out a precious window each morning and evening for the daily lesson in the *Course*. Soon I encountered one of its central tenets: forgiveness is the path to all we seek. Forgiveness is the path to freedom from illusions, to true happiness, to heaven on earth, to God.

Ron Roth had taught forgiveness. Bhagavan and the dasas of Oneness University had taught forgiveness. I was prepared to accept that forgiveness plays a critical role in all authentic spiritual paths. But the forgiveness taught by the *Course* seemed to be of a different nature, one I struggled to understand. It went beyond unplugging, beyond accepting the isness of what could not be changed, beyond offering to forgive another out of my own graciousness or because I had done some kind of internal work that allowed me to get over what the other person had done. Despite my efforts to grasp it, the essence of this new kind of forgiveness remained elusive.

Day after day, week after week, month after month, I opened to and wrestled with each lesson. Gradually I came to understand one of the *Course's* main teachings, that it falls to each of us to choose with our free will between love and fear in every moment, even in every perception. All fear is based in illusion, in projecting onto the world rather than grasping its essence. That projection makes the life we think we are living a dream, a dream from which we can choose to awaken.

I heard in this echoes of the Hindu concept of *maya*, that the world we perceive is all illusion, and that enlightenment is the act of waking up to this awareness. From my studies of Buddhism over the years, I recognized here parallels with the Buddha's central teaching that all suffering derives from desire, and desire arises from not grasping the nature of reality accurately. I gradually recognized the *Course* was teaching the same perennial wisdom as these and other great spiritual traditions. With each daily lesson, indeed with each step on the path I'd been walking since the earliest cracks in my armor of certainty, I experienced myself gradually awakening.

Many months into the *Course*, the key to forgiveness finally became clear. If all is illusion, there is nothing to forgive others for, because in their essence they have done no wrong. Only in this world of illusion does it appear to be wrong. I forgive others because I recognize the Divinity of others, I see them as just as much a manifestation of God as I am. This is a statement of what is, not a restatement of the Golden Rule, the "ought" that commands us to love another as oneself. To find within myself the capacity for this type of forgiveness is to free myself from all illusions of this world and open to an ever deeper oneness with God. Yes, forgiveness is the key to all I seek.

* * *

Shortly after this, I was on a call with Marsha discussing the latest wrinkle in Michael's life, which had improved much but which still bore the challenging ups and downs of young adulthood.

"Marsha," I began hesitantly, "we both know so much has transpired between us." I took a deep breath, and a profound calm came over me. "I want you to know that I forgive you." I paused and took another deep breath before going on, holding before me the image of the light of God glowing within her. "In fact, there is nothing to forgive, for you have done no wrong." And with that, I released the last remnants of all negativity I had carried from our shared past. I released her, and in so doing, I, too, found release…and joy.

* * *

Having opened to this profound level of forgiveness for all, I paused, troubled at the very moment I felt on the verge of embracing this newfound expansion. Did this mean all human acts lose their moral value? Did it mean how one person treats another has no consequence?

Once again I confronted the question that had burned within me ever since my days at Oxford. I had never stopped yearning for a foundation for ethics, for the moral guidance of human conduct, that did not depend upon any specific religious or historically relative set of cultural beliefs, whether about the purported will of God, the reasons we undergo reincarnation, or any of the myriad other justifications that have been used to try to ground ethical principles. Just as I despaired that forgiveness rightfully understood might render this question irrelevant, the *Course* provided a most startling answer. Love is WHAT we are. It is not something you do or don't do, give or don't give. The very nature of our being *is* love. If we simply allow the essence of who and what we are to manifest spontaneously, we will naturally act in loving ways. All human behavior that is to the contrary, all non-loving behavior, results from failures of individuals to connect to this truth within themselves. Such failures could come from experiences in family upbringing, culture, or a wide range of other influences, but each ultimately reflects how an individual chooses to exercise free will. If we choose to manifest our truest selves and make all choices from that consciousness, we will not only *act* in a loving way, we will *be* the love we already are.

For the first time in more than thirty years, I felt myself put down a heavy weight I hadn't realized I'd been carrying all that time. Ever since my studies at Oxford, I had felt a personal burden to prove that ethical behavior *should* be chosen over non-ethical behavior. I had felt it personally incumbent upon me to do all I could to find an unshakable fulcrum upon which to place the lever that would move my fellow human beings to behave morally. But much as my academic studies had led to ever more interesting questions without answers, my spiritual journey had produced the same regarding the foundation for moral choices. Yet if the very nature of our being is love, then my search had come to an end. I did not need to convince anybody they *should* make ethical choices. They only needed to wake up to who they truly are, and choices, loving choices, would naturally follow. In other words, the answer to why we *should* love another is not ethical but ontological.

I was beginning to see the wisdom of the opening words of the *Course.* "This is a course in miracles. It is a required course. Only the time you take it is voluntary."(In-1:1-3). Everyone has free will regarding when they awaken to the truth that their very essence is Love.

* * *

I reflected back on the myriad religious traditions that had become integral parts of my eclectic spiritual path. This path had begun in a swirling jumble of Jewish cultural identity and atheistic beliefs. I noted with irony that not only had I found my way from these roots to a spiritual path, but so had my younger brother, Daniel. He, too, had become a physician. He, too, had yearned for something more than the world of science into which he, our older brother (also a physician), and I had been inculcated. He had married into a family that lived Judaism based in love and rich traditions. This provided him a doorway through which he chose to step. He cut back his medical practice to attend Hebrew College in Massachusetts. He also pursued training in the Kabala, the centuries-old tradition of Jewish mysticism, and went ever deeper into the wonders of Kabalistic healing. Today he leads a congregation (without having become an ordained rabbi) that can best be characterized as an independent (unaffiliated) Jewish spiritual community, with renewal-style services.

I have had the opportunity to hear Daniel chant Torah and can only describe it as a transcendent experience. He prepares many days to perform this ritual, exploring the passage's countless interpretations by others, and then seeks his own. His religious leadership has evolved so that after all this preparation, when he stands before the congregation, he turns the words that will come out of him over to another source. It might be said he channels not just the Torah reading but the entire service.

My brother and I have taken different paths. He has found endless richness in the Jewish texts, traditions, and rituals, a richness that grows in depth and power year after year. While I eventually found meaning within Judaism, I found that no one religion, including Judaism, provided an adequate framework for my personal spiritual path. Yet my brother and I respect and appreciate each other's spiritual journey.

That we have both pursued our spiritual paths so deeply has perplexed our parents. One day, after I had just answered their questions about my most recent visit to John of God, my father turned to my mother and said, "Janet, Janet, where did we go wrong? We have one son who wants to be a rabbi...and the other is a mystic!"

My atheist father had referred to me as a mystic. Despite stumbling and lurching along an unplanned and unpredictable spiritual path for more than thirty years, I'd never seen myself in such a light. Did the label fit? I reflected on what I knew of the mystics who have arisen throughout the millennia. They all shared a passionate pursuit of direct communion with the Divine, with ultimate truth. They also shared a tendency to stand outside the orthodoxy of the organized religion of their day. On both counts, my father was right.

* * *

Virginia and I returned to another John of God event at the Omega Institute. As before, I was honored to serve in the Entity's current room. Heather assigned each current volunteer a specific seat to hold the current energy in a balanced and effective way. For the first two days I had been assigned to sit about halfway back on the right-hand edge, adjacent to the line of people coming before John of God. On the third and final morning, the volunteer who had been sitting directly in front of John of God was selected for a spiritual intervention (called spiritual surgery in Brazil), resulting in a need to fill her seat. Heather assigned a person to fill the empty seat and then asked me to take that person's vacated seat in the front row, leftmost corner of the Entity's current room.

As usual, I began my current meditation following the same preparation the Entity had called to the attention of others several years earlier. After completing the opening-the-chakras portion of the meditation, I shifted into opening myself to serve as a channel as I had the first time I'd felt the fire hose of energy pouring through me. I concentrated on letting go of any effort to control this energy, creating the intention that it flow smoothly through my entire expanded energetic being.

I heard John of God enter the large room. From experience, I knew that Heather walked at his side. His slow, methodical breathing as he stood just in front of me meant he had already incorporated. Knowing the Entity could see everything I did in current, the overachiever in me kicked in. I did all I could to open even further to allow the Divine energy to flow through me, releasing any last remnants of resistance. Opening... opening...with each breath opening ever more willingly, completely to all that coursed through me.

I heard the Entity take in a deep breath. This meant he was about to pronounce the words in Portuguese I had heard Heather translate so often as, "In the name of God, the children's spiritual intervention is complete." With the Entity standing directly before me, I sought even more to open to the Divine energy pouring down through my crown, through my entire being, and out to the world. Just when I thought John of God would make the pronouncement, I instead felt his large, heavy hand come down on the crown of my head. He uttered emphatic words in Portuguese, which Heather translated as "Open yourself to God!" A moment later, his hand was gone.

Stunned, I tried to take in that these words and the laying on of hands by the Entity had been directed specifically to me. John of God walked several steps away, and then I heard the familiar pronouncement, "Em nome de Deus..." as Heather translated, "In the name of God, the children's spiritual intervention is complete." Tears began to flow as I realized the Entity had seen my efforts to open to this Divine energy, to open to God, to open to what my web of belief now held to be the unfathomably loving consciousness and presence that is the source of all and penetrates every element of existence everywhere. Seeing this, the Entity had performed a spiritual intervention directly on me to help me open even more to God.

Since that moment, in every meditation, in every prayer, I have experienced ever more fully a deepened opening to the Divine. And each time I do, I experience inexpressible joy and gratitude.

* * *

On the last day of that same John of God event at the Omega Institute, Virginia passed before the Entity to offer gratitude and say good-bye. To her surprise, the Entity said words translated as "Do not worry. We are taking care of it." She returned to her seat, perplexed by what those words meant.

Two days later, while driving over a bridge near our home, she looked up and saw the sun spinning as we had in Medjugorje. Virginia said to herself, "Oh, Mary's here," feeling the warm sense of serenity and comfort her deepening relationship with Mother Mary now brought her. An hour later I got a phone call.

"Rick," one of our friends said rapidly into the phone, "something's wrong with Virginia. She's talking funny and she can't walk. You'd better come home right away."

I did not pause to think. The doctor in me gave way to the scared husband. Instead of telling our friend to call an ambulance and that I would meet them at the hospital, I threw everything together and raced to my car. The ten-minute drive from my office to home seemed to take forever. I found Virginia lying on the couch, drowsy, with slow, garbled speech. She seemed to be having a stroke, so I took her to the hospital. I waited anxiously for hours as she underwent a CT scan of her brain and then an MRI. Finally the emergency physician pulled me aside. Knowing I was a physician, he gave me the straight story. The MRI showed a 3.3 cm mass directly under her brain, a cranial floor tumor. The mass seemed to be partially in the cavernous sinus, a terribly complex collection of delicate structures. It abutted her carotid artery and jugular vein as well as multiple critical nerves passing through that area. It had severely eroded the bone of her skull. My heart sank. I didn't know if it was benign or malignant. I did not know if any treatment could help. I did not know if she would ever be neurologically normal again. Slowly I returned to her room.

To my surprise, her symptoms seemed to be clearing, and within a few more hours she was back to baseline, much to my great relief. But I knew her journey was just beginning. A neurologist diagnosed this event as a temporal lobe seizure caused by brain irritation from her tumor, an unusual presentation because her seizure had lasted more than six hours.

Over the next few weeks, driven by Virginia's courageous determination, we both learned more about cranial floor tumors than we had ever wanted to know. Soon we found our way to one of the top cranial tumor centers in the country. Myriad tests ensued. A guided-needle biopsy conducted while undergoing another CT scan determined she had a schwannoma of the fifth cranial nerve, thankfully a benign tumor but one involving a major nerve in a critical and vulnerable area. Her doctors weren't sure of the best way to treat her.

Then during one office visit, her neurosurgeon came into her examining room with a model of a skull and a big smile. "I've figured out a way to get to this tumor," he announced. He proceeded to describe how he would cut across and peel back the large temporalis muscle covering the side of her skull. He would then cut a hole in her skull to gain access to the area under the brain. During the same procedure, an ear, nose, and throat surgeon would take off her cheek bone and access the area just under her skull. They would meet in the middle, which would provide the best chance for taking out as much of the tumor as possible. As excited as he seemed, Virginia and I both knew how risky this procedure would be. It would involve taking down half her face. The surgeons might not get the entire tumor, meaning it could keep growing. She might be permanently neurologically impaired. She might even die during the procedure.

As word spread of Virginia's situation, prayers poured in from friends, family, and even strangers. We both took great heart in these, something I could not have done at a prior stage of my life. Several individuals told us they had received information that Dr. Augusto, one of the spirit beings who works through John of God, would be "doing" Virginia's surgery. I thought of the urologist who'd performed an eye scraping procedure with his hand guided by the Entity. Because of that data point and others, I held this news with hope but knew there were no guarantees.

The ten weeks between Virginia's initial diagnosis and her surgery dragged by. We each spent much of our waking hours in prayer. We supported each other, but we each also had solo journeys through this difficult time. When I finally left her in the preoperative area on the day of surgery, we both knew she had to walk the final steps of this path alone, which she did with breathtaking courage. She turned her life over to Mary and Jesus. While being wheeled into the operating room, she prayed for all those who had been praying for her, praying they be filled with light and the grace of God.

I waited with family members, continuing to pray. Then word came. Virginia was in the recovery room. Eventually, the nurses let me see her in the neurologic intensive care unit. Weak from surgery and medications, she managed to smile. "There is so much light surrounding you," she murmured as I took her hand. Tears fell from my cheeks with the knowledge she had survived and seemed to be neurologically intact. Minutes later the neurosurgeon came into her room.

"The surgery went very well!" he exclaimed. "We got in without a problem. When we got to the tumor, I was pleased and a little surprised to find the entire tumor located just outside the edge of the cavernous sinus. So I was able to get to it and shell it out. I think we got it all, but we'll have to wait for the post-op MRI to confirm." His excitement became contagious. For the first time in months, Virginia and I smiled with relief.

That relief turned to wondrous surprise at her amazing recovery. Two days after surgery, she came home with only over-the-counter pain medication. Two weeks after surgery, despite having had half her face taken off and put back on, she had no bruising or swelling. She was, however, left with severe chronic pain from nerve injury that couldn't be avoided when the tumor was removed. During the years that have followed her surgery, Virginia has made multiple trips to John of God. Each two-week period in Brazil has produced a dramatic improvement in her symptoms. She still lives with daily chronic pain, but with courage, determination, and grace, she now lives an almost normal life. And we are both filled with great joy at the miracle of her outcome and recovery.

Did Dr. Augusto, a disembodied, loving spirit somehow direct the surgeons' hands? Did that spirit play a role in the tumor being just outside the cavernous sinus instead of partially in it? I will never know. But my web of belief holds it may just be possible.

* * *

As I followed one step after another on my spiritual path, I became aware that one great world religion had not yet become part of that path: Islam. I had intended to read the Qur'an for many years, ever since a chance encounter during my days at Oxford with a young Muslim man from Egypt. We had spent an evening talking late into the night about all we held most dear. We had each been struck by the depth of the other's heart and how much we shared while our respective religious groups, Jews and Muslims, waged war with each other. As we parted, he gave me an English translation of the Qur'an as an offering he hoped would help me and help bring peace between our peoples. "I only request one thing of you," he had said. "Each time before you open this book, please wash your hands. Will you promise me this?" I had agreed to do so but without understanding the import of his request. Since my young student days I had kept this book with me. Every time I packed to move, I encountered the book again. And every time I chose to take it with me. But I had never opened it. Now it was time.

Yet I knew I needed a guide to read the Qur'an as it had been intended to be read. In English translation, I could not appreciate the beautiful Arabic in which it had been written, the very eloquence of the words providing evidence that Muhammad, whom Muslims traditionally believe to have been illiterate, must have channeled the Qur'an. I paused at that thought. Given the many exposures to channeling I'd already experienced, accepting the Qur'an as channeled information from the Archangel Gabriel, which is how Muslims understand its origins, did not at this stage feel like a stretch for me. Yes, I had come very far on my spiritual path.

In the absence of a personal teacher, I used Lex Hixon's *The Heart of the Qur'an*[9] as my guide. Before reading this book or the words of the Qur'an, I washed my hands as I had promised that openhearted young man I'd met in Oxford, creating an intention to receive with reverence whatever transmission was to come through. In my first reading, in the introduction to *The Heart of the Qur'an*, I learned the Arabic word *Islam* means *surrender*. Then I read the words, "Muslims are those who consciously and constantly surrender their lives to the single Source of the universe."[10] An electric sensation shot through me. These words expressed the same intention I had embraced when Ron Roth had baptized me into living a Spirit-directed life. *Yes,* I thought, *the spiritual journey truly is universal.*

---

[9] Hixon, Lex. 2003. *The Heart of the Qur'an: An Introduction to Islamic Spirituality.* Wheaton, IL: Quest Books Theosophical Publishing House.
[10] Hixon. *The Heart of the Qur'an.* 5.

In the weeks that followed, twice a day, morning and evening, I read first a passage in the Qur'an and then an interpretation of that passage from Hixon's book. Already having become familiar with the rich, varied connotations of Aramaic words from what I'd learned about the Lord's Prayer, I readily accepted the same applied to the closely related language of Arabic. Lex Hixon's soaring, poetic reflections did indeed take me to the heart of the Qur'an. I discovered there much that resonated with all I had already embraced on my spiritual path.

As with each religious tradition I'd encountered, I struggled with some of what I found, most notably the degree to which Allah was seen as a judging God. Was this in the original Arabic, or was it a casualty of the translation? Was it only a surface reading that missed the deeper resonance of the text? I realized any response to these questions could only reflect the level of the consciousness that answered. With a pause, I recognized I had indeed incorporated into my web of belief that as one conceives God, so God appears. I have experienced, and so conceive, God to be an all-present consciousness of unfathomably compassionate, generous love. Looking beyond the surface, I found such a God in the heart of the Qur'an.

* * *

One year after beginning the *Course*, I finally reached Lesson 365. I wondered where I had arrived now that I'd finished the *Course*. Obviously I realized one never really finishes the *Course*, at least not in this lifetime. I expect to continue studying and learning from the *Course* for many years to come.

My web of belief now included the likelihood that I had spent the past year of my life engaging the consciousness that had animated Jesus of Nazareth and diving deeply into one religion spawned by that consciousness through my trip to Medjugorje. I accepted that my web of belief now included opening myself fully and willingly to Christ consciousness in its universal, nonsectarian meaning. I sensed myself vastly expanded. I had explored Judaism, Christianity, Hinduism, Buddhism, Islam, and other spiritual traditions. Through all of this I had come to understand, respect, and appreciate the uniqueness of each religion's traditions. Yet I had also found a spiritual commonality in all of them.

Openness, humility, and tolerance teach us that there are many paths to spiritual truth. Some of these lead to God, some, such as Buddhism, to no God. My current web of belief includes that all of these paths, pursued with integrity, openness, and honesty, lead to the same universal truths. For those for whom the path leads to God, all paths lead ultimately to the same God, a God who does not take sides, a God of infinite compassion and love, a God for all.

I have come to appreciate the profound surrendering to a loving God that constitutes the spiritual essence of Islam. At the same time I embrace the Hindu-inspired concept of namaste, that when I meet and open to another, the spark of Divinity within me acknowledges, appreciates, and loves the spark of Divinity expressed in the unique consciousness and life of the person before me. These two principles reside easily side by side within my personal web of belief, linked together by yet a third principle, that love constitutes the highest essence of all I am, all that is, and all God is.

CHAPTER X: BROTHER RICK?

"I didn't see this one coming."

My spiritual path took yet another surprising turn one cool autumn evening. At a Celebrating Life Ministries retreat, now led by Spiritual Shepherd Paul Funfsinn, successor to Ron Roth following his death, I heard my name called to come forward. As I prepared one more time to say *hineni* to whatever would be next on this journey, I heard Paul solemnly intone, "You have shown great love of God and devotion to prayer. I now invite you, should you so choose, to become a novitiate in the Spirit of Peace Monastic Community that is part of our Celebrating Life Ministries family." All I knew of this monk order was that it required a commitment to pray at least two hours a day for the world, for healing and peace for all humanity. As a novitiate, I would get to try on the role of being a monk, including fulfilling this commitment. Me, a *monk?* Brother Rick? I didn't see this one coming. Given the starting place this journey had in my family of origin, I could think of no more unlikely outcome. Yet I had the now familiar feeling of facing what might be the next step on my path.

Pray for the world two hours a day…That would be a major commitment, especially given my demanding work schedule. But the more deeply I pursued a spiritual path, the simpler the path became, distilling down to two key elements: to love and to serve. Nothing else mattered as much as these. Was I now prepared to offer love and service to all humanity through dedication to prayer?

I took seriously all I'd absorbed from a now wide range of spiritual teachers and traditions that together painted a coherent picture, a picture that we are all one. I sensed that prayers, intentions, and all the work of raising my consciousness to the highest vibrational frequency possible had a loving impact far beyond what I had ever imagined. If this was how I was being called to love and serve, then I would say yes.

But before making this commitment I could see the wisdom of a six-month novitiate period. It would allow me to explore what it would be like to live with this decision More than that, I had to learn what I was committing to beyond praying two hours a day. Padre Paul, as everyone in Celebrating Life Ministries referred to our leader, directed me to readings about this monastic community. He also required me to speak with him once a month during this novitiate period. He wanted me to delve seriously into the commitment before making my decision.

"What did you learn in your readings this month?" he began on our first phone call.

"I was surprised to find the Spirit of Peace Monastic Community was a Benedictine order. I've been with Celebrating Life Ministries for almost a decade, but somehow that fact had escaped me."

"We don't advertise aspects of our monastic order. It is for those who feel called to it. Do you feel called?"

I wasn't sure. "You called me," I responded.

"I had prayed on this question and was shown that I was to offer you this novitiate opportunity. Whether you choose to profess the monastic vows is for you to decide. What guidance are you experiencing?"

"As you know, my spiritual path has been both unusual and highly eclectic. Right now I've been reading the Bhagavad Gita and commentaries about it. These are very much talking to me and seem to be the next step on my path. Frankly," I paused, hesitating to put my doubts into words, "the material you've directed me to on the Benedictine order and the Rule of St. Benedict doesn't seem to be where I'm feeling pulled."

"That's fine," the Padre responded easily. "If the Benedictine path isn't calling you, you are free to follow the guidance of Spirit wherever it leads you." And then with surprising finality he added, "If you don't want to join our monastic community, you can end the novitiate period now."

I suddenly felt I'd been punched in the stomach. Not join the monastic community? Only a few weeks earlier, this hadn't been on my radar screen. Now the thought of not joining…not taking this next step almost hurt. Why the sudden change? I thought the Padre understood how much I'd taken to heart Ron Roth's teaching that all great spiritual traditions had been founded on the singular principle of love. I thought he would be fine with my following whatever next step presented itself on my spiritual path, which in that moment was the Bhagavad Gita. Couldn't I be a monk in this spirit, committing myself to pray for the world, for healing, for peace every day? Wasn't that enough? Why did it have to be squeezed into one particular monastic tradition? Even the very term *rule*, as in the Rule of St. Benedict, smacked of all I had resisted in organized religion my entire life.

As my head swirled with these thoughts, a question formed somewhere on the periphery, slowly but insistently pushing its way to the center of my attention: Had I only been pursuing my spiritual path *as if* it were true? I thought of my original reaction upon hearing Tony and Hillary talk about reincarnation and energy. "You don't believe this crap, do you?" Now I had to confront that question for myself. Did I believe all I'd found on this spiritual path, or was I just playing at it?

"Padre," I responded, "I…I don't know how to answer your question. I'm not prepared to walk away from the opportunity to become a monk. But I'm also not sure it's right for me. I really want to use this novitiate period to do more than try it on. I want to be with my doubts, face them, and discover where they lead me."

"That's perfect," he said with complete acceptance. "This is exactly the intention for the novitiate period. But if you want to remain a novitiate, then I do expect you to complete the readings I've directed you to. Will you do that between now and our next call?"

I heard my voice say, "Yes." As I hung up the phone, I felt some regret at giving up the Bhagavad Gita to learn more about the Rule of St. Benedict. The Padre wasn't forcing me to choose between the two. He would be fine if I did both. Yet I knew I had to commit to the rule of this monastic order if I was to profess vows. I could always go back to the Bhagavad Gita or any other aspect of spiritual teaching at a later date. That was part of the beauty of Celebrating Life Ministries' ecumenical approach to living an authentic, Spirit-directed life. But for now, the Rule of St. Benedict was to be the next step on my spiritual path.

By our ensuing call I had read the Rule of St. Benedict much more carefully as well as additional information to which the Padre had directed me to begin learning about how to apply the rule in a modern setting. The call began with the same question from the Padre. "What did you learn in your readings this month?"

"I understand much better why you insisted I follow your instructions to read the material you assigned. You were asking me to walk the talk for one of the key Benedictine vows, obedience."

"Exactly! But let's be clear. This is not just obedience to me as abbot of our monastic community. This is freely committing to obedience to the will of God."

I thought of my baptismal decision to commit to a Spirit-directed life. My daily meditation and prayer consistently included the words, "Not my will, but Thy will." Was I again playing as if I were committed to these intentions, or was I prepared to affirm them with all my being? My decision whether or not to become a monk required answering this question with complete honesty.

I realized I was not yet ready to do so. So I responded, "Obedience has never been my strong suit. I've always prided myself on being an independent thinker, never taking things on the basis of authority." Then, catching myself, I added laughing, "Given what I read in the rule, 'priding myself' was definitely an unfortunate choice of words but probably pretty telling. Looks like if I become a monk, I'll have plenty of opportunity to work on the little challenge of pride, too."

"We all have to work on that one!" he responded laughing with me. Then he went on, "A related challenge comes from another of the key vows for our community, the vow of stability."

"I read about that. In the old days, and I guess now too, for any monastic community to succeed, monks needed to stick it out, to remain in the community even when it became challenging. If a monk could leave the monastery whenever he had a problem with a fellow monk or the abbot, there would quickly be nobody left. This leads to a question I need some help with. How does a rule designed to help residential monastic communities survive and thrive apply to our community that is nonresidential? The term I came across for my status is being a 'householder,' being married, having a job. How does the rule apply to me?"

"Great question, Rick. For the Spirit of Peace Monastic Community, we don't take every word of the rule literally."

"Including that one about not fulfilling the desires of the flesh?" I added hopefully.

"Yes, ours is not a community that requires a vow of celibacy" he said laughing again. "But that vow of stability means more than just staying in your current situation. It means finding a way to be fully present, fully open and loving, fully connected to God, without having to seek these things through a change in external circumstances. These all reside within you, not your circumstances."

"That's been a lesson it's taken me a long time to learn, but it's beginning to sink in." And then I added, "If a situation is truly abusive, is it OK to leave it?"

"That's always a judgment call. The vow is to remain where you are to do your work of opening your heart, opening to God, and serving others wherever you find yourself. If, after applying yourself fully to these intentions, you conclude the situation is truly abusive, of course it is OK to leave it and move on. That's one of the differences that comes from ours not being a residential monastic community."

"I read something else that hit home. While it's implied in the rule, one of the readings called it out as an important commitment. No grumbling. I take that to mean accepting with grace whatever is hard in any given situation without complaining. That's a real challenge. Do I have to take a vow of no grumbling?"

"It's not a formal vow," he said chuckling once again, "but it is important."

I thought of the intention I had created years ago for my time at Oneness University, to live each moment in joy. So much had changed since I'd uttered those words, but I could look back and see it all leading to this moment, all taking me deeper into the journey within, a journey to what I now found myself expressing with remarkable comfort and sincerity as the Kingdom of God, knowing this state of joy, love, and wholeness lies within every one of us. It's the reward at the end of all authentic spiritual paths, regardless of the particular religious tradition through which they are undertaken.

"It all fits together," I said, then added after a pause, "even the last major vow, the vow of conversion."

"Yes, that's your willingness to change EVERYTHING in response to the guidance of the Divine."

Change everything. That certainly described my experience of the previous forty years. Was I now ready to give up what felt like the last vestige of doubt, the part of me that held on to living *as if* all I had learned on this spiritual path were true? No, that wasn't the right way to come to peace with this question. I now understood truth to be far more complex and nuanced than I had ever envisioned when I began its passionate pursuit so long ago. It wasn't a question of whether I believed any of this. It wasn't a question of faith without evidence. Instead it was an expression of the inner knowing that came from all I had and would experience as I opened ever more fully and deeply to the spiritual path continuously unfolding before me.

I was still a scientist. I was not giving that up. I was still a skeptic. But I had also become a gnostic, in the non-sectarian sense, a knower of truths gained on the spiritual path.

So it came to pass that six months later I professed vows as a monk in the Spirit of Peace Monastic Community. Since then, early every morning I wake up in the dark, find my way to a place of silence and solitude, and embrace the world with my heart and all that flows through it.

CHAPTER XI:
WHEN SCIENCE MEETS GOD[11,12]

A Glimpse into the Coming New Paradigm

I opened this book with the words "I am a scientist and a skeptic." I remain both. But my journey over the last four decades has left me with data points that cannot be explained in the conventional scientific paradigm. I know we communicate at a distance during sleep. I know energy is palpable. I know through intention to manipulate another's energy one can experience subjective sensations (remember "Dad! Something inside my ankle is moving!"). I know John of God performs physical surgeries that defy our understanding of medicine and physics. I know a growing number of individuals have experienced healings at the Casa without any

---

[11] This chapter provides an abbreviated summary of some reflections on the coming new paradigm. For interested readers, a fuller discussion, including additional information about the integration of science and spirituality, is available for free download at www. ricksheffmd.com/joyfullyshattered/whensciencemeetsgod.

[12] Those interested in a deeper dive into the meditations described in this book rather than the science may download a free guided meditation on the oneness of all from www. ricksheffmd.com/joyfullyshattered/onenessmeditation.

physical surgery, healings that cause us to label them miracles because we lack any other explanation.

I am not the first person to identify undeniable data points that do not fit the conventional, dominant scientific paradigm. For countless individuals, including academically trained professionals, experiencing these data points changes *everything.* That's what happens when your web of belief is shattered by a data point that you *know* is impossible if the world works according to our current paradigm. Intellectual integrity calls for seeing the data point as evidence and revising your web of belief—yes even the web of belief in which our current scientific paradigm is embedded.

The data points are mounting. The time for revolutionary science is upon us. Countless scientists in diverse fields are taking these data points seriously and creating surprising, imaginative candidates for the new paradigm. As these activities expand and accelerate in the years to come, we will experience a period of competing theories to explain the new data points as well as the old. During this time, we must take to heart a warning from those who study the philosophy of science. All theories, they tell us, are underdetermined by facts. This means many different theories will be compatible with the available facts, but not all will be good theories.

The ferment at the boundaries of innovative, revolutionary science is palpable. In the space of this chapter I cannot hope to do justice to the outstanding work of courageous scientists who daily place their careers on the line by daring to challenge the current orthodoxy in their field with a wide range of mind-bendingly new theories. Instead, I will highlight one of the most compelling candidates for the coming new paradigm. In doing so, my goal is to whet your appetite for the exciting, creative, and challenging journey science will take us all on over the coming years as science and what we call spirituality become integrated into a grand, new synthesis.

* * *

William Tiller, PhD, a fully tenured professor and past chairman of the materials science department at Stanford University, had been puzzled. He had personally experienced many of the types of anomalous, seemingly inexplicable experiences I had. He, too, believed that science done well could produce valuable insights into the nature of reality, including what we call spiritual phenomena.

He posed the problem in the following way: "How might our universe be constructed so that a natural expansion of our conventional scientific constructs would allow this strange class of psychoenergetic phenomena to become both sane and rational within a larger conceptual framework?" This naturally led to a second question. "What assumed rigid constraints of our conventional worldview could really be relaxed to allow these two sets of experimental data to comfortably coexist?"[13]

In answer to these questions, he recognized that since the days of René Descartes, Roger Bacon, and Isaac Newton, research in the physical sciences has rested upon the unstated assumption that "No human qualities of consciousness, intention, emotion, mind, or spirit can significantly influence a well-designed target experiment in physical reality."[14] *On what basis do we know this to be true?* Tiller wondered. It is a core assumption of a widely shared web of belief, but not a proven "fact." Might our world be constructed otherwise? Yes, he realized, it might. Nothing other than shared beliefs keeps us from considering this possibility. But could this core assumption be tested scientifically? Could it be used to make predictions that could then be experimentally verified or disproved?

Those were exactly the questions Tiller set out to answer. He conducted a series of experiments[15] that could only have been conceived by step-

---

[13] Tiller, William. 2007. *Psychoenergetic Science: A Second Copernican-Scale Revolution.* Walnut Creek, CA: Pavior Publishing. 17.

[14] Tiller, *Psychoenergetic Science.* 2.

[15] For a description of Tiller's work accessible to the average layperson, see Tiller, *Psycho-energetic Science* and some of Tiller's white papers, which are available at www.tiller.org. For a deep dive into the experimental studies, theory, and surprisingly sophisticated

ping outside this assumption, this core piece of the conventional scientific web of belief. Tiller began by testing whether a group of people in meditation could, by holding an intention in their minds, create a change in a measurable parameter in the physical world.

The first such experiment he performed involved the meditators creating and holding an intention to raise the pH of a solution in a target experimental apparatus by 1.0. Since pH measures the negative logarithm of the hydrogen ion concentration in a solution, an increase in pH of 1.0 represents a ten-fold decrease in the hydrogen ion concentration. He was able to demonstrate such a change, but it happened slowly, over a period of several months.

Conventional scientists would find the experimental protocol utilized by Tiller somewhere between highly suspect and laughable. Yet the results proved reproducible, including achieving a decrease in pH by 1.0 purely through his intention experiment. He went on to demonstrate the same protocol could produce highly statistically significant, measurable changes in the in vitro (in the test tube) activity of a common biological enzyme, alkaline phosphatase. He and his coworkers took this one step further and demonstrated the protocol could impact experimental results in a living organism. They were able to produce increased growth in fruit fly larvae through the intention to maximize the ratio of ATP to ADP (a key factor in making energy biologically available to organisms). The larvae targeted with the intention matured faster and demonstrated higher ATP-to-ADP ratios than the group that did not, again with a high degree of statistical significance. (Details regarding these and other unexpected results are provided in the expanded version of this chapter available for download.)

For Tiller, data trumps theory. If a theory doesn't fit the data, the theory must be modified or discarded. So let us not underestimate the extraordinary import of these experimental results. *Tiller made the bold*

---

mathematics that constitute Tiller's fully fleshed-out candidate for the new paradigm, see Tiller, William, Walter Dibble, Jr., and Michael Kohane. 2001. *Conscious Acts of Creation: The Emergence of a New Physics.* Walnut Creek, CA: Pavior Publishing.

prediction that human intention could modify a standard, scientifically measured condition. He obtained experimental results consistent with this prediction and completely inconsistent with the predictions of conventional science. *If these results can be reproduced by others, this finding will be every bit as powerful in supporting Tiller's candidate for the new paradigm as predicting and confirming the existence of antimatter was for quantum mechanics.*

But what is Tiller's candidate for the new paradigm? He took a page from Einstein's breakthrough work in relativity. Einstein had noted that the Newtonian model made highly accurate predictions of physical events in our everyday world. But when objects move relative to each other at speeds approaching the speed of light, the Newtonian model's predictions, Einstein theorized, become inaccurate for common parameters such as mass and time. A different explanatory model was needed, which became Einstein's theory of special relativity and eventually his theory of general relativity, both of which were later confirmed by experimental scientific data. Seen through Einstein's eyes, Newton's model of our everyday world forms a special case of the theory of relativity. It is special because Newton's model holds only for the subset of phenomena which occur at speeds that are slow relative to the speed of light. The fact that our everyday experiences and most of what we measure with scientific instruments occur at these relatively slow speeds makes us think this is all that is possible. Einstein showed that assumption to be incorrect.

Tiller proposed a similar formulation to account for conventional scientific data *and* heretofore unexplained data points, such as my personal experiences and Tiller's experimental results. He proposed that conventional scientific data and experiences in our everyday world be understood as a special case for a more expanded model that includes spiritual phenomena. That expanded model theorizes that human intention, consciousness, and other phenomena we label spiritual are capable of impacting spatiotemporal phenomena, including measured scientific data and physical healing in the human body, to a varying degree. When any particular setting does not include these spiritual phenomena acting to a significant degree, the results will be exactly what science and medicine find today. But when these phenomena are present with adequate potency, additional causal relationships come into play, producing results not consistent with the dominant scientific paradigm.

Tiller proposes this explanation for his experimental results involving human intention. This formulation also provides a potential explanation for the efficacy of prayer and other forms of human intention. Furthermore, if our consciousness continues to exist after death in the form of a soul or spirit, the consciousness of such entities could, in this model, impact our physical world, producing the kind of healings occurring at the Casa.

Formulated this way, *Tiller's new paradigm could explain the anomalous data points that had challenged and eventually shattered my web of belief, convincing me that spiritual phenomena do occur and demand a new paradigm.* Consistent with good science, Tiller's model also makes predictions possible and testable.

The implications for those seeking to confirm or refute Tiller's findings by repeating his studies are highly significant. They must control, measure, or otherwise account for variables not recognized as relevant in the conventional scientific paradigm. These include the intention of the researchers and the level of spiritual development of both the researchers and those generating the intention to be tested.

During the coming period of revolutionary science, the goal should be to test Tiller's model (and other proposed models) with good science, not scientism. In this spirit I smile inwardly imagining a conversation between Tiller and a conventionally trained scientist regarding experimental design. It might run something like this:

> Tiller: How does your experimental design control or otherwise account for the spiritual development of the researchers themselves?

Conventional Scientist: Why would that be relevant?

Tiller: Because researchers who have years of experience with a regular spiritual practice such as meditation or prayer may have a greater capacity to affect measured data than those who have not.

Conventional Scientist: No they can't!

Tiller: How do you know that is the case if you haven't tested your hypothesis that they can't?

Conventional Scientist: ...um...

* * *

I've taken this dive into Tiller's extraordinary experimental data and proposed explanatory model to give notice that we have already entered the new period of revolutionary science. The time before us has the potential to be an exhilarating ride, filled with unpredictable twists and turns and flashes of brilliant intellectual and scientific creativity. I sincerely hope our generation and the ones to follow will witness a redrawing of the boundaries of science, medicine, and religion, giving us robust new configurations of science, healing, and spirituality. Unfortunately, this time also has the potential to play out as an exercise in power and prejudice in which creative researchers and their revolutionary ideas find themselves crushed under the weight of vested interests, tenure pressure, and grant-funding politics. Helping to avert this sad scenario serves as one of my motivations for writing this book.

* * *

One last question remains before this chapter on the coming new paradigm can be brought to a close. As a skeptic, I must now ask, "Why science?" In other words, why value science so highly? What value does science bring to that which we hold highest and most dear?

On an instrumental basis, science has provided humans an ever advancing mastery over our physical environment and a continuous flow of new ways to meet our bodily needs for physical well-being. We value physical well-being for ourselves and others, whether from having adequate food to eat, the trappings of comfort, or a long and productive life.

We also pursue science for a related but not identical purpose: power. The power science produces highlights two different meanings of the word. First, science provides the power to *do* something, such as the power to travel quickly from one place to another. Science also provides coercive power, meaning *power over another*, the capability for one person or one group to impose their will upon another. Science provides coercive power through a number of mechanisms, from generating wealth to the capacity to build more destructive weapons.

I have not returned over and over again to science because of its instrumental value or its capacity to produce power. Through my upbringing and academic training, I had come to believe that science provided the single, best available path to the Truth, with a capital T, meaning knowledge and understanding of all that *is* in its most fundamental nature. My current web of belief still holds this to be correct, but with a caveat. As I have repeatedly made the case throughout this book, I find good science increasingly demonstrating that what *is* includes phenomena of a non-spatiotemporal nature, phenomena that we call spiritual. As this current period of revolutionary science works itself out, I will be surprised if this does not become an ever firmer conclusion.

So far, science done well continues to prove itself capable of getting us closer to the most fundamental nature of what is. That journey can and should continue. But here's the caveat. I have experienced the ineffable. I have touched the Divine. I have joined the countless mystics through the ages who have direct knowledge of what I can best articulate as God. These experiences stand outside of science, as they should. They tell me more about what *is* than science can alone.

The scientific enterprise has yet another limit because science, in its essence, is an activity of the mind. Science can be understood as the dialectical dance between data and logic, beginning with data, interpreted through logic, which in turn leads to more data, and back to logic. (Yes, inspiration and creativity play a role in generating new ideas, but not in proving or disproving scientific truths.) At each step, data and logic mutually inform the other through activity of the mind.

In Western culture, we often confuse this particular activity of the mind with our highest intelligence. It is not. Science is all about mastery, but only mastery of the instrumental kind, mastery totally dependent upon left-brain thinking. Sadly we have learned that this kind of thinking is a lethal weapon when we allow the mind to be the master without informing it with the heart. Instead, science and all uses of the mind should serve the heart, should serve love.

We are not speaking here simply of the passions of the heart, the emotional reactivity of our personalities that arise from our biology and experiences (perhaps including lifetimes past). *Instead, we are speaking of the natural intelligence that flows from the heart's knowing who we truly are: beings whose very essence is love. The science of which I have been speaking throughout this book, the science we find on the verge of a new paradigm, the science I so highly value, properly understood, stands in service to the higher intelligence of the heart. This, too, is part of the coming new paradigm.*

CHAPTER XII: JOURNEY TO JOY

"Is It I, Lord?"

During every trip to John of God in Brazil, I participate in a weekly session of song on the grounds of the Casa. Someone suggests an entry from the songbook, and the group sings it together. Each time someone requests the song "Here I Am, Lord," the lines of the chorus catch in my throat. I am barely able to complete them.

> *Here I am, Lord. Is it I, Lord?*
> *I have heard you calling in the night.*
> *I will go, Lord, if you lead me.*
> *I will hold Your people in my heart.*[16]

The words reverberate, as if speaking directly to me. Is it I, Lord? Will I hold Your people in my heart? I think of all those I've held in my heart over the years, from a shivering cat, to family and friends, to my patients.

In fulfillment of my monk's vows, I daily hold *all* people in my heart with prayers for love and healing. *Yes,* I answer silently, *it is I.*

Looking back, I see how each step on the journey has helped me respond to this call ever more fully, respond *hineni*, opening my heart, my mind, my very consciousness. Along the way my web of belief and so much more has been shattered, and the result has been joy. I now see my whole life as a journey to joy. And I experience that joy most fully when I choose to love and to serve.

Each time I join in singing "Here I Am, Lord," I recognize I am not alone in my desire to hold all people in my heart. In spite of the violence and hatred that make the news every night, a great shift in consciousness is happening around the world. In every country, every culture, and every religion people are hungry for and opening to their own spiritual awakening.

At the core of this beautiful expansion in human consciousness lies a desire felt by ever more people to love and to serve. So it is not just I, Lord, for each of us is called to hold all people in our hearts, to be bearers of light and love and forgiveness to all. We have the choice to do so in the smallest encounters with others every day as well as in the crisis moments of our lives. How we respond to these opportunities is up to each of us. This is the gift of free will. Every moment is an opportunity to take another step on the journey to joy that we share. The growing number of people choosing love, service, and awakening around the world is, yes, a miracle.

* * *

I hope it is clear I do not feel I have arrived at some final state of enlightenment. I am in the process of awakening, discovering from both experiential and scientific frames of reference that wondrous, beautiful, loving phenomena exist beyond, and interface with, our physical world. I walk the path unfolding before me, as do you. As I seek to discern the next step on this path, it is my intention to manifest integrity, love, and service.

In doing so, at the center of my web of belief lies a glowing light, a still growing trust in the truth that the very essence of my being, the essence of all sentient beings including you, is love.

Namaste.

ABOUT THE AUTHOR

Rick Sheff, MD, is a family physician with over thirty years of experience in medicine. He chose the specialty of family medicine because he wanted to see and treat patients as whole people whose illness and wellness result from the complex interplay of their biological, psychological, social, and cultural circumstances. The years have taught him that to this must be added recognition of each patient's spiritual circumstances if they are truly to be seen as a whole person.

Dr. Sheff practiced family medicine in Massachusetts, seeing adults, children, and the elderly and, for the first part of his practice, delivering babies. Over the years he was asked to assume greater leadership responsibilities, eventually leaving clinical practice and becoming the senior physician executive for an integrated delivery system. He left there to launch a new company to help the US healthcare system integrate the best of complementary and alternative medicine with the best of conventional medicine. At the same time, he began to consult with hospitals and physi-